Opportunity
for Skillful Reading

Eighth Edition

Irwin L. Joffe

THOMSON
WADSWORTH

Australia Canada Mexico Singapore Spain United Kingdom United States

Opportunity for Skillful Reading
Eighth Edition
Irwin L. Joffe

Editorial Assistant: *Royden Tonomura*
Production: *Matrix Productions, Inc.*
Print Buyer: *Barbara Britton*
Copy Editor: *Victoria Nelson*
Cover Designer: *Madeline Budnick*
Printer: *Quebecorworld Fairfield*

Printed in the United States of America.
5 6 7 8 9   07 06 05 04

For more information contact Thomson Wadsworth, 25 Thomson Place, Boston, Massachusetts 02210 USA, or you can visit our Internet site at http://www.thomson.com

ISBN: 0-155-06588-2

Library of Congress Catalog Card Number: 96-8980

To Rose

Preface

College reading programs are becoming increasingly important as more and more students are exposed to upper-level textbooks. College materials demand reading skills that many students were not required to learn in high school—at least, not on as sophisticated a level. An effective college reading program, then, must help students develop a new set of reading skills. *Opportunity for Skillful Reading, Eighth Edition,* can help students achieve their higher-education goals by providing them with the tools needed to reach these goals.

This book provides information on and practice in the key skills necessary for the successful study and comprehension of textbooks. These skills help students become proficient in extracting the important information from their learning materials. The skills fall into three general categories:

1. Basic skills: comprehension, interpretation, and organization
2. Study skills
3. Critical reading skills

The text begins with a *Pretest* that samples the skills taught in Chapters 1–12. This test helps students pinpoint any areas where they need individual attention.

The *Basic skills* of comprehension, interpretation, and organization are addressed in the opening chapters. Each chapter begins with a brief discussion of the skill under consideration and then provides numerous practice exercises emphasizing that skill. These practice exercises are arranged in order of increasing difficulty and are taken from materials used in college courses.

Chapters 1–6 cover vocabulary improvement, main ideas, determining significant details, finding relationships between ideas, and outlining. Another basic skill, understanding graphic material such as tables, maps, and diagrams, is presented in Chapter 11.

Study skills are explored in Chapters 7–9. The PQ3R method of studying a textbook chapter is presented in Chapter 7. Chapter 8 deals with locating information within a chapter, Chapter 9 with following directions. The PQ3R skills can be reviewed and practiced in the *PQ3R Practice Selection* that presents a selection from a chemistry textbook. This selection acts as a bridge between *Opportunity for Skillful Reading* and the textbooks that students use in their various courses. Two sets of questions follow the selection, one to be answered after the students do a PREPARE, and one after they do the Q3R. If students can answer both sets of questions (after applying the skills learned in Chapters 1–12), they should have a good understanding of the material presented and, more important, be able to use the same approach with their textbooks.

Critical reading skills are explored in Chapters 10 (figurative language) and 12 (critical comprehension). Students are given practice in determining what an author really means and in deciding whether or not to accept those ideas.

Following the skill chapters is a section titled *Quizzes*. This part of the book provides three quizzes for each of the twelve chapters—thirty-six in all. Since the answers appear only in the Instructor's Manual, the material can be used as quizzes, tests, or practice material at the instructor's discretion.

The text's last instructional section, *Reading Rate*, begins with an explanation of rapid reading. This critique presents a philosophy of rapid reading consistent with the most recent research findings and suggests a methodology for success in this skill. Following this discussion are ten short reading selections chosen for their appeal to students. The selections are taken primarily from popular sources, and they provide historical, scientific, technological, and other types of information. Each selection is preceded by a short list of words or phrases that may cause difficulty and that instructors may want to preview with their students. Each selection is followed by two sets of questions: (1) ten short-answer questions to be used to test comprehension when the selection is used as a rapid reading exercise; and (2) ten skill-development questions geared to the skill chapters (that is, each question 1 tests vocabulary, Chapter 1; each question 2 tests main idea, Chapter 2; and so on.

The *Appendix* contains answer keys to odd-numbered questions in the practice exercises. It also provides all answers to the comprehension and skill-development questions in the reading rate section. In addition, a rate-conversion table allows students to quickly ascertain the rate at which they have read a particular selection and a progress chart on which they can chart their speed and comprehension scores.

SUGGESTIONS FOR USING THIS BOOK

Each chapter and each reading selection is complete in itself, so *any* sequence of presentation is appropriate if it meets the needs of the students and the instructor. The obvious sequence is Pretest, Chapter 1, Chapter 2, Chapter 3, and so on, with reading selections worked in at appropriate intervals. For students who need immediate help in studying college textbooks, the following sequence might be appropriate.

1. Give the Pretest
2. Go over PQ3R (Chapter 7). Do all the practice exercises, but save the section titled *PQ3R Practice Selections* for later.
3. Go over outlining (Chapter 6). Do all the practice exercises in the chapter.
4. Go over main idea (Chapter 2). Do the odd-numbered practice exercises.

5. Go over the subsection titled *Improving Reading Rate* in the *Reading Rate* section.

6. Read the first rapid reading selection, recording the elapsed time. Students should answer the comprehension and skill-development questions, recording the results.

7. Give Quiz 1 for the chapters covered so far: PQ3R, Outlining, and Main Idea.

8. Go over two more chapters, doing the odd-numbered practice exercises. Then do the second rapid reading selection, followed by Quiz 1 on the chapters covered.

9. Continue through the text covering one or two chapters, then a rapid reading selection, then Quiz 1 of the appropriate chapter or chapters.

Following this procedure omits the even-numbered practice exercises in the chapters. If an individual student notices that he or she repeatedly misses a certain number in the skill development questions, that student can self-assign the even-numbered practice exercises from the indicated chapter. If the instructor notices a general need for more practice, an assignment can be made to the entire class.

This format has several distinct advantages. First, additional practice work is easy for students to find because the chapter numbers for a particular skill are the same as the number of the question in the skill-development quiz that employs that skill. Second, students can spend time studying the skill they need most, rather than rehashing what they already know. Third, there is no chance for the students to "learn and forget." Each skill appears repeatedly throughout the semester in the skill-development questions accompanying each rapid reading selection. Also, the instructor can scatter the remaining two quizzes for each skill over the semester, obliging students to review and relearn.

NEW TO THIS EDITION

Because of suggestions from instructors, students, and reviewers, changes have been made in all chapters:

1. Explanations and examples as well as items in the practice exercises have been changed or added, enhancing clarity.

2. Definitions and procedures have been tightened up, especially in Chapter 9, *Following Printed Directions*, and Chapter 12, *Developing Critical Comprehension*.

3. A section of quizzes has been added, providing three quizzes for each of the chapters or thirty-six in all.

4. The sections on vocabulary, outlining, and PQ3R have been moved. They are now integrated with the other skills chapters.

5. The *Pretest* has been moved to the front of the book, and the answer key now has headings indicating the skill being measured.

6. The summaries at the end of each chapter have been rewritten and expanded, making them more precise and quantified.

ACKNOWLEDGMENTS

I would like to offer my thanks and appreciation to Dan Dramer and Austin Gelzer for their encouragement and their valuable suggestions at the time this book was conceived. In addition, I would like to thank my colleague Fred Patterson for his immeasurable help in manuscript preparation and my reviewers for their thoughtful insights: Barbara Boyd, Gadsden State Community College; Sharon Eggleston, West Georgia College; Chuck Hunter, San Jose City College; Jeannette Jabers, Luzerne County Community College; Bill Morris, College of the Redwoods; and Jacqueline Stahlecker, St. Philip's College. Finally, I would like to thank the Wadsworth staff for editorial direction—especially Lisa Timbrell.

TO THE STUDENT

You can count on certain things; they're natural laws. Bread always lands jelly side down. The phone only rings when you're in the shower. Two people in an otherwise empty locker room will have adjacent lockers. Understanding these natural laws can make your life easier, especially in college.

People who don't understand these laws think that the smartest students always get the best grades; that people who study longer know more than people who study less; that if you don't know an answer, you'll miss it on the test.

Wrong, wrong, wrong.

■ The people who get the best grades are the ones who know what it takes to get a good grade, then do what it takes.

■ The people who study long hours usually don't know how to study. Studying the right way means you'll learn the necessary material (instead of trying to learn everything), and do it in less time.

■ Trained readers, by knowing how to *read* a test question the right way, will answer correctly the ones they know, and then be able to guess accurately on the rest.

This book is about that sort of thing—reading. It covers various reading skills you'll need in your college classes. Some of them you already do, and do well; others will be new to you; still others you do a little but have never really mastered. You'll read about each skill, why it's important and how to do it; then you'll practice it on college-level material.

Give it a try. Books, especially textbooks, will be around a long time. The sooner you become really good at dealing with them, the sooner you'll be able to get the education you need, without spending thirty-two hour days trying to get it.

Then life will be perfect, right? Of course not; those natural laws are still at work. Planes will be late. Blizzards will howl during spring break. And the worst bad hair day the world has ever seen will occur on the day of your job interview. But those same natural laws say that *something* has to go right. And that something can be your education.

Contents

■ **PQ3R Practice Selection   309**

■ **Reading Rate   319**

■ **Improving Reading Rate   319**

■ **How to Use This Section   325**

Pretest

Do the following exercises carefully in order to discover how well you can handle the skills taught in this text. Then check your answers using the answer key that immediately follows. Use these results as a guide to help you discover which skills you need to sharpen.

Exercise

In the space provided write a sentence that expresses the main idea of each of the following paragraphs.

1. When we *own* property, we are more inclined to take care of it. This personal interest is a desirable outcome of the institution of private property. A proprietor of a retail store will put in long hours to see that an investment earns an adequate return. Stockholders who own a corporation will watch its executives to see that they manage the company properly. The head of a family will take better care of a house that is owned than of a house that is rented. The opportunity to care for our assets and try to make them grow is one feature of capitalism that has made it popular in America. _____

   _____

2. A shower is less expensive to buy and install than a tub. Also, a shower bath uses less water, involves no waiting for the tub to fill, and, because of the continuous spray of fresh water, is cleaner. Along with these advantages is the shower's adjustability. Your shower can soothe away the day's troubles and aches with a soft cascade of warm water, then put life back into your system with a needle spray of cold water. Try doing that in a tub. _____

   _____

3. The Homestead Act was supplemented by other acts. The old Pre-emption Act of 1841 continued in effect. The Timber Culture Act of 1873 gave additional Plains

land to owners who planted trees. The Desert Land Act of 1877 granted 640 acres to a claimant on condition that certain rather absurd irrigating conditions be met. The Timber and Stone Act of 1878, though ostensibly intended to apply to nonarable and nonmineral lands, enabled lumber and mining companies to engross vast areas with invaluable mineral resources.

_____

_____

Each of the following three paragraphs is preceded by a question that focuses on the main thought of the paragraph. Read the paragraph and then, in the space provided, answer the question by selecting the appropriate detail mentioned.

4. What is one advantage of learning to cope with mild stress in daily living?

Stress is inevitable in our daily living. Even young children meet frequent stress in their interactions with adults, with other children, and with their physical environment. Experience in meeting and dealing with this normal, day-to-day stress is not unhealthy for young children, assuming the stress is neither too heavy nor too frequent. As children learn to cope with mild stress, they gain in ability to cope with greater stress and are able to develop a self-concept as being competent and potentially independent.

_____

_____

5. How does a poor economy influence business leadership?

The state of the economy often has a tremendous influence on business leadership. Managers may be encouraged to experiment with different styles of leadership during profitable periods. But when the economy is in a state of recession, managements often revert to an autocratic approach. Although they realize that employees may be more highly motivated under democratic or laissez faire leadership, they also know that production often can be increased in the short run by using more forceful methods. And when managers are worried about the survival of their company, they are mainly concerned with short-term results. If the company fails, there will be no long-term results to deal with.

_____

_____

6. Why did Germany want to defeat the Allies quickly?

American Entry into the War

The effort came to nothing, for by now the German war lords were convinced that Wilson was pro-Ally and would probably enter the war; in that case Germany's only hope would lie in defeating the Allies quickly. Germany was now well supplied with up-to-date submarines and efficient crews, and on January 31, 1917, she set the next day, February 1, as the date for the renewal of unrestricted submarine warfare. The objective was to starve England out before the British blockade starved out Germany and before American power could make itself felt. Wilson countered (February 3, 1917) by breaking off relations with Germany.

_____

_____

A sentence below is followed by several statements. Decide how a statement is related to the sentence. Is it example, comparison-contrast, definition, or conclusion? Write your answer in the space provided.

7. Some people have strong, domineering personalities.

a. My friend George has a strong personality.

_____

b. Other people have weak, submissive personalities.

_____

c. These people probably like to control their families and friends.

_____

d. I imagine that they are very successful in life.

_____

The following two questions involve study skills. Circle the letter to the left of the answer you choose.

8. In studying a sociology chapter, when do you read the summary found at the end of the chapter?
  a. before reading the chapter
  b. after reading the chapter
  c. As you finish a part of the chapter, read the appropriate part of the summary.

9. In studying a chapter with four headings, what do you do after you finish reading the material under the first heading?
  a. Take a break.

> *b.* Close the book and say aloud the important parts of the material in that heading.
>
> *c.* Read the material under the heading again.
>
> *d.* Immediately read the next heading and its material.

The following two questions involve organization. Answer the questions in the spaces provided.

10. What are the two major thoughts in the following passage? (They would appear as I and II in an outline.) _____

_____

11. List the subpoints of the first major thought in this passage. _____

_____

_____

There is no doubt that flying from New York to California has many advantages over driving. For one, you will get there faster. Flying takes only a fraction of the time that driving does. Your trip will probably be more comfortable, especially considering the service on airplanes today. And you will arrive feeling less tired than if you drove.

Driving, on the other hand, offers opportunities and advantages that flying cannot provide. You can enjoy scenery not visible from the air and visit places that you have never been to before. If you plan your trip carefully, you can even stay longer in some places you've always wanted to see. Also, it is considerably less expensive if there are three or four people going.

Now reread this passage for purpose and tone, then answer the questions relating to it by circling the letter to the left of the answer you choose.

12. What was the purpose of this passage?
   a. to convince you to fly
   b. to convince you to drive
   c. to present information
   d. to confuse you

13. What was the tone of the passage?
   a. nonjudgmental
   b. formal
   c. excited
   d. amused

Reread the "shower" paragraph in question 2 near the beginning of the test.

14. What is the tone of the "shower" paragraph?
  a. formal
  b. matter-of-fact
  c. amused
  d. scornful

Each of the following paragraphs gives directions for a particular procedure. Following each paragraph is a list of some of the steps in the procedure. Number these steps in the order in which they should be followed.

15. To survey, follow this general pattern: Read the chapter title. If the author has provided an introductory paragraph, read it. Next, notice the pattern of the author's writing. Does the author put the main sentences at the beginning or end of each paragraph, or does he or she use a combination tactic? Once you determine the author's pattern, scan through the rest of the chapter rapidly, noting the main sentences. Finally, the author may have provided a summary statement that you should read carefully since it, too, will provide a good survey of the material.

_____ Note the main sentences.
_____ Note the author's writing pattern.
_____ Read chapter titles.
_____ Read the summary, if any.
_____ Read the introductory paragraph, if any.

16. After the class schedule is completed, the programmer asks the computer to determine whether there is another request for a completed schedule. If so, the computer checks the class desired with the list of classes still open. If the class is available, the student's name is added to the class list and the list is reduced by one. Then the schedule is printed and mailed to the student.

_____ The class list is reduced by one.
_____ A class schedule is completed.
_____ The schedule is mailed to the student.
_____ The computer determines that there is another request for a completed schedule.
_____ The schedule is printed.

Read each of the following paragraphs and, in the space provided, answer the questions preceding them.

17. Which words show why they needed to test the cohesion of the democratic powers?

To prepare the way for the final sharp blows that would put their program into effect, the dictatorships—and here we include Japan—needed to consolidate their position strategically and economically. They needed also to test the cohesion of the democratic powers. Three questions must be answered: (1) Would the League of Nations enforce collective security? (2) Would the European democracies support one another? (3) Would the United States come to the aid of the democracies as in 1917?

_____

_____

18. Which words tell why lights are needed on the console and control panel?

It is on the console and control panel that most of the control buttons and flashing lights are located. On election nights, the television cameras are often focused on them in order to give a dramatic effect. The lights help the operator to locate any source of trouble. For example, if something is wrong with the program and the machine stops, the lights (using a standard code) will flash a number indicating at what step in the program the stop occurred.

_____

_____

19. Which words tell why you couldn't have society, as we know it, without agreements?

I've asked you to look at the place agreements have in games because these agreements have the same characteristics as those that operate in the rest of social life. First, they are essential. You couldn't have society as we know it without them. Imagine what your daily life would be like if you and others did not agree on what language to speak and which side of the road to drive on. Agreements are necessary in thousands and thousands of similar instances.

_____

_____

In each of the following statements there is a figurative expression. From among the choices given, decide (1) what things are being compared, and (2) what likeness is being emphasized. Circle the letter to the left of the answer you choose.

20. A vacation does for a person what sharpening does for a knife.

What things are being compared?
a. the effect of a vacation and a person
b. the effect of sharpening a knife and a man
c. a vacation and a knife
d. the effect of a vacation and the effect of sharpening a knife

What likeness is being emphasized?
a. Both are nonproductive.
b. Both happen regularly.
c. Both rejuvenate.
d. Both waste time.

21. A person's reputation is a delicate piece of hand-carved glass.

What things are being compared?
a. a person's reputation and delicate glass
b. a person and his or her reputation
c. a person and glass
d. a person's reputation and good workmanship

What likeness is being emphasized?
a. Both can be seen through.
b. Both are unattractive when dirty.
c. Both are easily shattered.
d. Both are very revealing.

22. His bank account was the windshield wiper of his debts.

What things are being compared?
a. a windshield wiper and debts
b. a bank account and a windshield wiper
c. a bank and debts
d. a bank account and debts

What likeness is being emphasized?
a. Both are kept in storage until needed.
b. Both can be comforting.
c. Both are not used every day.
d. Both clear things away.

Read questions 23 and 24. Then answer them by referring to the graphic material that follows.

23. *a.* What is the capital of Montana?

_____

b. How many cities other than the capital are shown in Texas?

_____

c. According to the map, in which section of the country are most of the cities located?

_____

d. Which is the northernmost capital of the United States?

_____

24. *a.* What is the purpose of this graph?

_____

b. What do the numbers on the left side of the graph represent?

_____

c. Which occupational category has the greatest percentage of people using corrective lenses?

_____

d. Which occupational category has the smallest percentage of people using corrective lenses?

_____

In the following three questions, decide the meaning of each italicized nonsense word by using context and/or structure. Write the meaning in the space provided.

25. When you make an *endelment,* you use knowledge or experience you already have to understand what hasn't been directly stated.

Endelment _____

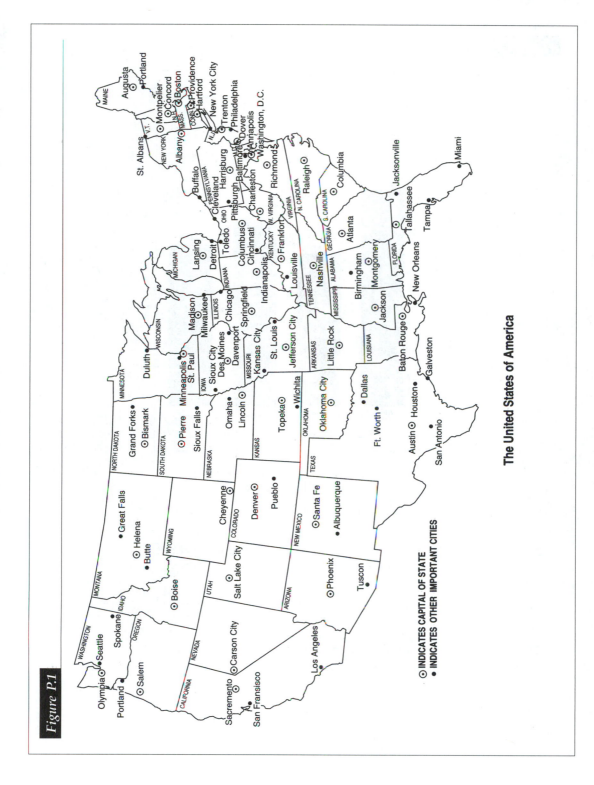

Figure P.1

The United States of America

⊙ INDICATES CAPITAL OF STATE
● INDICATES OTHER IMPORTANT CITIES

9

Figure P.2

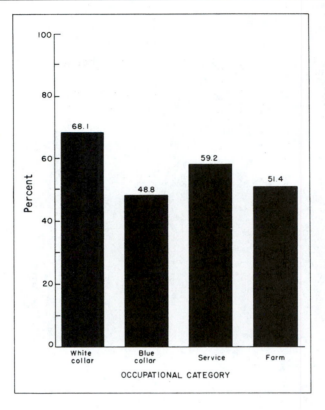

Percent of persons with corrective lenses,
by occupational category

26. Don't *droof.* Stay on the subject you have been talking about.

Droof _____

27. When an instructor (or a student) determines that help in a skill is needed, he can read the rationale and then do as many practice exercises as are necessary to make him *crellacious.*

Crellacious _____

Answer Key

Main Idea

1. We are more inclined to take care of property that we own.

2. A shower is better than a tub.

3. The Homestead Act was supplemented by other acts.

Details

4. It helps develop self-confidence; children learn to cope with greater stress.

5. Business leadership becomes autocratic.

6. To prevent the U.S. from entering the war.

Relationships

7. *a.* example
   b. comparison-contrast
   c. conclusion
   d. conclusion

Study Skills, PQ3R

8. *a.* before reading the chapter

9. *b.* close the book, say the important parts aloud

Organization, Outlining

10. advantages of flying from New York to California
    advantages of driving from New York to California

11. get there faster; a more comfortable trip; arrive feeling less tired

Critical Comprehension

12. *c.* to present information

13. a. nonjudgmental

14. b. matter-of-fact

Following Directions

15. 4, 3, 1, 5, 2

16. 3, 1, 5, 2, 4

Locating Information

17. to prepare the way for the final sharp blows that would put their program into effect . . .

18. . . . help the operator to locate any source of trouble . . .

19. . . . they are essential . . .

Figurative Language

20. d, c

21. a, c

22. b, d

Graphics: Maps, Charts

23. a. Helena
   b. 5
   c. east
   d. Olympia

24. a. to show the percentage of people in different occupational categories who wear corrective lenses
   b. percentage of people
   c. white collar
   d. blue collar

Vocabulary in Context

25. using knowledge or experience you already have, to understand what hasn't been directly stated

26. digress, stray, wander away from the subject

27. proficient, adequate, skilled

Chapter 1

Using Vocabulary in Context

In Chapter 1 you will learn how to improve your vocabulary ability. You will be able to use

- *context clues*
    synonym
    antonym
    example
    definition
    situation
- *structure*
    prefixes
    suffixes
    roots
- *derivation*

Why does true vocabulary improvement seem to take such a long time? Why is it so important anyway? Why is it that memorizing a list of words and their meanings doesn't mean that you really understand them?

Words by themselves are mere marks on a piece of paper or a chalkboard. Meaning is brought to them by people—by you. The meaning you bring to a word depends upon your entire life experience up to the moment that you see it. Thus the same word will have different meanings to different people. Does the word *fire* give you a positive or a negative feeling? Your own background might make you think of a cozy, warm fire in a fireplace while it's snowing outside. Perhaps, though, you recall your house burning down or being "fired" from your job. What would you think of if you read the magazine title *Driving Safely*? You might think of auto safety. On the other hand, your background and life experience could make you think of safety procedures on the golf course.

A major difficulty of written communication is that different people react to the same words in different ways, depending upon the background of the individual reader. Because of this, writers must somehow write in such a way as to make their point clear to all readers. How do they do this? Authors try to use words according to their most commonly understood meaning—that is, the meaning in keeping with the background and experience of most people. They then use *context* to make you more sensitive to the particular meaning. They also draw upon the *structure* of the word (prefixes, suffixes, roots) to make the meaning clearer to you. In addition, you can make yourself more sensitive to word meanings if you are familiar with their *derivations*. These three approaches to the study of words then—context, structure, and derivation—will be most helpful in understanding an author's meaning. Let us examine them in more detail.

CONTEXT

Authors often provide clues to the meaning of words in the context of their writing. If you are made aware of these clues, you will be more likely to notice them in reading. What are these clues to understanding vocabulary through context?

Synonym   Sometimes authors will provide a synonym in the same sentence in which an unknown word is used. The good reader will notice this and use it to help decipher the meaning of the word. What does the word *fallacious* mean in the following sentence? "My opponent's argument is fallacious, misleading—plain wrong." The construction of this sentence suggests that *fallacious* means something similar to the words following it: *misleading, wrong*. Read the following sentence: "A perambulator, or baby carriage, is very useful to mothers of young children." A perambulator is, of course, a baby carriage.

Read each of the following sentences, noticing the words in italics. Then, in the space provided, write the meaning of the word. Use the context only (each is restatement—synonym). Do not refer to a dictionary or other reference book.

   1. His *pertinacity,* or stubbornness, is the cause of most of his trouble.

   _____

   2. The girl was *churlish*—rude, sullen, absolutely ill-mannered.

   _____

The answers are (1) stubbornness and (2) rude or sullen or ill-mannered. Do you see how a synonym for the word in question is given in the context? This is restatement—synonym.

Antonym   Sometimes authors help you understand what they mean by using words that suggest an opposite meaning. Look at the following sentence: "Although some women are loquacious, others hardly talk at all." The context of this sentence (particularly the words *although*, *some*, and *others*) suggests that a loquacious woman is other than silent—that she is talkative. What does *nocturnal* mean in this sentence? "Nocturnal rather than daytime insects are attracted to light." The sense of this sentence suggests that nocturnal insects are nighttime insects.

Read each of the following sentences, noticing the words in italics. Then, in the space provided, write the meaning of the word.

1. The girl who used to be very *vociferous* doesn't talk much anymore.

_____

2. Rather than being involved in *clandestine* meetings, they did everything quite openly.

_____

The answers are (1) talkative and (2) secret. Notice how the meaning is suggested by the opposite sense given in the remainder of the sentence.

Example   Sometimes the unknown word names a group. If several examples from that group are given, the meaning of the unknown word becomes clear.

Celestial bodies such as the sun, moon, and stars. . . .
Piscatorial creatures, including flounder, mackerel, and sturgeon. . . .

Although a celestial body could be many things to one who doesn't know its meaning, the examples make the meaning clear. You may have never heard the word *piscatorial* before, but the the examples leave no doubt that it refers to fish.

Being sensitive to guide words can also help you here. Words such as *for example*, *including*, and *such as* suggest that an example will follow.

Read each of the following sentences, noticing the words in italics. Then, in the space provided, write the meaning of the word.

1. *Pedagogical* institutions, including high schools, kindergartens, and colleges, require community support if they are to function effectively.

_____

2. *Ecclesiastics*, such as priests, ministers, and pastors, should set models of behavior for their congregants.

_____

The answers are (1) having to do with teaching and (2) members of the clergy. Notice the use of guide words in these examples.

Definition   In textbooks or other fact-oriented reading materials, an author will often use an important word, then immediately define it.

> A *tropism* in moths is a tendency to fly toward the light.
> A *pentagon* is a five-sided figure.

Pay close attention to definitions like this; the author is telling you that this word is important and that an understanding of its exact meaning is necessary.

Situation   Often the meaning of an unknown word becomes clear when you examine the situation in which it is used. What does *somnolent* mean in this sentence? "The patient is so somnolent that he requires medication to help him stay awake for more than a short time." Do you see how the sentence tells you that *somnolent* means sleepy?

Read each of the following sentences, noticing the words in italics. Then, in the space provided, write the meaning of the word.

> **1.** He was so *parsimonious* that he refused to give his own sons the few pennies they needed to buy pencils for school. It truly hurt him to part with his money.
>
> _____
>
> **2.** Because the *conflagration* was aided by the wind, it was so destructive that every building in the area was completely burned to the ground.
>
> _____

The answers are (1) stingy and (2) fire. In each sentence the meaning of the word is explained by its context.

Sometimes, of course, an important word appears without any clue to its meaning. In this case you must look it up, either in the textbook's glossary—a list of important words and their meanings—or in a good dictionary. The glossary is the best place to look because there will be just one definition of the word: the one the author intended. Looking in a dictionary requires more care. Since most words have several dictionary definitions, you must be sure to match the definition to the context. Read the following statement.

> Tom was looking forward to his *date* with Sue. He would wear his best blue *suit* and a dark *tie*.

Let's assume that you do not know what the italicized words mean and that you have consulted a dictionary and discovered several possible meanings for each of the words:

date

1. the fruit of a palm tree
2. an appointment
3. a statement specifying a point of time

suit

1. an action in law
2. wearing apparel
3. to please

tie

1. to join together
2. a support to which rails are fastened
3. neckwear

How do you know which of the definitions applies in this particular sentence? The first word, *date*, refers to something that Tom is to share with Sue. He could conceivably look forward to sharing a piece of fruit or a February 15; but the context suggests something more important than a piece of fruit and more specific than a general point of time. Therefore, *an appointment* seems the most plausible choice. What about *suit* and *tie*? The word *wear* makes clear that both words refer to wearing apparel. But even without that clear clue, we would rule out "to please" for *suit* and "to join together" for *tie*, because action words (verbs) would not fit into the sentence (the word *his* signals a noun); we would then rule out "an action of law" and "a support to which rails are fastened" because such things don't belong in the situation described here—a situation in which Tom is looking forward to sharing something with Sue.

Notice that referring to a dictionary is not helpful in itself. The dictionary will supply you with various meanings for the word, but you must then decide which meaning fits the context. To make this decision, use your past experience, the "flow" of the sentence, and any context clues you can apply.

In each of the following sentences, determine the meaning of the word in italics from among the choices given. Circle the number to the left of your choice. In each case, the choices are actual dictionary meanings for the word.

1. His office is his *base* of operation.
   a. the bottom of something
   b. the main ingredient
   c. the locality
   d. a station on a ball field

2. A new class will be *formed* next semester.
  a. to shape
  b. to constitute or make up
  c. to acquire (as a habit)
  d. the appearance of something

The answers are 1(c), the locality, and 2(b), to constitute or make up. Notice how you must choose the correct meaning from among those given by using your knowledge and background and by the logic of the context in which the word appears.

STRUCTURE

Another way to recognize the meaning of an unknown word is to be sensitive to its structure. Understanding word parts gives you power. Knowing just a few prefixes, suffixes, and roots (and using this knowledge in combination with context) opens the door to understanding hundreds, perhaps thousands, of new words. What are these word parts?

Prefixes   Prefixes are syllables attached to a root word to give it a special meaning; they appear at the beginning of the word. *Bi* is a prefix meaning *two*. A *bi*cycle has *two* wheels. To *bi*sect means "to cut into *two* parts." Into how many parts do you divide something which you *tri*sect? How many angles are there in a *tri*angle, and how many children are *tri*plets? The answer to each of these questions is, of course, three.

Can you use the context to help figure out the meaning of *inter* in the following words?

We rested during *intermission*.
Do not *interfere* in the argument.
Do not *interrupt* me.

Did you guess that *inter* means *between*? If so, you are beginning to become sensitive to word meanings.

Suffixes   Suffixes are similar to prefixes except that they appear at the end of a word. *Able* or *ible* means *able*. If one is employ*able,* he or she is able to be employed. If what a child says is believ*able,* it is able to be believed. The suffix *less* means *without.* A person who is hat*less* has no hat. One who is speech*less* cannot speak; and when an astronaut is weight*less,* he or she is without weight.

Roots Roots of words (as the word *root* suggests) are the basic parts of words—"basic" because either they stand alone (*port*) or give vital support to prefixes (*import*) and suffixes (*portable*). The root *cred* means "to believe." When a story has *cred*ence, it can be believed. If it is in*cred*ible, it is unbelievable. Your *creed* is your political or religious belief. When you receive *cred*it, someone believes in you.

Why should you be satisfied learning individual words when learning a word part can teach you six, twelve, sometimes several dozen words? Understanding the meaning of the root *spect* (to see) also teaches you the meaning of *spectator* (one who sees something), *spectacles* (used for seeing), *inspect* (to look into), *specter* (a ghost, a vision), and *introspect* (to look within oneself). Knowing the meaning of the prefix *sub* (under, below, secondary in importance) helps you to understand the meaning of *submarine* (under water), *subordinate* (of secondary rank), and *submerge* (to go under). The power of word parts rests in your ability to combine the roots and affixes (prefixes and suffixes) with the context in which the word is used to develop sensitivity to the author's meaning. If you understand the meaning of *ambular* (walk) and *somn* (sleep) and see the sentence, *The somnambulist had to be locked in his bedroom at night for his own safety,* you will realize that a somnambulist is a sleepwalker.

DERIVATION

Etymology is the derivation or the study of the origins of words. It can also help you to become more sensitive to meanings. When you are aware of original meanings, you may have better understanding of the flavor of a word. Even when a word has changed considerably in meaning through the years, its particular *shade* of meaning often keeps some of the original meanings. This can help you to choose between synonyms when you want to express an idea exactly. It also can help you to understand an author's precise meaning. The word *eccentric,* for example, is derived from a Greek word meaning *away from the center.* This may help you to better understand what is meant by an eccentric person. The word *discover* comes from Latin words meaning *to uncover.* Something that is discovered has always been there but is now brought into open view (is uncovered), such as when a cave or other natural wonder is discovered or when the relationship between lightning and electricity was discovered. Notice that the derivation may help you to see how a discovery is different from an invention (which is created rather than uncovered).

Many of our English words come from Latin or Greek or from Middle English or Old English. Sometimes these words come to us through other languages, such as Old French or Scandinavian. We also get words from many other languages. Your dictionary has a list of abbreviations for the languages referred to in the word entries. Look at this list if you are not sure of the language being referred to. Now look up the derivation of the word *salary* in your dictionary. You will probably notice that it comes from a Latin word meaning *salt*. If you were to investigate further, you would find that Roman soldiers were paid (at least in part) in salt, a valuable commodity in those days.

HOW TO LEARN A VOCABULARY WORD

So you were able to figure out the meaning of that word by using context clues and structure. Now what? How can you make that word part of your usable vocabulary? How can you be sure that you will remember the meaning of the word next time you come across it?

You should consider two things when you try to remember the meanings of words. First, do not try to learn the words in a fixed order. Most people use association to help them remember. If the words are in a fixed order (as in a word list), you tend to learn them in that order. You may forget their meanings. Second, learn the words in context. For the reasons mentioned previously, you cannot learn the meaning of a word unless you see it in relation to other words.

Many individual systems have been worked out for learning words. The following method (which takes into account the two items just mentioned) is suggested as one that the author has found to be almost 100 percent successful among students who followed the directions exactly.

1. Obtain 3″ × 5″ cards. On one side of the card write the word to be remembered in a meaningful phrase or sentence. (A meaningful phrase is one that helps to bring out the meaning of the word.)
2. On the other side of the card write the meaning of the word *as it is used in the phrase or sentence.*
3. When you have made out eight or more cards, do the following once each day, every day, seven days a week. Shuffle the cards as you would a deck of playing cards. *This step is very important because it prevents you from learning the words in a preset sequence.* Then refer to the first side of each card (the one with the word in context). After reading it, try to tell yourself the meaning of the word. Check your answer by turning the card to the other side.
4. Place the cards in two piles—those whose meanings you knew and those whose meanings you didn't know. After going through all of the cards, pick up the pile of cards with words whose meanings you didn't know. Do step 3 again. Redo this step until all of the words are in the pile of cards whose meanings you knew.
5. Do this exercise every day. Do not remove a card from the pile until you know the meaning of the word *the first time* for four days.
6. Try to use the new word that you want to learn at least once a day for a week. You *can* improve your vocabulary. Allow this method to help you.

PREFIXES AND ROOTS

Root or Prefix	Meaning	Example
ab	away (from)	absent
acer, acr	sour, bitter	acrid, acerbity
ad	to, toward	adhere
ambi, amphi	both	ambidextrous, amphibian
ante	before	anteroom
anthropo	man, mankind	anthropoid
anti	against, opposed	antipathy
aqua	water	aquatic
aud	hear	auditory
auto	self	automatic
bene	well, good	beneficial
cede, ceed	go, move	proceed, recede
chron	time	chronological
circum	around	circumference
co, con, com	together, with	cooperate, conspiracy
cogni	know	recognize
counter, contra	against, opposite	counteract, contrary
cred	believe	credential
de	away, down	depart, descend
dent, dont	tooth	dentist, orthodontist
derm	skin	dermatitis
dic, dict	say	dictate
dis	apart, from, away from	distract
duc, duct	lead	aquaduct
ex, e	out (of)	exodus, emit
fid	faith, faithful	fidelity, confident
gamy	marriage	monogamy
graph, gram	write	graphology, telegram
gress	go, move	progress
hyper	over	hyperactive
hypo	under	hypodermic
inter	between	interrupt
man	hand	manicure
mega	big	megaphone
mis	wrong	misbehave
mis	hatred	misanthrope
morph	form, shape	amorphous

Root or Prefix	Meaning	Example
mort	death	mortality
mov, mob, mot	move	mobile, motion
neb	hazy, cloudy	nebulous
non	not	nonadjustable
path	feeling, disease	apathy, psychopath
ped, pod	foot	pedal
pel	push	repel
poly	many	polygamy
port	carry	porter
post	after	postpone
pre	before	preamble
pro	forward	propel
psycho	mind	psychoanalyze
re, retro	again, back	redo, retrospect
rupt	break	rupture
scrib, scrip	write	transcribe, script
sect	cut	dissect
spect	see, look	spectator, inspect
sub	under	submarine
super	over, above	superior, supersonic
syn, sym	with, together	synchronize, symmetry
ten, tain	hold	tenacious, contain
tend	stretch	extend
tort	twist	distort
trans	across	transport
vis, vid	see	visual, video
viv,vit	life	vivacious, vital

PREFIXES OF NUMBER

Prefix	Meaning	Example
uni	one	uniform
mono	one	monologue
du, duo	two	duet
bi	two	biped
tri	three	triangle
tetra	four	tetrameter
quad	four	quadruplets
penta	five	pentagon
quint	five	quintet

Prefix	Meaning	Example
sex	six	sexagenarian
hex	six	hexagon
sept	seven	septet
oct	eight	octopus
nov	nine	novena
dec	ten	decade
cent	hundred	percent
hect	hundred	hectogram
mil	thousand	millimeter
kil	thousand	kilometer
semi	half	semicircle
hemi	half	hemisphere
demi	half	demitasse

SUFFIXES

Suffix	Meaning	Example
able, ible	able to	readable
al	pertaining to	musical
ar, er, or	one who	teacher
ful	full of	hopeful
ic	pertaining to	allergic
ish	like, close to	foolish, twentyish
ist	one who	psychologist
less	without	hatless
logy	study of	cosmetology
ous	full of	cancerous

In Brief

A word can have different meanings; context lets the reader know which meaning the writer intended. Knowing word meanings and how to determine word meanings enables the reader to understand what the author really said.

Context clues help the reader understand the word.

Synonym: Another word with the same meaning appears in the sentence.
Antonym: Another word with the opposite meaning appears in the sentence.
Example: The unknown word names a group. Several items from the group are given, providing a clue to the word's meaning.
Definition: The word is defined.
Situation: The situation being described reveals the word's meaning.

Structure can reveal the meaning of the word.

Prefixes: A word part is attached to the beginning of a word.
Suffixes: A word part is attached to the end of a word.
Roots: This is the main word part. It can function alone or with one or more prefixes or suffixes. Example: *Unrepentantly.*

Derivation, the history of a word, can reveal a more precise meaning of a word.

How to Learn a Vocabulary Word

1. Don't learn the words in a fixed order.
2. Learn the words in context.
3. Learn words by using the six-step method presented on page 21.

Practice Exercises

Exercises A and B are designed to give you practice in finding meanings for words you don't know. But since finding words that nobody knows is impossible, these exercises use invented words, nonsense words. That's not really as strange as its seems. Whenever you see or hear a word you don't know, that word is a nonsense word to you until you find its meaning.

A. In The following passages, decide the meaning of each italicized nonsense word by using context and/or structure. Write the meaning in the space provided. Refer to the list of word parts if you need to.

1. The man and his wife celebrated their *semihectennial* anniversary. After so many years of *fidgamy*, they were very happy.

   Semihectennial _____

   Fidgamy _____

2. *Nebvidious* weather conditions made travel by automobile very difficult. John began to walk but a *pedsect* caused him to limp. After a while a *ruptderm* caused considerable pain. He had to sit down because he felt ill. He wanted to be *exoported*.

   Nebvidious _____

   Pedsect _____

   Ruptderm _____

   Exoported _____

3. Because of the *multimort* he had witnessed, the soldier became a misanthrope. He wanted a *beneviv*, but he could not undo his past. If only he could *retroceed*, things would be different.

   Multimort _____

   Beneviv _____

   Retroceed _____

4. When a person hears a joke, he *gleks*. When he hears sad news, he *slifs*. When he is hungry, he *cloops*, and when he is thirsty, he *radgems* a glass of water.

   Gleks _____

   Slifs _____

Cloops _____

Radgems _____

5. Being successful in college involves more than just sitting in a *gloop.* It involves more than just *runding* in a book. A good student runds hard and then must be able to communicate what he or she has learned. These two elements, runding and *sootuk,* are necessary for success. Without one, the other is inadequate.

Gloop _____

Runding _____

Sootuk _____

6. Don't *circumpel* that food on your plate. If you're finished, *retropel* your chair and *pedgress* to the other room.

Circumpel _____

Retropel _____

Pedgress _____

7. If I had a *chronotender,* I would never be late.

Chronotender _____

8. I was *cognious* of the fact that animals are *polydental,* but recently I was told about a *unidental* animal.

Cognious _____

Polydental _____

Unidental _____

9. Finding a job is a task that most youths face with a mixture of hope, fear, and even bewilderment. However, if they have a good educational background, they are more likely to find what they *gruck.* Attending *blim* certainly helps one in the world of work.

Gruck _____

Blim _____

10. Two communication systems exist in most animals. One of these is the nervous system. It consists of specialized cells, neurons, which transmit electrical impulses

from one part of the body to another. The other is the endocrine *resnic*. It achieves control of body functions through chemical substances, hormones, which are transported throughout the body in the blood. These two systems are not *bolat* of one another. As we will see in this chapter and those that follow, a close connection exists between their activities.

Resnic _____

Bolat _____

Practice Exercises

E. Use the entries in your dictionary to discover (1) the original meaning of each of the words below and (2) the current meaning. The first one is done for you.

		salt	*wages*
1.	Salary		
2.	Admiral		
3.	Alarm		
4.	Alimony		
5.	April		
6.	Atom		
7.	Babble		
8.	Companion		
9.	Comrade		
10.	Daisy		
11.	Eccentric		
12.	Escape		
13.	Fang		
14.	Lady		
15.	Monk		
16.	Mortgage		
17.	Nausea		
18.	Parlor		
19.	Planet		
20.	Pregnant		

Chapter 2

Finding Main Ideas

After you learn about main ideas in this chapter, you will be able to demonstrate

- *where main ideas are found in paragraphs*
- *a specific method for finding main ideas*
    if they are stated in the paragraph
    if they are implied in the paragraph

Perhaps you can recall baking your first cake from scratch. Spread before you were the various ingredients needed—sugar, salt, flour, shortening, milk, eggs, and so on. The thought and the taste of the cake were in your mind. Not one of the ingredients before you gave that thought or taste, yet you knew that if you put everything together correctly, you would have the cake. All of your efforts and all the ingredients would be used for the purpose of coming up with a finished cake. Each ingredient had to relate properly to the cake, or the whole thing would be a flop.

So it is with reading a paragraph. Each sentence in the paragraph is somehow related to the rest of the paragraph. Each sentence contributes to the total meaning. However, you must taste the flavor of the entire paragraph for good meaning and fast speed. If, somehow, you can find the main ideas of paragraphs quickly and efficiently when your purpose in reading is to get "the gist" of the material, you will read faster and with better understanding. How can you do this?

Read the following paragraph to discover its main idea.

Paula waited expectantly for her older brother, Joe, to take her to the circus performance in town. When they arrived she quickly found her seat. She tapped her foot to the music of the circus band. She sat at the edge of the seat as she watched the animal trainer putting wild tigers through their performance. She gaped with open mouth at the trapeze artists. She laughed with glee as the clowns put on their acts. Joe brought her a hot dog and she munched on it delightedly.

Which of the following sentences represents the main idea of the paragraph?

1. Paula went to the circus.
2. Paula enjoyed watching the clowns at the circus.
3. The circus comes to town once a year.
4. The circus band did not play.
5. Paula enjoyed her day at the circus.

Choice *1*, "Paula went to the circus," is *too general*. This paragraph is more specific, being concerned with only one aspect of the circus visit. It omits many aspects of the circus trip—for instance, the mode of transportation or how Paula was dressed. Choice *2*, on the other hand, is *too specific;* "watching the clowns at the circus" is only *one* of the things that Paula enjoyed. Choice *3*, "The circus comes to town once a year," is *irrelevant*. It is Paula's feeling that is being discussed, not the circus itinerary. Choice *4*, "The circus band did not play," is *false*. The paragraph specifically states that Paula tapped her foot to the music of the circus band.

Choice *5* expresses *the main idea*. A main idea should include the major consideration of the author. (Sometimes it will also reflect the author's point of view.) In this paragraph, the major consideration concerns Paula's favorable reaction to the circus.

How do you find the main idea of a paragraph? Sometimes the author is kind enough to actually state it in one sentence of the paragraph. This sentence can be found anywhere in the paragraph, although it is most often found at the beginning or at the end. However, you can't depend on a main-idea sentence. The best way to find a main idea is to ask two questions about the paragraph:

1. *Who or what is this paragraph about? The topic? The subject?* (In our paragraph the answer to this question is *Paula*.)
2. *What does the author want us to understand about the subject, the* who or what? (In our paragraph the author wants us to understand that Paula enjoyed the circus. This, then, is the main idea.)

Use this method in trying to determine the main idea of the following paragraph. Read it carefully with the two questions in mind.

> Not all insects are enemies of man. The silkworm spins threads of silk, which despite the popularity of synthetic fabrics is still an important textile material. In addition to producing beeswax and honey, the honeybee aids us immeasurably by pollinating many of the angiosperms upon whose seeds and fruit we depend for food. Also to be included among man's insect friends are

those species, such as the ladybird beetle and many others, that prey upon our insect enemies and thus help us to keep them under control.

1. *Who or what is this paragraph about? What is the topic?* It is about certain insects.
2. *What does the author want you to understand about certain insects?* The author wants you to understand that certain insects are friends of people. The topic, plus what was said about the topic, makes up the main idea.

In the exercises that follow, you will have the opportunity to practice finding the main ideas in many different types of paragraphs. Remember that each paragraph has one central thought and that it can be stated directly or it can be implied.

In Brief

A paragraph has a unifying idea to which all its sentences relate—the main idea.

Main ideas can be either stated or implied.

A stated main idea is usually found at the beginning or end of the paragraph.

Students skilled at finding main ideas

1. read faster.
2. understand the material better.

Finding Main Ideas

Main ideas consist of two elements: the topic (what the paragraph is about), and a statement about the topic.

These can be discovered by asking two questions:

1. Who or what is this paragraph about? (What's the topic or subject?)
2. What does the author want us to know about the topic? (What is said about the topic?

Because of the millions of travelers who depend on them, transportation workers must be *conscientious* in their work and *pay close attention to detail*. The shopworkers who build and repair railroad cars, for example, must do their work carefully so that cars don't break down while they're in use. Air traffic controllers have to pay strict attention to guide planes safely on their proper course. Long-distance truckdrivers must stay wide awake and concentrate on driving for hours at a time. Sailors, drivers, pilots, and railroad engineers all need to be alert while they're on the job.

For many transportation workers, the ability to keep calm and *work under pressure* is important. Meeting schedules—delivering goods or people on time—is very important in the transportation industry. Yet storms, accidents, traffic tie-ups, and other unexpected situations crop up from time to time. Transportation workers have to be able to think quickly and act decisively in order to get things back on schedule as soon as possible.

An *easygoing personality* is an asset for transportation workers who are in direct contact with the public. Local transit bus and taxicab drivers, for example, must have the patience to deal effectively with passengers—and rude ones as well as pleasant ones—and the steady nerves to drive in all traffic situations. Workers who sell tickets, answer questions, listen to complaints, or try to get new business need to be good at dealing with all kinds of people.

Some transportation workers need the *ability to work as part of a team*. In the merchant marine, for example, cooperation and interaction among the deck, engine, and steward's departments are essential for the "smooth sailing" of the ship. Not only do members of the ship's crew work as a team, but they eat, sleep, and socialize together too.

Others in transportation need to *be able to work independently*. Long-distance truckdrivers may spend days alone on the road. They must organize their time and set a steady speed in order to deliver goods on schedule.

The things that transportation workers do are not necessarily strenuous, but they require *good health and physical stamina*. Baggage attendants, for example, carry and load passengers' luggage on trains, buses, and airplanes. Parking attendants and flight attendants are on their feet and serving customers most of the time. Some jobs may not require much physical activity but demand excellent health just the same. Air traffic controllers, local and long-distance bus and truckdrivers, and locomotive engineers are some examples. These jobs all require workers who are levelheaded and have steady nerves. In many cases workers must pass strict physical exams to enter these occupations.

a. Main idea of entire selection _____

_____

b. Main idea of first paragraph _____

_____

c. Main idea of second paragraph _____

_____

d. Main idea of third paragraph _____

_____

e. Main idea of fourth paragraph _____

_____

f. Main idea of fifth paragraph _____

_____

g. Main idea of sixth paragraph _____

_____

h. Main idea of seventh paragraph _____

_____

Chapter 3

Determining Significant Details

In this chapter you will learn about details in paragraphs. You will be able to

- *distinguish between significant and relatively insignificant details*
- *understand the purpose of details.*

John smiled happily. It was his birthday. To celebrate it, he and his girlfriend Joan were being taken to dinner by his two best friends, Ted and Harry. John and Joan walked the six blocks to the restaurant at the corner of Main and Third. They met the boys and had a delicious dinner. Imagine the embarrassment of Ted and Harry when they found that they didn't have enough money to pay the bill. John had to save the day by chipping in.

There are many details in this little story: the birthday, the celebration planned, the people involved, the distance to the restaurant, the embarrassing incident at the restaurant. Which of these details are significant? Which of them are relatively unimportant? Certainly the fact that the boys didn't have enough money *is* important. The exact location of the restaurant is not important. Why are certain details more important than others? Because some details are necessary to the main point being made, and some details are not. The necessary details are those that help the story line along. Let us examine the following details from the story. Which are important to the story line and which are superfluous?

1. It was John's birthday.
2. He and Joan were being taken to dinner by Ted and Harry.
3. Ted and Harry were John's best friends.
4. Joan was the name of John's girlfriend.
5. It was six blocks to the restaurant.
6. The restaurant was at the corner of Main and Third.
7. The dinner was delicious.
8. The boys didn't have enough money to pay for the meal.
9. John chipped in.

The first three and the last two details are important because they are indispensable to the plot of this particular story. Details 4–7 are minor and incidental to the story; if these details were changed or even eliminated, the basic plot would remain the same.

You must be able to distinguish significant from relatively insignificant details if you are to read effectively. You must recognize that all details are not of equal importance and that if you are to become an efficient reader, you will pay less attention to the less important details and read the more important details carefully and attentively. In other words, knowing the difference between more important and less important details allows you to adjust your rate of reading and your intensity of concentration. It tells you what is important to remember and what doesn't require as much effort. The poor reader gives equal attention to all parts of a selection. The good reader is able to extract the "meat" from the selection and concentrate on it.

Do you try to remember *everything* when you study a chapter? Of course not. You study *selectively,* deciding which material is important and which is not. Being able to distinguish between important and unimportant details helps you to do this. Details are like the parts of a house. Each of the parts helps to make the house what it is. However, some items are absolutely necessary if we are to call it a house. Walls and a roof are absolutely necessary, but whether there are pictures on the walls or green shingles on the roof would not change the picture significantly.

"The Three Bears" is a fable about a girl who enters a cottage owned by three bears while they are away. She eats some of their porridge, breaks one of their chairs, and falls asleep in one of their beds.

In that story, which of the following details is significant?

1. The heroine's name was Goldilocks.
2. The fact that the porridge was too hot caused the bears to leave the house.
3. The chair was too fragile for Goldilocks.
4. The bears' house was a two-story house.

As you have probably guessed, answers 2 and 3 are significant, while 1 and 4 are not. The reason for the three bears' leaving the house is necessary to the story line. So, too, is the fact that the chair was fragile because if it hadn't broken, the chain of events would not have continued. On the other hand, the girl could have had any other name without changing the story line. The fact that the bedroom was on the second floor would also not affect the story line.

Read the following paragraph.

We know now that in the early years of the twentieth century this world was being watched closely by intelligences greater than man's and yet as mortal as his own. . . . Across an immense ethereal gulf minds that are to our minds as ours are to the beasts in the jungle, intellects vast, cool, and unsympathetic, regarded this earth with envious eyes and slowly and surely drew their plans against us.

This paragraph describes certain beings (apparently on some other planet or somewhere in space) who were making plans to harm or destroy the inhabitants of the earth. Which of the details in the paragraph point up the dangerousness of these beings?

1. These beings were more intelligent than humans.
2. They were mortal.
3. They were unsympathetic.
4. They were envious.

The details that spell danger (items *1, 3, 4*) are significant to this paragraph because they carry along the main thought of the paragraph—the possible threat to humanity. Certainly the statement "These beings were more intelligent than man" helps the reader to realize the danger because the enemy can outwit people. The fact that these beings were unsympathetic and envious helps the reader to realize the danger because these qualities suggest possible aggression against people. However, the fact that the watchers were mortal does *not* help us to recognize danger. If they were *not* mortal and had the above attributes, they would still be dangerous.

The following practice exercises are designed to help you become more aware of the significance of certain details. In order to be successful at finding these details, you must ask yourself which details help further the story line or are pertinent to the main idea. Do each exercise carefully.

In Brief

Some details are more important or significant than others.
To determine significant details, do the following:

1. Decide which details help to further the story line.
2. Decide which details help you understand the main idea.

More attention should be given to the important details.
Giving attention to involves changes in

1. rate
2. concentration

Giving more attention to certain details results in better recall of those details.

REPETITION

Sometimes writers try to help you understand their point by saying it in different words. They provide a REPETITION of their idea, usually in brief, easier-to-understand language. Read the following groups of sentences:

1. I wish you would discontinue constantly annoying me. Please stop calling me on the phone, writing letters to me, and waiting for me when I leave my place of work. In other words, please stop bothering me.
2. Just because there are laws prohibiting murder doesn't mean that there are never any situations where one is not justified in committing murder. What I am really trying to say is that sometimes it is permissible to kill someone.

In *1* above, the main idea is stated in the first sentence. This is followed by examples of the point and finally, in the last sentence, a REPETITION of the main idea. In *2*, the second sentence is a REPETITION of the first.

You may occasionally find it difficult to decide whether a particular relationship is example or repetition. One hint may help. Recall the idea of a thought being a pie, suggested in the last chapter. In EXAMPLE, the author zeroes in on a piece of pie. In REPETITION, he repeats the entire pie.

Look at the following two lists. Decide whether the item in column B is an EXAMPLE of the idea on the same line in column A or a REPETITION of it. Write your answer in the space provided.

A	**B**
1. The states in the United States	_____ Wisconsin
2. The states in the United States	_____ All fifty states
3. The sexes	_____ Males
4. My parents	_____ My mother and father
5. My parents	_____ My mother

You should have written EXAMPLE on the first line. Wisconsin is a piece of the pie, an example of just one of the fifty states. The second line, however, is REPETITION. *The states in the United States* and *all fifty states* refer to the same idea. Lines 3 and 5 are EXAMPLE. *Males* refer to just one of the sexes, and *my mother* would refer to only one of my parents. Line 4, on the other hand, is REPETITION because it refers to both parents.

The following sentence is followed by four statements. Write *E* in the space provided if the statement is EXAMPLE and *R* if it is REPETITION.

Some TV programs are educational.

_____ In other words, you can learn things by watching certain TV programs.

_____ *Sesame Street* is an educational program.

_____ A college TV course is educational.

_____ Certain programs on TV provide educational experiences.

The second and third sentences are examples. They specifically mention some of the TV programs that are educational. (They are a piece of the pie.) The first and fourth sentences are repetition. They repeat the whole idea in the same general terms as the lead sentence. They are not specific.

CAUSE-EFFECT

In CAUSE-EFFECT, writers refer to the idea that one thing happened or came about only because something else happened or came about first. One thing occurred as a result of something else occurring. Read the following groups of sentences:

1. It is raining outside. The ground is getting wet.
2. Professor X is very boring. Because of this, few people like his class.
3. Courses in African-American history are being offered in many schools. As a result, more people than ever before appreciate the African-American's contribution to society.

In *1* above, the ground is getting wet as a result of the rain. The second thing happened because the first thing happened. It is CAUSE-EFFECT. Sentence 2 is also CAUSE-EFFECT for the same reason. So is 3. The cause-effect relationship is really the reverse of explanation. That is, if you turned the order around, you would have explanation. Look at *1* above. Turn the sentences around. The ground is getting wet. Why? Because it is raining outside (EXPLANATION). Cause-effect has the sense of *because of this*. . . . Explanation has the sense of *this is because*. . . . Try to reverse 2 and 3 above. It will help you understand this concept better.

In the following groups of sentences, determine whether the relationship is EXPLANATION or CAUSE-EFFECT. Write your answer in the space provided.

1. He was late to work three days in a row. He was fired.

   _____

2. He was sick all night. He had eaten food that didn't agree with him.

   _____

3. Her car stopped running. She was out of gas.

_____

4. She ran out of gas. Her car stopped running.

_____

Do you understand why *1* and *4* are CAUSE-EFFECT and *2* and *3* are EXPLANATION?

CONCLUSION

Sometimes authors will offer a conclusion. Simply stated, a CONCLUSION is a guess or an opinion. Even if it's dressed up with words like *inference, theory*, or *hypothesis*, a CONCLUSION means that the author is guessing. Read the following groups of sentences.

1. It's raining outside. The ground will probably become soaked.
2. Jim spends most of his spare time listening to the musical group called the Brothers. He spends most of his money buying their records. He certainly must enjoy their music.
3. Roslyn has been studying very hard in her science course. She should take a break.

In *1* above, the second sentence talks about what will *probably* happen. This looks like a cause-effect relationship, but the author uses a "maybe" word to let you know he is guessing. Maybe words, such as *maybe, perhaps, can, might*, and *probably*, indicate that the relationship is a CONCLUSION. In *2* above, the relationship is more subtle, but it's still given as a guess. If the sentence had stated, "Jim *enjoys* their music," it would be reporting fact. But since it uses "certainly must," we know that the author is guessing. In *3* above, the second sentence gives an opinion. The writer thinks that Roslyn should take a break. Others, including Roslyn herself, could have a different opinion. "Opinion" words, such as *should, best, good*, and *ugly*, let you know that the relationship is a CONCLUSION.

Examine *1* again. If we remove the maybe word, the second sentence reads, "The ground will become soaked." It sounds factual, but it's still a guess; we don't *know* that the ground will become soaked, because nobody knows the future. Whenever a relationship extends into the future, the author is guessing and the relationship is a CONCLUSION.

Read the following sentences to determine whether the relationship is CAUSE-EFFECT or CONCLUSION. (Remember that CAUSE-EFFECT is something you're sure of, whereas CONCLUSION is a guess or opinion.) Write *CE* in the space provided if it is CAUSE-EFFECT and *CN* if it is CONCLUSION.

_____ Jerry has become very busy in the past few weeks. As a result, he doesn't see his friends as often as before.

_____ Sarah just got a job in addition to her other responsibilities. You won't get to see her as much as you used to.

The first sentence is CAUSE-EFFECT. Do you see that the second thing happened as an outcome of the first thing? Sentence 2 should have been answered CONCLUSION. It is an opinion, a guess that you won't get to see her as often.

As in the last chapter, the thought relationships discussed in this chapter can often be recognized by signposts. Some of the more significant ones are as follows:

definition: *by . . . I mean*
repetition: *in other words*
cause-effect: *because of this, as a result, consequently*
conclusion: *perhaps, good, will*

Although they can be helpful, it is important not to be misled by the guide words. It is the *thought pattern* that determines the relationship. What is the writer really trying to say? In understanding the difference between cause-effect and conclusion, for example, it is the existence or nonexistence of a sense of probability that should guide you to a decision. The guide words could be the same.

Once again, as you do the following exercises, try to discover the relationships of *ideas* as well as the signposts to help you better understand the writer's message.

study. And the best way to study is to make your own outline or concept map from their material.

Making your own outline or map of the material you need to learn helps you in three ways: (1) You will understand the material better. (2) You will spend less time studying. (3) You will have handy material to review later.

Besides helping you study, becoming skilled at outlining or mapping helps you take class lecture notes. You can distinguish quickly between main points and supporting material, between new material and repetition. This means less writing and better notes.

OUTLINING AND MAPPING

Outlining and mapping are two different ways to do the same job. Both systems take the author's ideas and put them on paper where they can be seen. But they don't just list the ideas; they show how these ideas relate to each other—how many main points there are, and which details go with each main point. Outlining and mapping show all the ideas of the original, but they eliminate many of the words. An outline presentation of this paragraph would look like this:

Outlining and Mapping

> *I.* Ways of representing an author's ideas on paper
>   *A.* Outlining
>   *B.* Mapping

Notice how the outline organizes the ideas and eliminates most of the words.

Both outlining and mapping show the same ideas and the same interrelationships. OUTLINING, as you know, uses indentation to show relationships, then adds Roman numerals, capital letters, and Arabic numerals, like this:

Title

> I. Major Idea
>   A. Detail
>   1. Support

In an outline, details are listed under the appropriate main idea, then indented to show that they are part of the idea directly above them.

MAPPING uses circles or other shapes and shows relationships by the size of the shapes and the lines connecting them, like this:

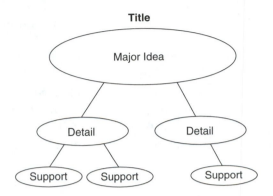

Unlike an outline, the map has no "correct" place to put information. In one map, the title could be in the center of the page, with the major ideas in a starburst arrangement around it. In another, the major ideas could be arranged down the left side of the paper, similar to an outline. A third map arrangement, such as a time line, could have the major ideas marching across the page. The details for these maps can be in any arrangement, just so their shapes are smaller than the major idea shapes and have a line connecting them to the right major idea.

The same major ideas, details, and support will appear in both outlining and mapping. An outline with three major ideas will have three Roman numerals. A map with three major ideas will have three large circles (or rectangles, or whatever shape you choose.) The Roman numerals or large circles, along with their information, are called headings, and referred to as the first level. An outline or map with no details, just a title and some headings, is called a one level outline or map.

So which is a better system, outlining or mapping? It depends. Some people are familiar with outlining and don't want to learn a new system. For them, outlining is better. Others have had bad experiences with outlining and want something new. And some find that they can see the overall structure of the material more clearly with a map. These people will choose mapping.

But choosing isn't all personal preference; each system has its own advantages. Since there is no fixed placement of material in mapping, information can be added to a completed map more easily than to an outline. If you map a textbook chapter, then find additional material in a lecture or outside reading, adding to the map is simply a matter of drawing another line and circle. Adding to an outline, in contrast, means rewriting the entire thing. On the other hand, almost everyone, including instructors and employers, understands and accepts outlines, a statement that cannot be made about concept maps. So which method will you choose? Many people use both, first roughing out ideas on a map, then making a finished outline.

WHAT IS ORGANIZING?

Organizing is simply putting ideas that are alike into groups, with a heading to identify the group. These groups are then written down so they can be referred to later.

Look at the following list of items: *apple, hot dog, hamburger, spinach, peach, carrot, plum, steak, corn.* If you had to divide them into three groups, which items would you keep together? Did you put *apple, peach,* and *plum* in one group? Did you put *hot dog, hamburger,* and *steak* in another, and *spinach, carrot,* and *corn* in another? If you did, you have just organized the material. Now try dividing the following items into three groups: *dog, robin, cow, salmon, eagle, trout, dove, horse, whitefish.* Write the three groups of items in the spaces provided.

_____   _____   _____

_____   _____   _____

_____   _____   _____

(Be sure to do the exercise before reading on.)

Did you put *dog, cow,* and *horse* together? Were the other two groups *robin, eagle, dove* and *salmon, trout, whitefish*? Once again, you have organized the material. How did you do this? What must you have understood in order to have organized the groups correctly? You must have realized that certain of the creatures listed have something in common with one another. You must have understood that three of them are birds (or at least flying creatures), that three are fish (or at least creatures that live in water), and that three are land animals. In the first groups you must have understood that the categories are fruits, meats, and vegetables. You had to understand these relationships before you could group them. In other words, you had to understand how big ideas and little ideas related to one another. Is it difficult to make an outline or map? It can be when you work with difficult-to-understand textbooks, but you can learn to outline more easily if you follow the steps suggested in this chapter.

HOW TO ORGANIZE INFORMATION

When you wish to organize a chapter in a textbook for outlining or mapping, do the following:

Try to discover the most important idea. In textbooks this has usually been done by the author—it's the chapter title. This chapter title becomes the title of your outline or map. If you would rather reword the title or write it as a thesis statement, do so.

Look at the following list of words. Which item includes all of the other items? *Shirts, coats, articles of clothing, shoes, dresses, hats.* Do you understand why *articles of clothing* is the correct answer? If you do, you have taken a first step toward being a skilled outliner or mapper. Now take the next step. Think in exact terms. Read the following list: *aunts, sisters, mothers, wives, grandmothers.* Think about a term that would include all of those terms. Now, which of the following terms would most exactly include every one of the above: *females, young girls, people, human beings?* The correct answer is *females. Young girls* is incorrect because we can reasonably assume that *grandmothers* will not fit that category. (It is likely that mothers and wives do not either.) Everyone on the list could be included in the two remaining categories, *people* and *human beings.* However, *men* and *little boys* could also fit this category. *Females* is more exact. It describes the terms more precisely. It is essential when you look for important or major ideas that you describe them as precisely as you can.

Try to discover how the author develops or subdivides the most important idea.   Frequently, the author has done your work for you by dividing the chapter into sections with *headings.* These headings, or the ones you compose, become the major headings of your outline or map.

Sometimes authors will develop their main point chronologically. They will tell about the early years of a person's life, then the middle years, and finally the later years. These, then, are your major headings. Sometimes authors will enumerate. They may talk about three reasons or four methods or six advantages. This again is a clue to your major headings. Sometimes they use cause-effect relationships (as in the discussion of a war in a history book or an experiment in a chemistry book). Sometimes they go from general to specific or from specific to general or from easy to difficult or from known to unknown. Sometimes they use comparison-contrast. Although this is not an all-inclusive list, these are the major ways in which authors develop their topics. To review briefly, these ways are chronological order, enumeration, cause-effect, general to specific, specific to general, easy to difficult, known to unknown, and comparison-contrast. When you can discover these relationships the difficulties of outlining and mapping melt before you and understanding becomes easy.

Which of these methods is used to develop the topic in the following paragraph?

There are six factors that contribute to a good memory. First, there is *association.* When you associate, you make ideas belong to one another—you relate them in some way. The second factor that contributes to a good memory is *visualization.* When you visualize, you try to form pictures in your mind of what you wish to remember. If you can create a strong, intense picture, then all you need do is recreate that picture when you wish to remember the information. Visualization also forces you to practice the next item, which is *concentration.* What is concentration? It is the ability to focus attention on one thing, thus eliminating attention to anything else. Learning to concentrate forces you to pay attention to what you want to remember. The fourth factor is *repetition*. Repeat information that you wish to remember by saying it over and over in your mind. This will help you to overlearn it, thus helping memory. The next factor in memory improvement is *intensity of impression*. You should realize that the more vividly, the more intensely the information is presented to you, the longer you will remember it. Seeing movies of how people lived in eighteenth-century England helps you to remember this information longer than if you just read about it. Witnessing or being involved in an accident helps you to remember the details longer than if you read about it. The last factor in memory improvement is the realization that *we tend to remember longest those things that we see first*. You may have heard the expression about first impressions lasting longest. This is probably related to two of the other items. The first idea that you come across when you study probably comes to you more intensely because your mind is uncluttered. For the same reason, you will probably concentrate better.

Before answering the question, let us do Step 1 first. What is the main thought in this paragraph? Your answer should make the point that there are six factors that contribute to a good memory. Which of the techniques mentioned does the author use to develop the information given? Your answer should be *enumeration*. The author numbered, named, and spoke briefly about each memory factor in turn.

If you chose to use outlining to organize the ideas in the preceding excerpt, your outline's first level might look like this:

Factors Contributing to a Good Memory

    I. Association
   II. Visualization
  III. Concentration
  IV. Repetition
   V. Intensity of impression
  VI. First impressions are long lasting

If you chose to map the concepts, your map's first level might look like Figure 6.1.

Figure 6.1

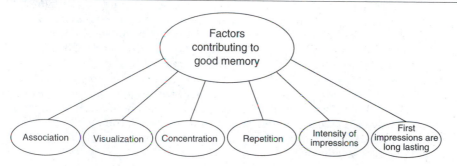

Try this exercise once more. Read the following paragraph to discover the technique the author uses for developing his point.

> I was born to very poor parents in the middle of a city ghetto teeming with people. Even when I was very young I was conscious of all the people around me. I played in the street on a block that must have contained 300 kids. At five I began to do odd jobs for whatever I could earn. At six, I was sent to school, but I hated it and couldn't wait for each school day to end. When I was nine, I had all sorts of after-school jobs until I quit school at sixteen. Then I worked full-time as a helper in a restaurant. At twenty I joined the Navy. For the first time in my life I felt uncrowded. When I left the Navy, I didn't want to go back to what I had run away from. Also, I realized for the first time what training could do for me. I enrolled in a school for barbers and graduated at 25. I also married that same day. At 30, after working as a barber for five years, I opened another shop, and still another two years after that. By the time I was 40 I had a string of twelve shops. Today, as I celebrate my sixtieth birthday, I think fondly of my four sons, who are managing the shops.

The main point of this paragraph concerns a man who became successful after overcoming a background of poverty and little education. Which technique does the author use? Notice how chronological order is used to develop the point. This, then, is the basis for the headings of your outline or map.

Try to discover the author's details. How does he or she develop major ideas? Which ideas are given the most attention? These are ordinarily clues to what the author thinks is important or complicated and in need of more detailed explanation. Always connect these details to the major points that they explain or develop. It is very important not to allow the detail to become a fact by itself, but to connect it instead to some major point. Read the following paragraph. Try to discover the title, the three major ideas, and the details related to them. Write these items in the spaces provided in the outline and in the concept map (see Figure 6.2).

> There are three major kinds of programs offered in the junior or community college. One kind is the terminal program. Among the purposes of this program is to prepare students for a career or a job, to train students in particular skills, or to provide organized general education beyond high school. Then there is the college transfer program. This program provides the courses required for the first two years of college. It also helps to relieve the congestion and need for added facilities for the freshman and sophomore years at the four-year college. The third kind of program is the community service program. Two major purposes of this program are to provide community special-interest courses for adults and to train students in particular skills needed by local business or industry.

Title _____

    I. (First major idea) _____

        A. (Detail) _____

        B. (Detail) _____

        C. (Detail) _____

    II. (Second major idea) _____
        A. (Detail) _____

        B. (Detail) _____

    III. (Third major idea) _____
        A. (Detail) _____

        B. (Detail) _____

Figure 6.2

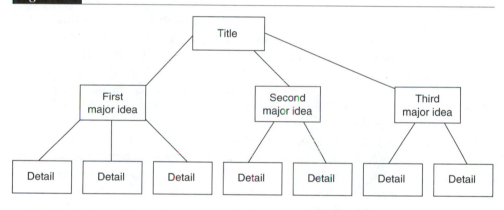

As you can see from the outline and concept map, the details make up the second level, so an outline or map with a title, some headings, and some details is called a two level outline or map.

(Be sure to do the exercise before reading on.)

    What did you say was the title? A correct response would focus on the statement that there are three kinds of programs in many junior or community colleges. What are the major ideas? You should have noted the three kinds of programs (terminal, transfer, and community service) and should have written them in the correct spaces. How should the spaces provided for details have been filled in? Under "terminal programs," you should have mentioned preparing students for careers or jobs, training students in particular skills, and providing organized general education beyond high school. Under "transfer programs," you should have mentioned providing needed courses for the first two years of college and relieving congestion and the need for more facilities at the four-year college. Under "community service programs," your details should have included providing adult special-interest courses and training students in skills to meet business or industry needs.

You may not have been able to do this last exercise well. Do not be concerned. The exercises following this chapter will take you to this level of skill in easy-to-understand steps. Before going on to these exercises, however, it is important to talk about notation in outlining and hierarchy in mapping.

NOTATION IN OUTLINING AND HIERARCHY IN MAPPING

Skill in outlining and mapping depends upon an ability to understand how ideas are related to one another. Once you can do that, you will probably find it quite easy to learn the notation symbols and their relative ranking positions. Following are some of the important points that you should understand about notation for outlining and hierarchical arrangement in mapping.

The importance of an idea determines its placement.   In outlining, the more important an idea is, the closer to the left you should place it. You should place the most important ideas (the major ideas) closest to the left-hand margin of the page. Also, in order to follow the standard system for notation, you should assign a roman numeral to these major ideas. In other words, the most important ideas are placed farthest to the left as headings and are notated I, II, III, and so on. These make up your first level of ideas.

You should place the next most important ideas—the details that explain or develop the headings—to the right and below the headings, and you should notate them with capital letters (A, B, C, etc.). These make up your second level of ideas.

You should place the support material, or lesser ideas that explain or develop the details, to the right and below these details, and you should notate them with arabic numbers (1, 2, 3). These make up your third level of ideas.

Most outlines need not go beyond this third level of ideas. If you must do so, however, as in very complicated or highly developed outlines, less important ideas are placed below and to the right and are notated

    a.

       (1)

         (a)

In making a concept map, the ranking of ideas is also important. An outline is a linear sequence of major ideas and details, whereas a map is a more horizontal arrangement. This horizontal ranking of ideas results in a hierarchical pattern that is easy to follow and remember.

In the typical map, major ideas are reduced to key words or phrases, then are put into large boxes or circles arranged left to right across the top of the page. Details are shown in smaller shapes and are linked to the major ideas by lines or arrows. These lines or arrows are sometimes labeled with a word or phrase to explain the relationship. The details form the second level of the hierarchy. Support material is written in still smaller shapes and linked to the appropriate detail with lines. This support material makes up the third level of the hierarchy.

As in outlining, most maps do not exceed the third level. If there is a need to do so, less important ideas are shown by still smaller boxes, with additional branching.

Read the following list: *aunts, sisters, females, mothers, wives*. Which term should be placed farthest to the left? What should its notation be? The term *females* is the major idea here in the sense that it includes the remaining terms. You should have placed it farthest to the left, and you should have assigned the notation I to it. When outlined, it should look like this:

I. Females

    A. Aunts

    B. Sisters

    C. Mothers

    D. Wives

When mapped, it should look like Figure 6.3.

Figure 6.3

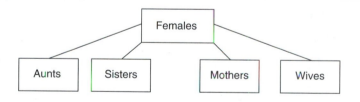

Now read the following list and outline it in the spaces provided: *aunts, uncles, sisters, females, brothers, males, mothers, fathers, wives, husbands*.

I. _____

    A. _____

    B. _____

    C. _____

    D. _____

II. _____

    A. _____

    B. _____

    C. _____

    D. _____

If you organized this correctly, you would have realized that *female* is once again the first major idea. It should have been placed next to I. You should have placed the items that name females under I, next to the capital letters (A, B, C, D). You also should have realized that the term *males* is the second major idea. You should have placed it next to II. Then you should have placed the items that name males under II, next to the capital letters (A, B, C, D). The completed outline should look like this:

    I. Females

        A. Aunts

        B. Sisters

        C. Mothers

        D. Wives

    II. Males

        A. Uncles

        B. Brothers

        C. Fathers

        D. Husbands

A concept map could take one of the forms shown in Figure 6.4.

All ideas of the same importance should have equal prominence. In other words, in an outline you should begin all major ideas (headings with Roman numerals assigned to them) farthest to the left. You should begin all details (ideas having capital letters assigned to them) in the column to the right of the headings, and you should begin all support material (ideas having lower-case letters assigned to them) in the column to the right of the details. If you think about this for a moment you will realize that in an outline, any stated idea is smaller than and part of, or a development of, any stated idea that is above it and to the left of it. It is equal to any stated idea that has an equal rank or

Figure 6.4

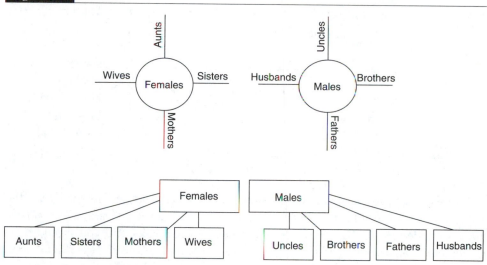

indentation (whether above or below it) and is a bigger idea than any idea that is stated to the right of it (whether it is above or below it).

The same system of ranking ideas holds true when making a map. The size of the box (or chosen shape) differentiates the most important ideas and the major and minor details. These different sized boxes form the basis for the ranking of ideas. The major ideas are shown in a left-to-right sequence (in order of occurrence) across the page, forming the top level of the hierarchy. Details follow in smaller boxes and under the appropriate major idea box. Support is next, in still smaller boxes placed under the appropriate details.

Figure 6.5

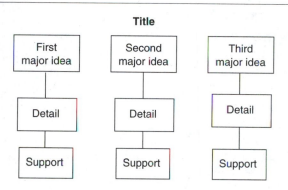

Examine the following list of items. In the space to the left of each one, mark I if it should be ranked as a roman numeral, mark A if it should be ranked as a capital letter, and mark 1 if it should be ranked as an arabic number.

_____ Uncle Joe	_____ Sister Jean	_____ sisters
_____ Sister Rose	_____ Aunt Paula	_____ aunts
_____ males	_____ females	_____ Uncle Marty
_____ Sister Lucy	_____ fathers	_____ brothers
_____ mothers	_____ Uncle Abe	_____ Aunt Sarah
_____ wives	_____ husbands	_____ uncles
_____ Brother Harry	_____ Brother Tim	

You should have marked two items with a *I* (*males, females*) because they are the major ideas. You should have marked eight items with an *A* (*mothers, wives, fathers, husbands, sisters, aunts, brothers, uncles*) because they are details, and you should have marked ten items with a *1* (*Uncle Joe, Sister Rose, Sister Lucy, Brother Harry, Sister Jean, Aunt Paula, Uncle Abe, Brother Tim, Uncle Marty, Aunt Sarah*) because they are support material. Now use the same items to finish the partially completed outline below.

I. Males

   A. _____

       1. _____

       2. _____

       3. _____

   B. _____

       1. _____

       2. _____

   C. _____

   D. _____

II. _____

   A. Aunts

       1. _____

       2. _____

   B. _____

       1. _____

       2. _____

3. _____

C. Mothers

D. _____

Use the same information to complete the map in Figure 6.6.

Figure 6.6

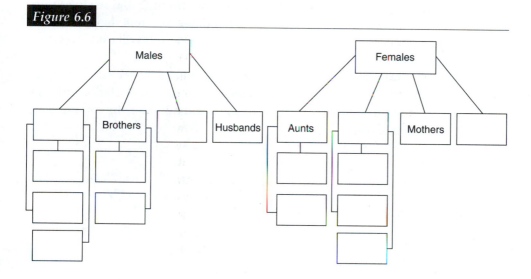

Items in an outline or map should balance. In organizing the above material, there is no reason to list *uncles* first under *males*. The outline or map would have been correct with *fathers, husbands,* or *brothers* first. But once the pattern is set for one major idea, the other major idea must follow that pattern. If *husbands* is the first detail under *males*, then *wives* must be the first detail under *females*. This balance, or parallel structure, makes the ideas easier to understand and remember.

You may write items in an outline as either phrases or sentences, but the entire outline should be one or the other. In other words, don't mix phrases and sentences in the same outline.

Always capitalize the first word of each item in an outline.

Always place a period after each notation symbol (numbers and letters) in an outline. In concept maps, key words and phrases are used within the geometric shapes, without regard for capital letters and punctuation (except for proper names).

These are the most important rules for outlining and mapping. Remember, the main purpose of outlining and mapping is to help you understand how an author or a speaker has organized a book or a speech. Used this way, both methods will help you study effectively and will provide you with better and faster understanding.

Many exercises in organizing information follow this skill-development presentation. Do them carefully. They will—in gradual, easy-to-difficult steps—provide you with an opportunity to develop the skill of outlining and/or mapping. Learning this skill can be difficult. You must take time, you must have patience, you must put forth effort, and above all *you must practice*. You will find, however, that it's worth the effort.

Following is an outline based on the information contained in the discussion in Chapter 1, Using Vocabulary in Context. Notice the use of the notation rules as they are described in the summary below. Use it as a model to help you improve your own outlining skills.

Using Vocabulary in Context

    I. Nature of word meanings

   II. Approaches to improving word meanings

      A. Context

        1. Synonym

        2. Antonym

        3. Example

        4. Definition

        5. Situation

      B. Structure

        1. Prefixes

        2. Suffixes

        3. Roots

      C. Derivation

Notice how the same information is organized in a concept map (Figure 6.7). You can use this as a model to help you improve your mapping skills.

Figure 6.7

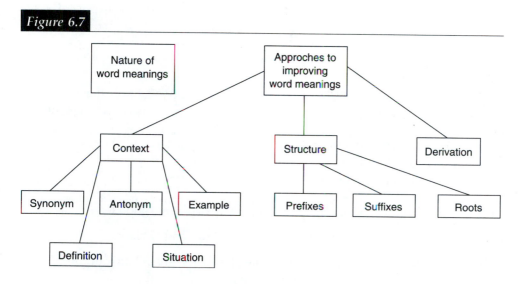

In Brief

Outlining and mapping give a visual representation of a writer's ideas and their interrelationships. Making an outline or map has certain benefits:

1. You understand the material better.
2. You save study time.
3. You have good review material.

Becoming skilled at outlining or mapping helps you take good lecture notes.

Outlining shows organization by (1) indentation, and (2) labels.

Mapping shows organization by (1) the size of the shape surrounding the idea, and (2) the lines that connect the shapes.

Outlining has two advantages: (1) You already know the system. (2) Most people accept it.

Mapping has two advantages: (1) Information with shapes is easier to remember. (2) The overall structure (organization of the material) is easier to see.

How to Organize Information

1. Find the most important idea (title).
2. Find the subdivisions (headings). Relate them to the title.
3. Find the details. Relate them to the headings.

Notation in Outlining and Hierarchy in Mapping

The importance of an idea determines—
In outlining: how far to indent, and the notation to use.
In mapping: the size of the shape surrounding the idea.
Ideas of equal importance should be placed—
In outlining: on the same level of indentation.
In mapping: inside boxes or circles of the same size.
Parallel structure (balance) should be maintained in both outlining and mapping.
In outlining: Don't mix phrases and sentences. Capitalize the first word in each item. Place a period after each notation symbol.

Practice Exercises

A. Each of the following lists represents a particular topic. Decide what the topic is and write it in the space provided. You may not be familiar with items in some of the lists. Check these in an encyclopedia or a dictionary. The first one is done for you.

1. **Countries**
   Holland
   Japan
   Brazil
   Greece
   Argentina

2. _____
   Toyota
   Buick
   Chrysler
   Oldsmobile
   Datsun

3. _____
   Pies
   Cakes
   Bread
   Cookies
   Brownies

4. _____
   Elm
   Redwood
   Maple
   Spruce
   Birch

5. _____
   Horse
   Cow
   Cat
   Goat
   Dog

6. _____
   Hudson
   Congo
   Rio Grande
   St. Lawrence
   Yangtze

7. _____
   Noun
   Verb
   Adverb
   Adjective
   Pronoun

8. _____
   College
   High school
   Elementary school
   University
   Junior high school

9. _____
   Living room
   Dining room
   Kitchen
   Bedroom
   Bathroom

10. _____
   Rain
   Snow
   Tornado
   Hurricane
   Sleet

11. _____

    Tin
    Copper
    Nickel
    Cobalt
    Zinc

12. _____

    Trombone
    Clarinet
    Harp
    Organ
    Cello

13. _____

    Prime Minister
    President
    Chancellor
    Czar
    King

14. _____

    Chemistry
    Biology
    Zoology
    Physics
    Astronomy

15. _____

    Dollar
    Pound
    Shilling
    Mark
    Yen

16. _____

    New York
    Nevada
    California
    Georgia
    Maine

17. _____

    Doctor
    Lawyer
    Engineer
    Musician
    Architect

18. _____

    Alexander Graham Bell
    George Washington
    Marie Curie
    Napoleon Bonaparte
    Sigmund Freud

19. _____

    Smell
    Taste
    Touch
    Sight
    Hearing

20. _____

    Jungle drums
    Smoke signals
    Semaphores
    Hand signals
    Magazines

Practice Exercises

B. For each of the lists in Part II, find the topic in Part I that describes it most exactly. (Although more than one topic in Part A may fit a particular list, only one will fit it most accurately.) Write your answer in the space provided. You may not be familiar with items in some of the lists. Check these in an encyclopedia or a dictionary. The first one is done for you.

Part I

Animals
Carpenter's tools
Clothing
Domestic animals
Famous people
Female names

Inventors
Measurements
Measurements of length
Measurements of volume
Names of people
Technical terms

Terms used in chemistry
Terms used in science
Tools
United States presidents
Wild animals
Women's clothing

Part II

1. __*Women's clothing*__
   Dress
   Skirt
   Woman's jacket
   Blouse
   Pantyhose

2. _____
   Mary
   Sue
   Agatha
   Roslyn
   Margaret

3. _____
   Plane
   Wrench
   Hammer
   Electric drill
   Electric sander

4. _____
   Jack
   Helen
   Anna
   Dick
   Kenneth

5. _____
   Jefferson
   Monroe
   Truman
   Cleveland
   Kennedy

6. _____
   Thomas Edison
   Alexander Graham Bell
   Eli Whitney
   James Watt
   Samuel Morse

7. _____

    Bobcat
    Jaguar
    Horse
    Cobra
    Bear

8. _____

    Pint
    Quart
    Dram
    Ounce
    Gallon

9. _____

    Millimeter
    Bushel
    Ton
    Gram
    Liter

10. _____

    Hydrolysis
    Meteor
    Leukocytes
    Metabolism
    Atom

Practice Exercises

C. To the right of the items below are lines *showing* three different levels of indentation or ranking of ideas. Copy each of the items and show how they relate to each other by indenting them at the correct level of indentation. All items are in the proper order. Some lists require two levels of indentation while others require three levels. Following each listing is a map that shows how the ranking of the same information can be represented in a different way. If you are not familiar with an item, check it in an encyclopedia or a dictionary. The first listing and map are completed for you.

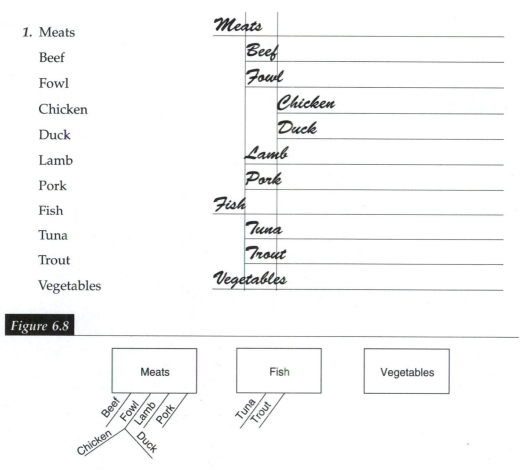

1. Meats
   Beef
   Fowl
   Chicken
   Duck
   Lamb
   Pork
   Fish
   Tuna
   Trout
   Vegetables

Meats
  Beef
  Fowl
    Chicken
    Duck
  Lamb
  Pork
Fish
  Tuna
  Trout
Vegetables

Figure 6.8

| Meats | Fish | Vegetables |

Beef · Fowl · Lamb · Pork · Chicken · Duck

Tuna · Trout

2. Famous painters
   Da Vinci
   Goya

Rembrandt   ————— | —————————————

Famous sports personalities ————— | —————————————

Baseball   ————— | —————————————

Joe DiMaggio   ————— | —————————————

Babe Ruth   ————— | —————————————

Track   ————— | —————————————

Jesse Owens   ————— | —————————————

Jim Thorpe   ————— | —————————————

Figure 6.9

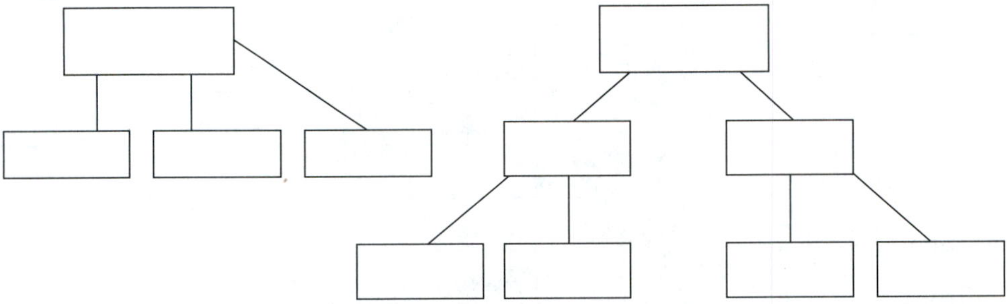

3. Christmas

   Giving gifts

   Sending cards

   Easter

   Sending cards

   Attending church

   Displaying clothes

   New hats

   New dresses

   New accessories

Figure 6.10

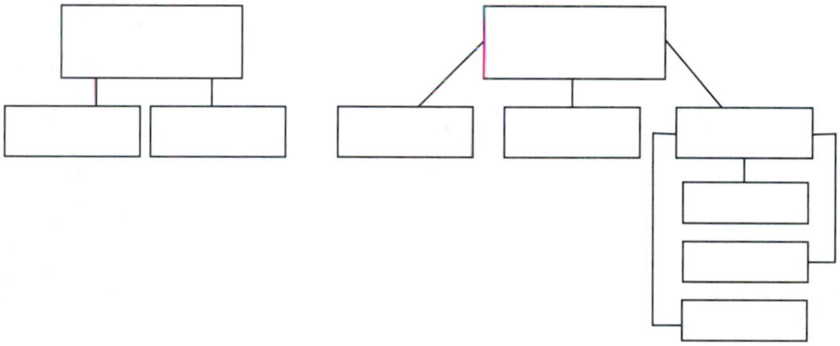

4. Inventions

   Communication

   Telephone

   Printing

   Transportation

   Railroad

   Airplane

   Discoveries

   Electricity

   Planets

Figure 6.11

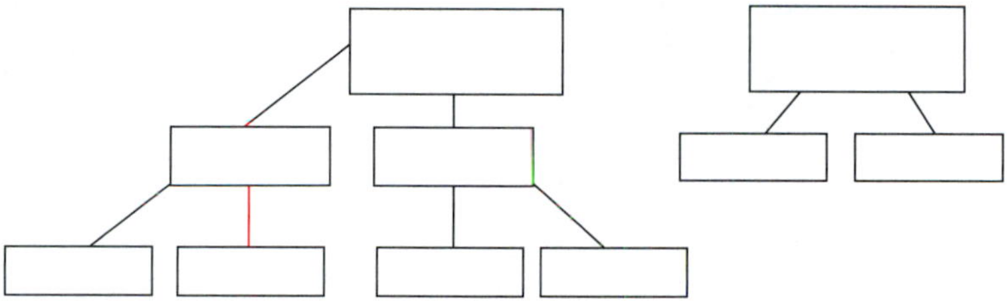

Now try this one, which shows four different levels of indentation, or ranking of ideas.

5. How to study

 Survey the chapter

 Read titles

 Read illustrations

 Pictures

 Maps

 Charts and graphs

 Turn titles into questions

 Read subsections

 Recite from memory

 Review

 How to take tests

 How to take notes

 From lectures

 In textbooks

Figure 6.12

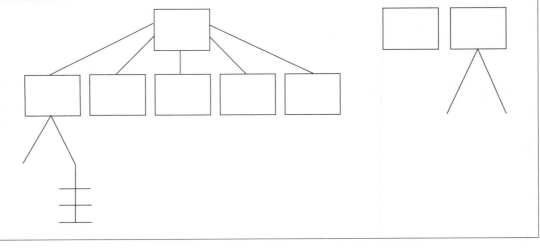

Practice Exercises

D. *In the following lists, major ideas and details are mixed together. Rewrite them in the proper order by filling in the outline or map following each one. Begin each item with a capital letter. If you are not familiar with an item, check it in an encyclopedia or a dictionary. The first one is done for you. Some of the others are partially completed.*

1. *Ebony, New York Times,* magazines, *Chicago Sun-Times, Dead Man Walking, Time,* books, *Washington Post, Reader's Digest, Moby Dick,* newspapers, *A Brief History of Time*

   I. *Magazines*
      A. *Ebony*
      B. *Time*
      C. *Reader's Digest*
  II. *Books*
      A. *Dead Man Walking*
      B. *Moby Dick*
      C. *A Brief History of Time*
 III. *Newspapers*
      A. *New York Times*
      B. *Chicago Sun-Times*
      C. *Washington Post*

Figure 6.13

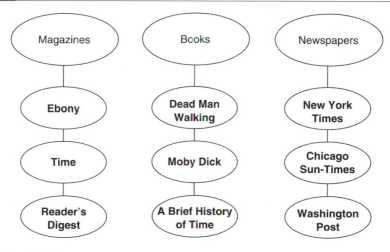

2. Electrician, carpenter, cement, bricklayer, wood, building tradespeople, building materials, pipe, brick, plumber

    I.

        A.

        B.

        C.

        D.

    II. *Building Materials*

        A.

        B.

        C.

        D.

Figure 6.14

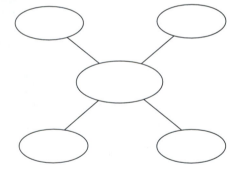 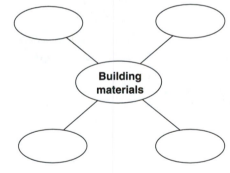

3. Cataract, glaucoma, lens, retina, structure of the ear, eye conditions, vision, structure of the eye, optic nerve, outer ear, hearing, inner ear, ear diseases

I.

    A. *Structure of the eye*

       1.

       2.

       3.

    B.

       1.

       2.

II.

    A. *Structure of the ear*

       1.

       2.

    B.

Figure 6.15

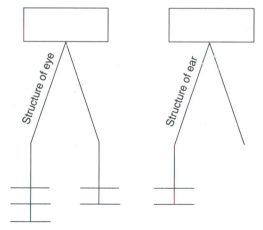

4. In bronze, popular song, instrumental, music, opera, painting, in stone, vocal, sculpture

    I.

       A.

       B.

         1.

         2.

    II.

    III.

       A.

       B.

Figure 6.16

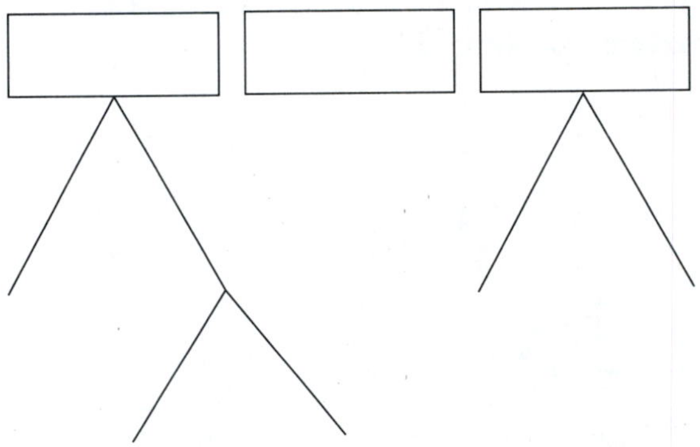

Practice Exercises

E. *Read each of the following paragraphs or groups of paragraphs and complete the outline or map that follows it. The first one is done for you. Some of the others are partially completed.*

1. Students select major fields for many different reasons. Although most choices are based on vocational goals, some students turn to a particular major because of avocational interests: because of a favorite instructor, or because they think it will be easy. Sometimes the choice is made simply because the student is interested in the field, without a particular goal in mind.

   There is no single answer to the question "When do I have to select my major?" The student who feels confident of his or her vocational goals and who recognizes the relationship between these goals and the college program may choose a major before entering college. On the other hand, many students do not know which way they are headed vocationally. Perhaps because of pressure to declare themselves, they begin to tell people that they are majoring in something or other, but the basis for their choice is vague and inadequate. Such students may be better off postponing their final decision as long as possible.

   I. Reasons for selecting major

       A. Vocational

       B. Avocational

           1. Favorite instructor

           2. Easy to learn

           3. Interest in field

   II. When to select major

Figure 6.17

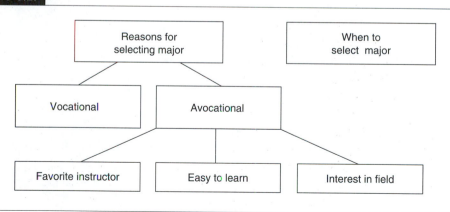

2. A marriage may be legally terminated in our society only by the civil actions of legal separation, annulment, or divorce.

Legal separation. A legal separation, which is not an alternative in some states, does not really "terminate" the marriage in that neither partner is permitted to remarry as long as the legal separation is in force. Legal separation merely limits the privileges of the two persons; for example, it provides for separate maintenance—the couple may not cohabit under penalty of law—but the husband is still financially responsible for the "separate maintenance" of his wife and family.

Annulment. The concept of annulment has its origins in the canon law of the Catholic Church—which takes the position that marriage is indissoluble except by death. Because of this position, the church had to have some means of ending a marriage that, in its view, was fraudulently entered into or maintained. Thus, annulment, which formally declares that the marriage never existed in the first place, was conceived.

Divorce. Divorce—the legal abrogation of a valid marriage contract—not only ends the right of the couple to cohabit and limits the legal obligations of the husband but also permits remarriage. Property is divided by court action, and rights of visitation, physical custody, legal custody, and support payments for any children are assigned by the court. The husband may be required to pay alimony as well—either for a specified number of years or until the woman remarries. Alimony payments from the woman to the man are extremely rare.

Legal Termination of Marriage

    I. Legal separation

        A.

        B. Limits

   II.

        A.

        B. Purpose

   III.

        A. Definition

        B.

Figure 6.18

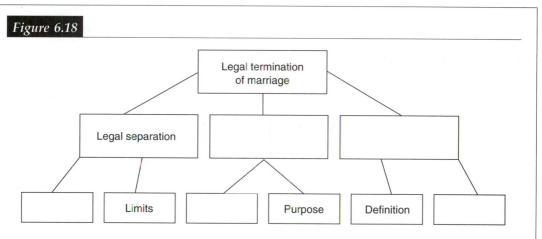

3. **Plan your play.** Playing any round of golf calls for intelligent thinking and planning to achieve the best results. A player who uses good judgment will score better than one who shoots with reckless abandon and with little concern for strategy.

Avoid tension. Many times when a golfer is playing before a group, tension can cause a poor shot. Always take practice swings to ensure a good stroke. Blot out the spectators from your mind. Hit the ball as though it were a practice shot. Frequently, overstudying a putt causes tension and thus stroking off line. If tension is felt at the address, walk away from the ball and relax.

Take the offensive. Hit all shots so they will force your opponents to try to do as well or better. Don't be concerned if an opponent hits a longer drive than you do. You have the opportunity to hit the green in position for a par or birdie, while the burden of getting as close as your ball rests with your opponent. Play the course, and induce your opponent to play your game.

Allow for mistakes. A match is no place to experiment with your game. If you are slicing, play to the left side so that the ball will come to rest in the middle of the fairway. If you are pulling your pitch shots consistently, aim for the right side of the green. If the error is a minor one, make the correction, but don't experiment; you may lose the match.

Don't gamble. When the opponent has the advantage, too many players attempt shots of which they are incapable. For example, an opponent may be on the green in two strokes, 20 feet from the flagstick, while you may be in the bunker in the same number of strokes, with the flagstick quite near the edge of the bunker. If you try to play the ball close to the pin rather than merely to the green, you may find the next shot still in the sand. Trying to hit the flagstick every time is too risky and may add extra strokes All long approach shots should be played to the center of the green; short pitch or chip shots may be aimed at the flagstick without as much chance for error.

When in the deep rough, don't try for distance, but play for position on the next shot. Be more concerned with getting a decent shot from the rough than with attempting to hit the green.

Concentrate. Play each shot as it comes. Attempting to figure too far ahead may cause a poor shot. Think each stroke through, visualize the ball in flight, think positively. If you are convinced you can't hit a shot, or sure it will slice or hook, in all probability it will. Decide how the shot should be played, then play it that way. If on your backswing you feel you have too much club, trying to compensate with an easy swing will probably result in a poor and inaccurate shot. A poor shot should be forgotten and not allowed to influence the next stroke. Be careful in selection of club.

I.
   A.
   B.
   C.

II.

III.
   A.
   B.

IV.

V.

Figure 6.19

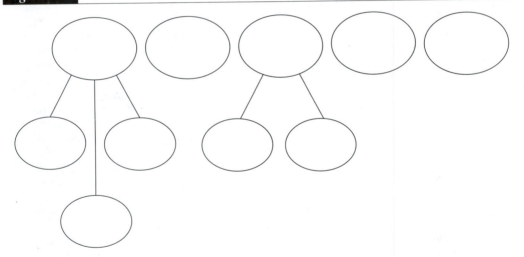

4. Every woman has her own body build (somatype), depending on her muscular-ity, linearity, and fat distribution. The three main body types are:

   The endomorph (the big square). This type is square-shaped, has a large frame, and is well padded with fat around the stomach, hips, upper arms, and neck. She usually has small hands and feet, short arms and legs. Because of her excessive bulk, she moves slowly, has slow reaction time, and tends to be sluggish. Her weight will be a problem throughout her life.

The mesomorph (inverted triangle). This type has a firm, well-proportioned body with broader shoulders than hips. She is usually active, likes sports, and tends to excel in those that require balance, endurance, strength, and speed.

The ectomorph (frail, pencil-thin). This type has a long, thin body with underdeveloped muscles, sloping shoulders, a low waistline, long arms and legs. Less strenuous individual sports appeal to her more than more active team games. She tires easily and may eat well, but will likely remain thin and wiry throughout her life.

Body Types

I.

    A.

    B.

    C.

    D.

II.

    A.

    B.

III.

    A.

    B.

Figure 6.20

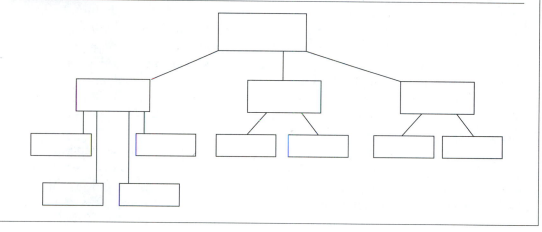

Practice Exercises

F. Now try to prepare an outline or concept map without any help at all. Read the following short selection and outline it in the space that follows.

Four main woods are used in making self bows. A *self bow* is made entirely from one piece of material, in contrast to the *laminated bow*, which is made of several pieces of wood or other materials glued together.

Probably the smoothest shooting self-bow wood is yew, a type of cedar that grows in the Pacific Northwest. It is becoming rare, consequently expensive, and market conditions seem to indicate its coming obsolescence. Yew makes a wonderful longbow, especially for target archery, and will not soon be forgotten, for its records have left their imprint for centuries. A yew bow should have some sapwood on the back of the bow, for its elastic quality. The heartwood, better under compression, is used on the belly side.

A good hunting bow can be constructed from osage orange (*Bois d'Arc*), a hardwood tree sometimes called hedgewood, for it is planted in rows to make hedges on many farms ranging from Indiana to Texas. The tree is thorny and develops a warty, green, nonedible fruit the size of grapefruit. Selection of this wood for bows presents problems in both manufacture and use. The wood is extremely hard, sawing and planing are difficult, so scraping and sanding are often resorted to. The wood is better under *compression* than it is under tension. Consequently, it is better used in the belly of the bow and backed with another wood, such as hickory, or some elastic material. However, good short bows made of osage orange will withstand the abuse they often get under hunting conditions. It does not make an especially good target bow, because it is rather *rough-in-hand*—that is, it tends to kick or recoil.

A third wood commonly used for self bows is lemonwood, named after its creamy, lemon color rather than after the tree it comes from. The tree is *degame*, which grows around the Mediterranean and in Cuba. Even though this wood is imported, it is reasonably priced and is recommended to the beginning hobbyist for a first homemade bow. Although the wood is extremely hard and close grained, it works rather easily. The finished bow may hold up for years of rough use. Lemonwood may be used for target and field or hunting bows. Since it is a hardwood, it has *recoil* tendencies. Also, this wood has a tendency to follow the string, as it is not adept at withstanding stretch or tension. Therefore, better bows can be made by backing lemonwood with a more elastic wood or other material.

Hickory is the fourth most commonly used self-bow wood in the United States. It is fairly abundant, but it is the least desirable of the four woods, because it does not stand compression, is slow in action, has much kick, has poor recovery, and follows the string badly. The best thing that can be said for hickory is that it has excellent stretch qualities;

consequently, it can be used successfully to back other bow woods, especially osage orange.

Other self bows are made of solid or hollow fiberglass, steel, and aluminum. Aluminum bows have lost popularity because of the personal danger involved when the bows break. At the present time, fiberglass bows are very popular, especially for schools, camps, beginners, and children. They are durable, have good shooting qualities, stand up well under mistreatment; but they lack that smooth-in-hand quality that the more experienced archer seeks. Low cost and ease of production favor the future of fiberglass bows.

Chapter 7

Using the PQ3R Method of Study

After you learn about the PQ3R method of study in Chapter 7, you will be able to use

- *Prepare*
- *Question*
- *Read*
- *Recite*
- *Review*

as a powerful aid in studying textbook chapters.

Imagine that on a very dark night a friend takes you to the door of a room you have never seen before. Your friend explains that the room is a fully furnished living room. At the other end of the room is a door that leads out onto a patio. Your task is to go through the room (alone), open the door, and step out onto the patio. There is only one problem. It is very dark in the room, and you may *not* turn on any lights. What will probably happen? Not knowing the location of the furniture, you will begin to grope your way slowly, very slowly, until—bang! You hit your shin against the sofa, fall down, perhaps bruise yourself.

Now imagine that instead of having to grope your way without *any* knowledge of where you are, your friend had turned a light switch on (before you started) for just a brief moment. Would this have helped? Most certainly. In the fraction of time that the light was on, you would have seen the sofa and the lamp and, most important, the path that leads to the patio door. Even after the light went off, you would be able to find your way in the dark more quickly, with less difficulty, and with less damage to yourself and to the furniture.

Trying to study a chapter in any textbook without PREPARING the chapter first is like groping your way in the dark without any idea of where things are. You finally come to the end of the chapter with your mind disarrayed, not sure how you got there and not sure what you have been through. This is why the *P* of the PQ3R method of study is so helpful. What is this technique and how can it be helpful?

The PQ3R method of study allows you to study a textbook chapter in less time, with better understanding and better recollection of the information than you are used to experiencing. The results of research in both learning and memory are incorporated into this technique.

To be a good reader, you need to become actively involved in what the author is saying. You must listen to the author and try to understand the ideas being presented. Then you must react to them. The PQ3R method forces you to do that.

P stands for PREPARE. Successful students prepare the chapter for study before they read it. Runners on a starting line get on their mark and get set before they "go." Their whole bodies become prepared for the task ahead. Readers must prepare their minds for the study task ahead. How do they do this?

PREPARE

Research in learning tells us that you learn new information best when you can relate or associate this new information with something that you already know. When you PREPARE your textbook for study, you reach back into the warehouse containing millions of bits and pieces of information you have stored in your mind during your lifetime up to the moment that you apply this technique. These connectors or associations are then lined up ready for use *before you actually read the chapter.* To prepare a chapter for study, *actively* read five things. (*Actively* means *read and think about,* not just stare at.)

First, actively read the TITLE. What does it tell you about the content of the chapter? What do you *already* know about this topic? Don't be afraid to guess. Even if you guess incorrectly, you are reading actively and will correct your error as you proceed. Thinking about the title helps to bring to the forefront of your mind any information you may have stored away on this topic. It helps commandeer and organize all of this information *before* you begin to actually read the chapter.

Read each of the following textbook or article titles. Then answer the questions that follow it.

American Government in Colonial Days

1. What school subject would this be a textbook for?

_____

2. In this book, which of the following would you expect to read about? Circle the letter before each correct answer.
   a. the first two presidents of the United States
   b. the settlement of Virginia
   c. Columbus

Do you understand that probably this would be a history textbook? In question 2, only choice *b.* (the settlement of Virginia) is correct. Choice *a.* (the first two presidents of the United States) is not part of the colonial period in our history. The presidents served after the colonial period. Choice *c.* (Columbus) relates to his voyages and the discovery of America. This occurred in history before the colonies were founded.

Driving Safely

This selection is probably about driving your car in a safe manner. What kinds of information would you expect to read about? Be as specific as you can.

_____

_____

_____

Even though you haven't read the article yet, you would expect it to suggest that in order to drive safely you should obey speed limits, avoid driving if you are tired or under the influence of drugs or alcohol, use seat belts, and be sure that such things as tires and brakes are in proper working order. Do you see how much you know about the article before you read it?

How to Make Money Make Money

What do you expect the author to talk about in this article? Be as specific as you can.

_____

_____

Do you realize that this is probably about investment strategies or how to invest your money successfully? Your answer should have mentioned such things as areas of investment (i.e., types of businesses, stocks, bonds, real estate), the relative safety of different kinds of investments, and what to watch out for—the pitfalls.

Next, carefully read the INTRODUCTION to the chapter. If there is no introduction, read the paragraph(s) before the first heading. Authors often give a brief outline of the chapter in their introduction. They tell you where they are going and how they are going to get there. Try to relate the introduction to the title. Doing this should either (1) reinforce your guess (after reading the title) as to what the chapter is about, or (2) help you to realize that your original thought was incorrect.

Here is an introductory paragraph to Chapter 10 ("Dividing the Workload") from *Fundamentals of Modern Business*, by Robert Swindle. List, in the space below that, the kinds of information that you expect to read about in the chapter.

Teamwork is vital in business. A plan must be developed for dividing work among the members of the management team. Each member must be given enough authority to be able to accomplish the assigned task. Moreover, for the greatest efficiency the authority of each member must be expanded by various means.

_____

_____

_____

The author says that a plan must be developed. Don't you expect, then, to find out what the plan is? The author also says that managers must be given authority that must be expanded by various means. This should suggest to you that the author will tell you what the "various means" are and perhaps even the advantages of each means of expansion. Remember that you haven't read the chapter yet, but you already have a good idea of what will be discussed.

Here is the title and introductory paragraph from Chapter 1 ("What Is Data Processing?") from the second edition of *Data Processing—Computers in Action*, by Perry Edwards and Bruce Broadwell.

Computers are invading our lives more and more. They have already changed society more than the wheel, which merely extended our "muscle power." Computers have extended our "mind power." Just what is a computer? What can it do? What can it not do? What do we mean by *data*? This chapter answers these questions and more.

Before reading the chapter you should try to think of the answers to the questions asked in this paragraph. As far as you know, just what is a computer? What can computers do or not do? What do you think is meant by *data*? What has all this to do with the title? Were you able to realize that data (facts or information) are processed by a computer? Think carefully about all of this before reading further. If you can come up with some answers, reading and studying this chapter will become easier.

Here is the title and introductory statement from Chapter 5 ("Personal Conflicts and Problems in College") of *The Search for Independence*, by Joseph B. Cook, Marvin A. Hoss, and Robert Vargas.

In this chapter, we will present a few problems and conflicts that have been faced by students at one large junior college. These case histories will show the kinds of problems that students may expect to run into in college, as well as the role counseling can play in handling such problems.

Stop and think first about the kinds of problems and conflicts you may have. Did you seek counseling for these problems? As you read the chapter, what questions will you look for answers to? Are you curious to see if the problems and conflicts mentioned are the same as yours? Do you wonder if counseling can help, and if it might be something for you to consider? Even if you can't personally identify with the contents of this chapter, do you realize that you already know what it is going to talk about?

Third, turn to the end of the chapter and actively read the SUMMARY (if any) or questions about the chapter (if any). A summary will outline the important points made in the heart of the chapter, and questions at the end of a chapter will be geared to material that the author thinks is important. Again, try to relate the ideas in the summary and/or the questions to the information gathered in the title and the introduction. People who read murder mysteries are often told *not* to look at the last page or two of the book because that will spoil it for them. They will discover who the murderer is, and this takes away all of the suspense and excitement of the book. In study, however, you *want* to be able to predict the author's ideas *before* you actually read the selection. The summary separates the fat from the meat. It gives you the highlights *before* you actually read the chapter.

Before reading on, choose a chapter you haven't read yet, from one of your textbooks (one that has a summary and/or questions at the end). Read the end material and relate it as much as possible to the title and the introductory material. This will give you a good idea of the important information in the chapter itself. Even though you haven't read the contents of the chapter, you already know some of the information it contains. Studying in this way also helps you remember the information because important items are highlighted and then repeated when you later read the chapter.

Fourth, read (and think about) the first HEADING. How does it relate to the title and the introduction and the information at the end of the chapter? What will the subsection *probably* be about? Read actively, trying to correlate everything you have read so far.

Fifth, actively read the FIRST SENTENCE of each paragraph in the first subsection. Although first sentences of paragraphs are not necessarily main idea sentences, reading *all* first sentences will usually furnish you with all of the main points the author makes. Don't be concerned, however, if even doing this does not seem to provide much information. The background it provides will be helpful when you do the Q3R.

Now redo Steps 4 and 5 for each subsection. In other words, read and think about the *second* heading and then read the first sentence of each paragraph in the *second* subsection. Then do the same for the *third* heading and *third* subsection and so on through the entire chapter.

When you go through the subsections and read the first sentences of paragraphs, you should also examine any ATTENTION GETTERS. Attention getters can be either *graphics* or *outstanding print*. *Graphics* includes pictures, maps, charts, graphs, tables, cartoons, and all other illustrative materials. *Outstanding print* is just that—any print that differs from the normal print being used: underlines, italics, capital letters, boldface, and the like.

These attention getters are not decorations; they are important aids to understanding the material quickly. Authors emphasize words with outstanding print because those words are important. Authors use graphics because they know that "a picture is worth a thousand words." Readers who examine attention getters before reading the entire subsection get a quick view of the important ideas. Also, because people remember best what they see first, they'll remember these main points better.

Look carefully at the information from *The World in the Twentieth Century*, by Geoffrey Bruun.

Part I EUROPE: 1900–1914
Chapter II GREAT BRITAIN
Headings 1. *Resources: The Problem of Supply*
2. *Defense: The Problem of Naval Supremacy*

How much information do we have here? First, the book's title (*The World in the Twentieth Century*) suggests that this is a history book limited to world history since 1900. The title to Part I ("Europe: 1900–1914") indicates that *this* section is limited to the history of Europe from 1900 to 1914. Think ACTIVELY about this title. What do we already know about Europe from 1900 to 1914? What special significance do these years have? Many readers would realize that these were the years just before World War I. What do we know about these prewar years in Europe? What would we expect an author to say about them? Certainly the immediate events leading up to the war would probably be included here. The more remote causes and background would also be discussed. Now let us look at the chapter title. This tells us that Great Britain, in the years immediately preceding World War I, will be the focus of attention in this chapter. Notice that we are taking the time to relate past knowledge to the current material in order to become better acquainted with the content. Doing this allows us to predict what is coming and to fit new information into an already organized structure of knowledge.

Look at the first heading ("Resources: The Problem of Supply"). What will this subsection probably be about and how does it relate to the chapter title? It suggests, of course, that Great Britain (in the years preceding World War I) had a problem getting an adequate supply of resources. Searching our prior knowledge still further, we would probably conclude that Britain's high degree of industrialization and limited land area are related to this problem somehow.

Now let us look at the second heading ("Defense: The Problem of Naval Supremacy"). Notice how it fits into the entire picture. Knowing that Britain is an island and knowing that it has a supply problem, we can conclude that some of its supplies must come from outside the country—therefore (since it is an island), from across the water. Thus, Britain vitally needs free and undisturbed access to shipping lanes. Therefore, naval supremacy is vital to Britain's defense—and was, we assume further, especially vital in 1900–1914, when airplanes were not available for shipping. A good reader becomes aware of all these interrelationships just by previewing carefully. Although the chapter content itself has not yet been read, notice how much information we have *before* reading.

Now PREPARE a short section of a business book used in many colleges today: "Getting into Business: Organizing the Company's Structure," from *Fundamentals of Modern Business,* by Robert Swindle. First, note the section title, "Getting into Business: Organizing the Company's Structure." What does it suggest that the section is about? Think about it. Doesn't it suggest that this section will be concerned about how you organize a company when you go into business? Perhaps the author will talk about different ways in which companies might be organized. What else might be discussed? What kinds of information would you want if you were forming a company? (Perhaps the laws regarding starting companies, and what your costs and obligations might be.) Stop and think about this before continuing to read.

Now read the two introductory paragraphs.

> The manner in which a company is organized is of great importance not only to the owners, but also to those planning to do business with the company. Just as the owners hope to profit from their business, so do the employees, suppliers, creditors, and customers who enter into transactions with the firm.
> Accordingly, this chapter describes and compares the three basic forms of business organization—the sole proprietorship, the partnership, and the corporation. Because the corporate form of ownership is so important in modern business, a description of corporate structure and expansion is also included.

How does this introductory statement relate to the title? What does it tell you about what will probably be covered in the section? Have you learned that this section will tell you about three different forms of business organizations and will compare them? What does it mean to "compare" them? Do you understand that the author will probably tell you about the advantages and disadvantages of the sole proprietorship, the partnership, and the corporation?

What do you know about these forms of business organizations? Before reading on, you should stop and recall whatever you may happen to know about these types of businesses. Doing this helps you to read with better understanding, attention, and concentration.

The next thing you should actively read is the summary or questions at the end of the section. Because this is a practice exercise, in this instance *only* do not look at the questions at the end. (There is no summary.) You will be asked to answer these questions after doing the PREPARE even though you have not read the selection completely. This will be a test of the effectiveness of this technique. Now read on.

Sole Proprietorship

Any business owned by one person is a sole proprietorship. If Joe Jones opens a hamburger stand at the beach, for example, he is a sole proprietor. If Joe eventually acquires a chain of hamburger stands across the country, he is still a sole proprietor—so long as he maintains complete ownership of the business. The definition of a sole proprietorship does not depend on the size of the business, therefore, but on its ownership by just one person.

The subtitle, "Sole Proprietorship," introduces this part of the section. The paragraph is also an introductory statement and should be read completely. Here, the author defines a sole proprietorship and explains it somewhat.

Advantages of Sole Proprietorships

Some of the characteristics of sole proprietorships are explained in the following list of advantages commonly associated with this form of organization.

Ease of entry. The primary advantage of a sole proprietorship is usually referred to as "ease of entry," which means that it is relatively easy to go into business by yourself. In some states, Joe would have to pay a nominal fee for a license before he could legally sell hamburgers. In other states, no license would be required. However, most states do require an inspection and an approval from their boards of health for permission to sell food products.

Retention of profits. The cost of food (ground beef, buns), overhead (rent, lights), and wages for employees Joe may have hired must be deducted from the money received from his sale of hamburgers to the public. The profits remaining belong to Joe, however. He does not have to share his money with anyone; the profits are all his.

Freedom of action. As a sole proprietor, Joe has the freedom of action so often necessary to get a job done quickly. If he decides to lower the price of hamburgers as a way of competing with other restaurants, for example, or if he wants to remodel or expand his operation, he doesn't have to seek anyone's permission. Such decisions are his alone.

Ease of exit. Finally, Joe can quit the business at any time he might decide to do so. No red tape is involved, providing he settles all outstanding bills. He need not secure permission from his employees or from any government agency. He may simply close the business or sell it to someone else.

Personal satisfaction. Sole proprietors have the personal satisfaction to be gained from owning their own business. For a variety of reasons, many people dream of someday being in business for themselves. They may relish the idea of not having to take orders from others or, just the opposite, of being able to tell their own employees what to do. Also, the statement "I have my own business" has a rather pleasant ring in the ears of many people.

The heading "Advantages of Sole Proprietorships" indicates that the author is going to tell you about the advantages of a sole proprietorship (which you now know means a one-owner business). The subheadings below that tell you what the advantages are. Read the first subheading, "Ease of Entry." Then read the *first sentence only* of the paragraph that follows. It tells you that an important advantage of this form of business organization is that it is easy to go into business by yourself.

Now read the second subheading, "Retention of Profits." What does this mean? It suggests that in a sole proprietorship the owner can keep all of the profits. Now read the first sentence of the paragraph that follows. It doesn't really seem to help you understand the subheading. If you think about it for a moment, however, you might guess that the next sentence will explain that the owner retains the money left after expenses. The third subheading, "Freedom of Action," suggests that the owner can make and act upon decisions quickly without having to discuss them with anyone or get anyone else's permission, and the first sentence confirms this. The next subheading, "Ease of Exit," suggests that the owner can close up or leave the business easily; when you read the first sentence that follows the subheading, you discover that this is correct. The last subheading of this section, "Personal Satisfaction," suggests that there is personal satisfaction to be gained from owning your business. Read the first sentence following the subheading. It says exactly that. Reading and thinking about subheadings help you to read and study more efficiently.

Now PREPARE the next subsection.

Disadvantages of Sole Proprietorships

The freedom inherent in a sole proprietorship also produces some important disadvantages in management difficulties, size limitations, unlimited liability, and limited life.

Management difficulties.   If Joe were to become ill, or if he wanted to keep the hamburger stand open around the clock, he might experience management difficulties. For example, it probably would be difficult for him to hire someone who could manage the employees properly and also treat the customers in the same manner that he does. It might be even more difficult for Joe to find employees whom he can trust with the money that must be handled.

Size limitations.   These difficulties of management tend to limit the size of sole proprietorships. If Joe experiences problems in keeping the one place open twenty-four hours a day, imagine how those problems would multiply if he decided to sell hamburgers at several locations. Also, the size of a sole proprietorship is often financially limited. The owner may not have sufficient funds of his own for expansion; and, unless he has extensive properties to offer as security for a loan, lenders may be reluctant to extend the necessary funding.

Unlimited liability.   Sole proprietors have unlimited liability. Let's imagine for a minute that Joe does decide to expand his operation to include several hamburger stands. As an *entrepreneur* (business organizer, owner, and manager), he expects to assume the risk of loss if the business should fail. Under sole proprietorship, however, Joe would risk much more than the loss of his investment in the hamburger stands. Unlimited liability means that if his business venture should fail, his creditors could claim ownership of his personal and business properties. If sale of the restaurant equipment would not bring in enough money to satisfy his debts, for example, the creditors could take such personal belongings as his home, auto, and savings to settle his business debts.

Limited life.   Joe will eventually grow old and die, of course. Or he may zig on the freeway when he should have zagged and meet with a fatal accident. Either event will end the sole proprietorship. Surviving relatives may continue to operate the business. Legally, however, it will be a different business than before Joe's death.

The heading of this section tells you that the author is going to discuss the disadvantages of sole proprietorship. The one-sentence introduction that follows mentions what they are. Now read the first subheading, "Management Difficulties." Think about this subheading. What management difficulties could be a disadvantage to a one-owner business? You may be able to think of some. If you can't, read the first sentence that follows the subheading. This sentence suggests an answer. It is saying that the business depends on the owner alone for proper management. In a business that has a partner, for example, the partner could fill in if Joe were ill or if longer hours were required. Now read the second subheading, "Size Limitations." This suggests that a one-owner business can't get too big because if it did, the one owner would have even more problems in management. The first sentence says just that. Think about the next subheading, "Unlimited Liability," and the first sentence after it. They seem to say that there is no limit to how much one owner might be liable if there are any financial problems in the business. The last subheading, "Limited Life," and the first sentence after it seem to say that a one-owner business has a limited life. That is, the business dies when the owner dies.

Without reading on, you are fairly sure that the author will discuss the advantages and disadvantages of the partnership next and then the advantages and disadvantages of the corporation. Even though it is not included here, you are *prepared* to read it.

Now answer the following questions based on the short selection you have just PREPARED. Answer the questions without looking back at the material.

1. What is meant by a sole proprietorship? _____

_____

2. What are three advantages of the sole proprietorship?

   a. _____

   b. _____

   c. _____

3. What are two disadvantages of the sole proprietorship?

a. _____

b. _____

4. What are two other forms of business organization in addition to the sole proprietorship?

a. _____

b. _____

Now check the correct answers by looking back at the selection. Were you able to answer most of the questions? You probably were. Notice how much information you can acquire just by PREPARING a selection for study.

Preparing a chapter for study is often enough to give you all of the basic information you may need for general learning of that chapter. What is the value, then, of the Q3R steps? Q3R helps you to learn the details in the chapter more thoroughly. It checks your understanding and memory of what you have learned, and it forces you to concentrate. It then double-checks these items. What is Q3R?

QUESTION

A QUESTION provides a purpose for reading the subsection, and it's easier to keep in mind than just a statement of purpose. Also, a question is a starting point in learning. Ask yourself why the author has expressed this heading in this way. Once again, how does it relate to the information given so far? What will the author probably talk about in the subsection?

Here are some titles and headings from various books. In the space provided, write questions for these titles. Try to make up questions whose answers can be discovered by reading the selection. Then guess at the answer to each question.

1. *Human Needs: Physical Needs*

   Question: _____

   Answer: _____

2. *Advantages of a College Education*

   Question: _____

   Answer: _____

3. *Types of Auto Insurance*

   Question: _____

   Answer: _____

Do you see how asking and answering questions helps you to focus on what is important in the reading material?

READ

READ the subsection to find the answer to the question and for any other important information. Again, ask questions. What does the information presented have to do with what you are trying to learn? Does the information follow logically from what you may already know about the subject? If not, why not? What do you still need to have answered in your own mind? Have a conversation with the author as you read. Agree or disagree with what is said, and if you disagree, tell yourself why. If the author does a great job of explaining a point, say so. This forces *active* reading, which keeps you thinking and helps you to concentrate and learn and understand. You will already have an idea of what is being said from having done the PREPARE step, so you should be able to learn this material more quickly than otherwise. Wherever you can, use any graphic materials (maps, charts, graphs, tables, pictures, etc.) or outstanding words (boldface, italics, capitals) to reinforce your learning.

RECITE

Look away after finishing the subsection. Now tell yourself (from memory) the answer to the question and any other important information. This RECITE step has two very important advantages. First, it forces you to *concentrate*. When you know in advance that you will have to *recite*, you will pay more careful attention to what you are reading. Second, if you are unable to do the recite step, you know it immediately. You catch yourself right away and should then repeat QRR until you can do it. You are not lulled into a false sense of security, thinking that you understand something that you really don't.

QRR should be done for each subsection individually until the chapter is finished. In other words, look at the first heading; change it into a question; read to find the answer to the question; try to recite from memory. Then follow the same procedure for the second heading and subsection, and so on to the end of the chapter. Only after this is done should you do the third *R*: REVIEW.

REVIEW

Active REVIEW is an important part of learning, but many students don't do it well because they review at the wrong time or in the wrong manner.

Good review occurs after a break of at least an hour, preferably half a day. After this time, you realize which items you haven't adequately learned, so you can concentrate on them. Two excellent times to review are right before you go to sleep at night and right after you awaken in the morning. For various reasons, reviewing at these times locks the material in your memory.

The process of REVIEW is similar to the RECITE step: Look at the first heading. Look away. (Do not read the subsection.) Try to tell yourself what the subsection was about. Try to remember the questions that you had. Are they now satisfactorily answered? Did your questions help you to get a better understanding of the points the author made? If so, go on to the second heading. Follow the same procedure with the second heading. Look away and tell yourself (actually *explain* to yourself) the information you feel you need to know from the second subsection. If you can do that, do the same with the third heading and subsection. Continue this procedure until you reach the end of the chapter. If there is any subsection that you cannot review in this way, don't continue. Redo QRR on this heading and subsection before continuing. When you can do QRR, continue the review.

This procedure has a very special advantage. When you review, you spend the bulk of your time on the material you don't know. Too often, students review by merely rereading the chapter, thus apportioning as much time to what they *do* know as they do to what they don't know. In Q3R you allot your study time to the different sections of the chapter according to how well you understand them. The less you understand something, the more time you give to it.

In Brief

▼

PQ3R comes with a three-part guarantee: a textbook chapter can be studied in less time, with better understanding, and with better recollection. To achieve this, PQ3R demands your *active* involvement in the study process.

Prepare a chapter by actively reading five things:

1. *Title:* Speculate on what will be covered.
2. *Introduction:* Read the area between the title and the first subheading.
3. *Summary and Questions:* Read these parts, usually found at the chapter's end.
4. *Headings:* Speculate on what will be covered.
5. *First sentences and attention getters:* Read these in every paragraph under each heading.

   Attention getters consist of:

   Graphics (charts, pictures, etc.)

   Outstanding print (boldface, italics, etc.)

   Graphics should be examined *before* reading the verbal explanation because people remember best what they see first.

Question Change the title and headings into questions.

Read Relate the material to what has been learned so far. Pay attention to graphics and to outstanding print.

Recite Say the information in the subsection out loud, from memory.

   Advantages to reciting:

1. You are forced to concentrate.
2. You catch mistakes right away.

Read/Recite is done as a set for each subsection:

Read the heading, then READ/RECITE the material under it.
Read the next heading. READ/RECITE the material under it, and so forth.

Review REVIEW is similar to RECITE, but it's done after reading the entire chapter.

   Material that has been forgotten should be relearned at this time. Advantage to the REVIEW step: Time is spent relearning material that had been forgotten.

Practice Exercises

A. This exercise covers just part of a chapter, so there is no title, introduction, or summary to deal with. Do the appropriate PREPARE steps, then answer the questions.

INSURING AGAINST RISK

Even when we are very careful in the things we do each day, the risk of loss or injury is always with us. Starting the day with a shower, we risk slipping and falling through the glass door. Riding to work, we risk collision. While we are away from our homes, the risk of fire or burglary is greater. Going to school, our children risk being injured. We also risk loss through unintentional actions of our own that might injure others.

Such events may occur regardless of how careful we may try to be, and they can cost us a lot of money. Rather than taking the chance of being wiped out financially, we transfer some of our risks to others. We buy insurance.

Uninsurable Risks

The risk of incurring a business loss is generally an uninsurable risk. Entrepreneurs enter into business ventures with the hope of making profits. Many businesses fail, however, and the entrepreneurs lose the money they have invested.

The risk of loss because of changes in the economy is uninsurable. Jim Brown may have an excellent plan for success in business. He has a unique product, an ideal location, and extensive business experience. As the economy goes into a recession, however, many people who would have bought his product cannot afford to do so. They are without jobs. Since insurance coverage for fluctuations in the economy is not generally available, Jim must suffer the resulting losses.

The risk of loss because of changes in consumer behavior is uninsurable. Rosy Rosen decided to order two more truckloads of the fast-selling Hula-Hoops. By the time the Hula-Hoops were received at Rosy's warehouse, however, kids had turned to yo-yos and Frisbees. Rosy may decide to give the Hula-Hoops away, if she can find some organization that will accept them, or she may store them and hope for a renewed demand for Hula-Hoops next year. Since storage costs money, she may decide simply to destroy the hoops and suffer the loss.

The risk of loss as a result of changes in the population is also uninsurable. A manufacturer of baby products may have expanded plant facilities in response to a growing demand for his products, only to learn the following year that American women are having fewer and fewer babies. The manufacturer may convert part of his factory to the production of something other than baby products, but there still will be a huge loss of money involved. The risk of such losses is uninsurable.

Insurable Risks

Many business risks, however, are insurable risks. Instead of taking a chance on being forced out of business because of a natural disaster or a lawsuit, for example, business owners may transfer such risks to others by purchasing insurance.

Insurance companies do not sell coverage automatically, however. To be insurable, a risk must have five specific characteristics. First, it must be a predictable risk—that is, the losses from a particular kind of risk must be calculable. For example, insurance companies do not gamble on the number of people that are going to die each year. The number of deaths can be predicted quite accurately.

Second, risks must exist in large numbers to enable the prediction of losses through the law of averages. As an example, take a coin and toss it into the air. There is a 50-50 chance that the coin will come up heads, and a 50-50 chance of it coming up tails. When you toss the coin ten times, however, it may come up heads on three times and tails seven times. But when you toss it 1,000 times, the tally will come close to 500 heads and 500 tails. The greater the number of tosses, the closer the tally will be to one-half heads and one-half tails.

The law of averages works the same way with business risks. Assume, for example, that on a national basis insurance companies receive loss claims averaging 5 percent of the value of all fire insurance policies sold. If an individual insurance company were to sell thousands of such policies, representing millions of dollars of fire insurance, the company could predict losses of approximately 5 percent of the total coverage. If, instead, an insurance company were to sell only ten policies for $100,000 each (totaling $1 million), the complete loss of just one building would represent a claim payout of 10 percent—twice the national average. Insurance companies can use the law of averages to predict losses, therefore, only if risks are insured in large numbers.

Third, risks must be scattered over a *wide geographic area* to be insurable. If an insurance company were to confine insurance sales to a particular city, a natural disaster such as an earthquake or flood could result in losses that would ruin the company.

Fourth, risks must be *selected* by the insurer. If insurance companies are to remain in business they must earn a profit. A company will not continue to be profitable, of course, if forced to insure those businesses and persons who, on the basis of their past record or present condition, are almost certain to suffer losses.

Fifth, a risk is insurable only if the person buying the insurance has an insurable interest in whatever is being insured. For instance, you cannot legally purchase insurance on another person's property unless you have a legal claim on all or part of the property. Neither can you legally insure the life of any person you choose. You must have an insurable interest. If the person is a member of your family or a business partner, for example, you do have an insurable interest in the life or death of that person.

PREPARE Questions

1. Business losses that occurred because of various changes are not insurable. List the three types of change mentioned.

    a. _____

    b. _____

    c. _____

2. What are the five characteristics of an insurable risk?

   a. _____

   b. _____

   c. _____

   d. _____

   e. _____

B. This exercise covers just part of a chapter. Do the appropriate PREPARE steps, then answer the questions.

INSURANCE COVERAGE

There are many types of insurance coverage. Movie stars have purchased insurance that would pay them if anything happened to destroy their beautiful faces or bodies, and women have insured themselves against the possibility of multiple births (twins, triplets, and so on). Some insurance companies, especially Lloyds of London, specialize in very unusual types of insurance coverage.

The more common types of insurance that relate to business—life, property, auto, and liability insurance, as well as commercial credit insurance and several types of employee coverage—are presented here.

Life Insurance

Life insurance is important to businesses. Partners often buy life insurance that is payable to the surviving partner, with an accompanying agreement that the surviving partner will use the money to buy the deceased partner's share of the business from the deceased partner's surviving family. Similarly, corporate managers often buy key man insurance to protect the company against losses that might result from the death of important employees. If a leader in the development of a new and important product should be killed in an accident, for example, the company could lose an important segment of the market because of the delays this person's death would produce.

Life insurance protection is also stipulated in many loan contracts. Lenders often require borrowers to buy credit life insurance to guarantee repayment should the borrowers die before repaying the debts.

When you decide to buy insurance on your life, the insurance company usually insists that you demonstrate your good health by taking a physical examination. The insurance company pays for the examination and includes the doctor's fee in the premium that you must pay.

Insurance companies usually investigate the applicant's lifestyle before issuing a policy. Does the applicant live alone? Where does he work? How does he drive? What kind of person is he? They obtain the answers to such questions from talks with employers, neighbors, and other acquaintances of the applicant.

There are four basic types of life insurance: term, straight life, limited payment, and endowment. Term insurance is usually for a period of from one to ten years. The rates for term insurance are the lowest for any type of life insurance, but coverage ceases when the term has ended. If the policy has a conversion privilege, the person may extend his coverage for another term. The rate for the extended coverage would be higher, since the person has grown older, but a physical examination to demonstrate good health would not be required.

A straight life policy provides coverage for the insured person's entire life, but payments must also be made for a lifetime—even if he lives for 100 years or longer. Like term insurance, the insured person must die before anyone can collect anything from the insurance company. Unlike term insurance, however, straight life insurance provides an element of savings. After the first year or two of coverage, the policy has a cash value. The insured may borrow some of the cash value at a relatively low rate of interest, or he may decide to cancel his policy and take the money.

A person who dislikes the idea of making payments to an insurance company for the rest of his life may buy limited payment life insurance. He or she may buy a ten-, twenty-, or thirty-year policy, or one that will be paid at the precise time of retirement age. The person still must die before anyone collects a penny from the insurance company, but will not have to pay premiums after retirement.

A person who dislikes the idea of having to die before the insurance company pays off may buy endowment insurance. An endowment policy includes life insurance, but places a greater emphasis on savings. If the endowment is for twenty years at $10,000, for example, the person is insured for $10,000 if he or she dies or is killed during the twenty years. But if the person is alive at the end of twenty years, the insurance company must pay him $10,000.

The main advantage of life insurance, of course, is the financial protection that it provides the survivors—the spouse, the children, and (in some cases) the business associates of the deceased. Also, straight life, limited payment life, and especially endowment insurance provide a method of forcing the insured person to accumulate savings.

The main disadvantage of life insurance is inflation. During periods of inflation, which seem to be characteristic of our economy, the premium dollars that go to insurance companies are more valuable than the dollars insurance companies pay out in later years. A dollar paid to an insurance company in 1977, for example, may have a purchasing power of 50 cents or less when the insurance company pays a related claim in 1987.

Property Insurance

Businesses usually have several kinds of property that ought to be insured: office equipment, supplies, inventories, machinery, buildings. Such properties are vulnerable to losses from such perils as accidents, theft, fire, floods, hurricanes, tornadoes, and earthquakes.

The value of the property to be insured helps determine the size of the premium that must be paid. If the fire department is right down the street from your business, it might occur to you to underinsure the property, since a complete loss of the building would be unlikely. Instead of insuring the building for its replacement value of $200,000, therefore, you might decide on coverage of only $80,000.

Insurance companies discourage this kind of thinking by specifying the appropriate amount of coverage in a coinsurance clause. Assume that the business that insured the $200,000 building for only $80,000 suffered fire damage of $5,000 and that a coinsurance clause of 80 percent is in effect. Divide the amount of insurance carried by the amount of insurance that should have been carried, and the amount of the loss is multiplied by the resulting fraction:

$$\frac{\text{Amount of insurance carried}}{\text{amount should carry}} \times \text{its actual loss} = \text{payment}$$

$$\frac{\$80,000}{.80 \times 200,000} = \frac{80,000}{160,000} = .50 \times 5,000 = \$2,500$$

Since the business carried only one-half of the $160,000 insurance specified in the coinsurance clause, the insurance settlement was for only one-half of the loss. And if the entire building were to burn to the ground, the insurance company would be liable only for the amount of insurance carried, regardless of the amount of the coinsurance clause.

Auto Insurance

Auto insurance is divided into four main categories: collision, medical, uninsured motorist, and liability coverage. To understand each type of coverage, imagine a situation in which you are driving an auto owned and insured by your company. As you pull into an intersection, another driver runs a red light and slams into your company car. But when the police arrive, the other driver insists that you, not he, ran the red light. If the other driver is declared right, your company's collision insurance will cover the repair or replacement of the company auto.

A deductible clause is usually included in the collision section of auto insurance policies. If your company policy had a $50-deductible clause, for example, your company would pay $50 toward repair of the company car, and its insurance company would pay the balance. If the policy had a $100-deductible clause your company would have to pay the first $100. The higher the deductible, however, the lower the premium; a $100-deductible clause is considered a much smarter buy than a $50-deductible one. If the other driver is declared at fault, on the other hand, his insurance company must pay the entire bill.

If the accident caused you to suffer a broken arm or other bodily injury, either your firm's insurance company or the other driver's will pay any resulting doctor or hospital bills, depending on who ran the red light. If the other driver is found responsible for the accident but has no insurance coverage, your firm's insurance company will pay for your medical bills and the damage to the company car—as provided in the uninsured motorist coverage in the policy. Insurance companies are required by law to offer such coverage at low cost to all applicants for insurance.

If the impartial witness to the accident insists that the accident was your fault, either you or the company that you work for will be held responsible for any damage to the other person. However, the liability coverage in your policy transfers this risk to the firm's insurance company.

Your firm's insurance company must attempt to settle liability claims within the limits of the policy. The policy may state, for instance, that the insurance company is responsible for liability coverage not exceeding $50,000 per claimant or $100,000 per accident. These limits may be raised or lowered, depending on the amount of money your firm is willing to pay for insurance protection.

Liability Insurance

Liability insurance is important to business in many ways besides insuring automobiles. Customers have been known to injure themselves on products, falling off chairs, walking through glass doors, and many other ways. If it can be shown that such accidents resulted from negligence, the business may be sued for large amounts of money.

For example, was the business negligent in designing or producing the product? Was the chair in disrepair? Should the glass door have been marked in some way to make it more obvious? These are questions that must be answered in the courts, and juries tend to be generous in their awards to plaintiffs who have suffered bodily injury. Because the results of such litigation could mean financial ruin for many businesses, it is common practice to protect against such losses by purchasing liability insurance.

PREPARE Questions

1. What four types of insurance are given?

a. _____

b. _____

c. _____

d. _____

2. What are the four main types of automobile insurance?

a. _____

b. _____

c. _____

d. _____

3. What is the difference between limited payment life insurance and straight life insurance?

_____

_____

4. What kind of life insurance could pay you before you die?_____

Practice Exercises

C. Answer the following questions by writing the answer in the blank or drawing a circle around the letter of your choice.

A chapter in a biology textbook is titled "Preservation of Foods." The first sentence of the introductory paragraph is

> The preservation of foods is largely a problem of preventing the growth in them of the agents of decay: bacteria, yeasts, and molds.

Three headings appear after the introductory paragraph:

> *Heat*
> *Cold*
> *Chemicals*

1. Since there are three agents of decay and three methods of preserving foods, is the material under the headings likely to identify one method for each decay agent? (For example, heat for bacteria, cold for yeasts, and chemicals for molds)
   a. yes
   b. no

2. Explain your answer to question 1.

   _____

   The paragraphs under the heading *Heat* will probably tell (a) the foods suitable for this treatment, and (b) the length of time to expose each food to the heat.

3. What is the third thing these paragraphs will probably tell?

   _____

   The paragraphs under the heading *Chemicals* will probably tell the foods suitable for this treatment.

4. What else will they probably tell?_____

Practice Exercises

D. *Answer the following questions by writing the answer in the blank, or drawing a circle around the letter of your choice.*

A sociology textbook contains an article titled "Our Modern Revolutions." There are no headings. The first five paragraphs begin with these sentences:

> This generation is living in a time of three major revolutions.
> Every day we read of new scientific wonders.
> Someday we may be able to fly airplanes and heat houses with atomic energy.
> It even seems possible that we can someday control the weather.
> The revolution in warfare is equally impressive.

1. What is the first revolution?

_____

2. What is the second revolution?

_____

> The next paragraphs begin with these sentences:

> The third revolution confines itself to several isolated locations across the globe, but its effects are felt worldwide.
> Countries that have relied for generations on profits from their colonies are having to reorganize their economies along different lines.
> Former colonies are also experiencing major shakeups as they adjust to open trade in a world-wide marketplace.
> Countries that had once enjoyed an agriculture-based economy, where the materials for production were all located within their own borders, are now focused on manufacturing, with the accompanying complications of foreign suppliers and a bewildering array of foreign customers.

3. What is the third revolution?

_____

> The next paragraph begins with this sentence:

> Here another difficulty arises.

4. To find this difficulty, where should you look first?
   a. in the next sentence
   b. at the end of the paragraph
   c. in the next heading
   d. under the next heading

Chapter 8

Locating Specific Information

In this chapter you will learn how to locate specific information in reading material. After learning this material, you will be able to

- *scan the selection; keep in mind what you are looking for*
- *look for key words or phrases*
- *read the section containing the key word or phrase*
- *decide which words provide the information that you are seeking.*

In your reading assignments you often are asked to locate *specific information*—the answer to a question asked by your teacher in class or the answer to a question asked at the end of a chapter. How do you do this? First, you must glance over the selection, with your specific purpose in mind—that is, the specific information you are being asked to locate. Then, by looking for a key word or phrase, you must determine the specific section or page or even paragraph in which the information being sought is probably located. Notice that you don't read all the words; just sample enough of the text to get an idea of what is there, and where your answer is likely to be found. This is called *scanning*—partial reading in order to locate specific information. Third, you must read the section decided upon. Finally, you must decide which particular words in the section will answer the question.

Read the paragraph below. As you do, keep in mind the following question: Which words indicate the circumstances under which the people have a right to change their form of government?

> We hold these truths to be self-evident, that all men are created equal, that they are endowed by their creator with certain inalienable rights, that among these are life, liberty, and the pursuit of happiness. That to secure these rights governments are instituted among men, deriving their just powers from the consent of the governed. That whenever any form of government becomes

destructive to these ends, it is the right of the people to alter or abolish it, and to institute new government, laying its foundation on such principles and organizing its powers in such form, as to them shall seem most likely to effect their safety and happiness.

How does the method we have just described apply in this paragraph? First, you *glance over the paragraph,* keeping in mind the specific question: Which words in the paragraph indicate the circumstances under which the people have a right to change their form of government? To answer this question, you do not have to know what truths are self-evident or what inalienable rights people are endowed with; but you probably *do* have to know what is said about "the rights of the people to *alter* or *abolish*" the government. After *locating this key phrase,* you *reread* this particular section of the paragraph. Finally, you *decide which particular words answer the question.* In this instance the correct answer is found just before the words "right of the people to alter or abolish it." The answer is "whenever any form of government becomes destructive to these ends."

The specific key words that you must find depend on the information you are looking for. The traditional six questions—*who, what when, where, why,* and *how,* plus one more, *how many*—are usually involved in finding the information. You must place the appropriate question firmly in your mind; then, as you read, you must test each idea you encounter to see if it answers that question. Sometimes you need to find out *why* something happened. Fix the *why* firmly in your mind and start reading. (Looking for the key word *because* may help you locate the specific information you are looking for.) When the author gives you a reason that it happened, you have your information. Sometimes you need to know *who* did something or was somewhere. In that case, you are looking for a *name.* Sometimes the question tells you that the key word will be a *number* (*how many*), and sometimes it tells you that the key word will be a *location* (*where*). By the way, the author won't always use the key word you're expecting, so you need to keep the *sense* of the question in mind as you read.

The following exercises provide practice in applying this method. Do them carefully. If you make an error, analyze it. At which step in the sequence did you err? Did you fail to keep in mind the specific information you were asked to locate? Were you unable to locate the section containing the information? Perhaps you could not find the exact words that answered the question. Think each error through before going on to the next question.

In Brief

Scanning is partial reading intended to locate specific information. Steps in scanning:

1. Locate the general area that might contain the information
2. Glance over the area, looking for key words
3. Read the section that contains the key word
4. Decide which words provide the needed information

The traditional six questions:

1. *Who?*
2. *What?*
3. *Where?*
4. *When?*
5. *Why?*
6. *How?*

Plus one more: *How many?*

Practice Exercises

1. Column A below lists the kinds of information you may be asked to locate. Column B lists key phrases. Find the key phrase in column B that gives you the information you are looking for in column A and place its letter in the space provided.

A	B
_____ In what geographical location?	A. because it's late
_____ When should she go?	B. a dozen eggs
_____ Why can't I?	C. 14
_____ Where is it?	D. he will go home
_____ Under what circumstances?	E. my friend
_____ Who is it?	F. in the kitchen
_____ What is in the bag?	G. in about a year
_____ How many are there?	H. when it's cold
_____ What will happen?	I. in the ocean

Read each of the paragraphs below and, in the space provided, answer the questions preceding them.

2. Which words tell two ways in which special-purpose fans are helpful?

Ventilate the house when outside air is drier than that inside. As the air comes in, it takes moisture from the damp interior walls and furnishings. Then the moisture vapor is carried outdoors. Since cool air holds less moisture than warm air, take advantage of cool nights to freshen the air in the entire house.

Run an electric fan in places that cannot be exposed to outdoor breezes. Special-purpose fans, such as adjustable window fans, can be used to help remove moisture and keep the house well ventilated.

_____

_____

3. Which words tell how you should cook seafood so that it will be tender, flavor-ful, moist, and appetizing in appearance?

Although raw fish is enjoyed in various countries of the world, cooking fish and shellfish is necessary to make it acceptable for most Americans. You can easily learn to cook any seafood so that it will be tender, flavorful, moist, and appetizing in appearance. Just use a moderate temperature and short cooking time—and you have won the battle.

_____

_____

4. Which words tell why some people have difficulty remembering the names of people they are introduced to?

There is possibly no sweeter sound to the human ear than the sound of one's own name. If you don't know the interviewer's name prior to meeting her, concentrate on it when she introduces herself and remember it. For some people this is very difficult. They are concentrating on themselves so much and thinking about how nervous they are that they completely forget the name or don't pay close attention when they hear it for the first time.

_____

_____

5. Which words tell why people would have to help each other during an emergency?

A nuclear attack on the United States would cause great numbers of casualties, and there would be fewer doctors, nurses, and hospitals available to care for them. Even in areas where no nuclear weapons exploded, radioactive fallout could prevent doctors and nurses from reaching injured or sick persons for a considerable period of time.

_____

_____

6. Which words tell why you should store flammable materials outside the home?

Store explosive or flammable fluids carefully, outside the home if possible. Never use gasoline, benzine, naphtha, and similar fluids indoors—if their vapors mix with air in a closed space, they will ignite readily from any kind of a spark. Rags soaked with oil or turpentine sometimes catch fire by themselves (this is called spontaneous combustion), and therefore should never be left lying around.

_____

_____

7. Which words tell why vegetables should not be allowed to stand after they are gathered?

When to gather vegetables is a very important part of good gardening. Many people let vegetables get too ripe before harvesting them. Vegetables should be eaten while they are young and tender. They taste better, and many of them have more protective food value then than they do when they get too mature.

Vegetables like beans, peas, okra, and lettuce should be gathered every day or two. Vegetables should not be allowed to stand after gathering. When they become wilted or dried out, they are not as good. All vegetables should be cooked, eaten, or preserved in some way as soon after harvesting as possible.

_____

_____

8. Which words tell a good way to learn the chemical symbols?

It is important that the student begin to learn the symbols immediately. Since they represent the basic building blocks of matter, they will be used extensively in the remainder of this book and in future chemistry courses the student may take. To write chemical equations, one must know the chemical symbols. One way to learn the symbols is to practice writing them a few minutes every day, by first making a list of the names and the symbols side by side and then alternately writing the names and the symbols.

_____

_____

9. Which words tell why it is important to explore the world?

To find your own identity, you must face the real world and explore it. You must discover what you can do and how well you do it. You must build things—cars, boats, racers, stereos. You must pit your physical strength against your peers in football, swimming, and mountain climbing. You must earn money and make friends. You must organize and master whatever you can. Such seeing, exploring, and doing must be of your own choosing. Then society, too, will observe what you can do and who you are and what you are becoming. Meanwhile, you will be finding your way and your personal identity.

_____

_____

10. Which words give the relative positions of the sun, earth, and moon at the time of spring tides?

Twice each month, when the moon is a mere thread of silver in the sky, and again when it is full, we have the strong tidal movements—the highest flood tides and the lowest ebb tides of the lunar month. These are called the spring tides. At these times, sun, moon and earth are directly in line and the pull of the two heavenly bodies is added together to bring the water high on the beaches, and send its surf leaping upward against the sea cliffs, and draw a brimming tide into the harbors so that the boats float high beside their wharfs. And twice each month, at the quarters of the moon, when sun, moon and earth lie at the apexes of a triangle, and the pull of the sun and moon are opposed, we have the moderate tidal movements called neap tides. Then the difference between high and low water is less than at any other time during the month.

_____

_____

11. Which words show why listening skill is important?

You learn in school through your ears as well as through your eyes. Experts who have studied human communication thoroughly have come up with some revealing facts. They show that the average individual spends approximately 70 percent of his or her time communicating. Only about 9 percent of this time is devoted to writing, 16 percent to reading, 30 percent to talking and 45 percent to listening. However, in spite of the large amount of time spent in listening, the average person does not do it well. Estimates of listening efficiency show that the average skill is only about 25 percent of what it should be.

_____

_____

12. Which words tell why negativism is important?

Frequently this exploration manifests itself by a period of negativism. Every parental suggestion is greeted by "No." While this is frustrating to the parents, it probably is an important step in the development of self-awareness and independence. Such negativism typically reaches its peak between the ages of two and a half and three and a half and then normally declines. Although negativism is annoying, parents who know that such a stage is common can tolerate it with some amusement. For other parents, however, negativism represents a severe threat to parental authority and the parent may act vigorously and forcefully.

_____

_____

13. Which words show why squadrons were stationed in the West Indies?

The ships of the new navy were soon at sea. In December they numbered fourteen men-of-war properly armed, and eight converted merchantmen. Some of them were small, but most of them were fast and well manned. They were well able to deal with the French privateers; and the frigates, the pride of the fleet, showed that they could meet successfully ships of equal size from the French navy. Squadrons were stationed in the West Indies, where our commerce suffered most, with orders to seize privateers wherever found.

_____

_____

14. Which words suggest why rapid recognition of pictures of aircraft doesn't give skill in recognizing real airplanes?

Research showed that students who had practiced recognizing dots and numbers with brief exposure did not develop a general efficiency which helped them in aircraft recognition. Their recognition learning scores were no better than those of students who had not had special training. This suggests that practice is most efficient when carried out in a situation as similar as possible to that in which training is applied. In fact, even training on rapid recognition of pictures of aircraft had little relationship to skill in recognition of real airplanes.

_____

_____

15. Which words indicate how phytochrome behaves like a protein?

Phytochrome has been isolated from plant tissue, although not yet in purified form. It behaves like a protein (its activity is destroyed at high temperatures) and is probably an enzyme. It has not yet been concentrated sufficiently to make its color visible, but the fact that it absorbs strongly in the red and far-red end of the light spectrum suggests that it is a blue pigment.

_____

_____

16. Which words tell under what circumstances the cowboy was a board-whacker?

The cowboy was a board-whacker. Each time he held superior cards, he whanged them, one by one, with exceeding force, down upon the improvised table, and took the tricks with a glowing air of prowess and pride that sent thrills of indignation into the hearts of his opponents. A game with a board-whacker in it is sure to become intense. The countenances of the Easterner and the Swede were miserable whenever the cowboy thundered down his aces and kings, while Johnnie, his eyes gleaming with joy, chuckled and chuckled.

_____

_____

17. Which words tell why they were there?

But it was the ship all right, the ship they had been sent to find. They came upon her suddenly: she was masked until the last moment by the gently whirling snow, and then suddenly she emerged and lay before them—a small untidy freighter with Swedish funnel-markings. She was derelict, drifting downwind like some wretched tramp sagging his way through a crowd: she listed heavily, her bridge and forepart were blistered and fire-blackened, and her forebridge itself, which seemed to have taken a direct hit from a bomb or a shell, looked like a twisted metal cage from which something violent and strong had ripped a way to freedom. One lifeboat was missing, the other hung down from the falls, half-overturned and empty. There was nothing else in the picture.

_____

_____

18. Which words tell why golf can be as strenuous as you want to make it?

Golf can be as strenuous as you want to make it. Since the golfer sets his own pace, golf can be stimulating or relaxing. Endurance and strength may be improved by increasing the number of holes played and the distance of balls hit. Golf offers the opportunity to be out-of-doors, to walk or ride while enjoying nature and fellowship. It can be challenging, satisfying, and relaxing, even if played during a short period of leisure time. Because it is challenging, golf offers opportunity for sportsmanship, whether alone or with a group.

_____

_____

19. *a.* Which words tell three disadvantages of television advertising?
    b. Which words tell what hours are called "driving time"?
    c. Which words tell what is meant by "lead time"?
    d. Which words tell why "prime time" costs more?

Advertisers must consider two main disadvantages in magazine advertising. First, the ads cost significantly more than newspaper ads. Second, the element of timeliness is sacrificed. The lead time (time between placement of an ad and its publication) for magazine articles is often as long as two months, which means that copy and artwork must be submitted to a magazine two months before the date of publication. The whole marketing pattern of a product may change during a two-month period, however.

The broadcast media include television and radio. Advertisers may demonstrate their products to large audiences with *television* commercials, and they may appeal to certain marketing segments by placing their commercials with certain types of programs. The hours between 8:00 and 11:00 P.M. are considered prime time, when the largest number of people have their TVs turned on; advertisers must pay higher prices to have their commercials broadcast during these hours.

High cost is the greatest disadvantage of television. Because of the wide audience this medium reaches, however, the cost per viewer is sometimes lower than with magazine advertising. Television commercials have a very limited life; once they are viewed, they are gone. Also, television commercials are wasted on many viewers who have no interests in the products being advertised.

Advertisers may also reach large audiences with *radio* commercials, and they may select their audiences to some degree by choosing from a large variety of stations, programs, and times. The most expensive advertising time on radio, known as "driving time," are the hours between 6:00 and 10:00 A.M. and between 3:00 and 6:00 P.M., when people are driving to and from work with their radios turned on.

The lead time for radio commercials is relatively short, depending on the hour and programming desired, and radio personnel tend to be flexible in responding to last-minute changes in advertising. However, radio commercials suffer from two major disadvantages. As with television advertising, radio commercials are short-lived. Additionally, the lack of visual communication makes it impossible to demonstrate consumer products on radio.

a.　(1) _____

　　　(2) _____

　　　(3) _____

b. _____

c. _____

d. _____

20. *a.* Which words give two advantages of public education of all classes?
　　　b. Which words tell why people wanted to own property?

c. Which words tell what happened to the country town?

d. Which words tell what, besides a growing demand for white-collar workers, resulted in a longer school term?

e. Which words tell why the Gilded Age seems leisurely to us?

On the whole, there was a rise in the American standard of living. Since ownership of property was a badge of respectability, even the working class strove to acquire title to their cottages, while the better-to-do lived in houses decked out with cupolas, bay windows, pillared porches, jigsaw scroll work, and spacious enough to accommodate large families. Still, even for the well-to-do, servants were getting scarcer, and the effect was seen in a growing simplicity of furnishings and a lighter diet. Improved plumbing made bathrooms possible, and improved furnaces made central heating possible.

Though the Gilded Age seemed fevered to itself, to us it seems leisurely. There was time for the manufacture of one's own pleasure and less dependence on mass entertainment than there is now. But the change was under way. Even before the Civil War the nation had been participating in sports such as wrestling, boxing, and racing. Team sports now entered: rowing, baseball, basketball, and football. Baseball began to take on commercial and professional status. Tennis and golf became excuses for social gatherings. By 1900 there were ten million bicycles in use, and manufacturers and bicycle clubs were promoting a good-roads movement.

The Gilded Age may have devoted its main attention to the city, but it was also the heyday of the country towns, and the country town was to be remembered with nostalgia by the generation that rose to power in the business, political, and intellectual realms. That world was rooted out by the automobile, and something fine, unhurried, and neighborly went out with it. While it was true that social pressures were more powerful in the town than in the city, yet there were compensations. Everyone knew everybody else, and if community opinion was a powerful rein on personal behavior, the residents supported one another against strangers and gave help in time of need.

Democratic education. The nation was happily able to spare young people from production and service in order to give them a chance to broaden their education. Education of all classes in the public schools was presumed to advance democracy by weakening class-consciousness; moreover, it was a means of assimilating immigrants to American culture. With this higher valuation of education there was a growing disapproval both by society and by labor organizations of child labor in industry. These, combined with the growing demand for white-collar workers, resulted in lengthening the school term and adding to the years the child was compelled to attend school. Public high schools began to displace private academies, and promotion of scientific education was stimulated by the growing need of industry for chemists, mathematicians, and engineers. The movement was encouraged by the influence over American colleges and universities of German universities with their attention to science. State universities had been neglected during the antebellum era, but the Morrill Land Grant Act of 1862 . . . together with increased appropriations by state legislatures, had given them a new lease on life, clearly evident by the 1890s.

a. (1) _____

    (2) _____

b. _____

c. _____

d. _____

e. _____

Chapter 9

Following Printed Directions

This chapter will offer you various suggestions for following printed directions found in tests, in textbooks, in lab manuals, and elsewhere. Learning this material will enable you to

- *identify the purpose*
- *visualize*
- *note guide words*
- *know the order.*

Even when you know most of the answers, you may do poorly on important examinations because you have difficulty understanding printed directions. Even when an examination is not at issue, you may have had trouble following directions in other academic situations: the directions for experiments in science laboratories, directions for preparing foods in home economics classes, directions on the athletic field, directions and/or procedures in nursing education. In all these instances, students often go astray because they do not follow the given instructions.

Why do printed directions cause so much difficulty? Mainly because people get only a *general* idea of what is wanted and do not attend to every step in the directions. Sometimes people who are familiar with a procedure read lightly through the directions, assuming that the directions will tell them what they already know. If the directions differ from their expectations, these people don't notice it and perform the procedure incorrectly. Other people, who haven't really committed themselves to following the directions, read as if they are reading a magazine article and miss some of the procedure. In both cases, these readers went wrong because they got only a general idea instead of a precise understanding of the directions.

Your first step in following directions is to commit yourself; decide that you will do exactly as the directions indicate, even if you already know a better way. Your next step is to read through the directions to discover what they are trying to accomplish and whether any special tools or materials are required. (Well-written directions will often contain a list of tools and materials, along with the estimated time you'll need to do the job.) If there are words or procedures you don't understand, clarify them now. Since certain procedures occur again and again, authors will not explain them each time and the directions may confuse you. A cookbook may say, "To a basic white sauce, add . . . " without telling you what a white sauce is. An auto repair manual may tell you, "Tighten the studs in a crisscross pattern, torquing them in stages to 95 foot pounds." Unless you understand the words and procedures already, find out what they mean.

After you gather your tools and materials and have an understanding of each part of the process, you're ready to start doing things. Read through the first step in the procedure, do it, then read again to make sure you did it correctly. Often the steps will be numbered; if not, you need to divide the procedure into steps. When the first step is finished, go to the next, then on through the procedure. Don't try to do the procedure by memory. Airline pilots have a checklist that they read aloud before every takeoff, even if they have flown almost daily for twenty years.

To follow directions, you must understand each step in the directions, in its proper order. You must also use other skills, particularly visualizing, seeing relationships, and utilizing guide words. Guide words are words and phrases such as *first, then, after that, next, now, finally,* and the like.

Read the following directions for taking a pulse count.

> Place the first three fingers of your hand on the inner surface of the patient's wrist just above the thumb. Press down gently but firmly with the fingertips until artery pulsations can easily be felt.
>
> Now count the pulsations that occur in a half-minute period, using a watch with a second hand for timing. Wait a few seconds and then repeat the count for another half-minute period. The two figures should be almost identical. If there is a difference of more than one or two between the counts, repeat the procedure. Then add the two counts together for the pulse rate, which is customarily expressed in pulsations per minute.
>
> Note the pulse rate on the patient's record together with his temperature. Note any irregularities in rhythm, and state whether [the pulse] appears strong or weak.

Were you able to follow the directions? If not, you probably had difficulty in visualizing them. When this happens, you may find it helpful to act out (or, for some instructions, to draw a picture of) each step in the procedure. How many steps are there in these directions for pulse taking? What must you do first? What must you do next, and next? Try to list the steps in the directions now, before reading further. Check your list by rereading the directions and numbering the steps as you read. (You should find seven steps altogether.) Note any steps that you omitted or put in the wrong order. If your list is incorrect, do you understand why you made an error? For example, did you recognize the guide words *now* and *then,* which indicate that a new step should be taken?

Read the following directions for taking a test.

      This test covers four pages, beginning on Page 9, and has six parts. If you finish Part 1 before time is called, go right on to Part 2 on Page 10, and then to Parts 3 and 4 on Page 11, and then to Parts 5 and 6 on Page 12. However, if you have not finished Part 1 (or any part) before time is called, go right to the next part when told to do so. Do not guess on Parts 1, 3, and 6. However, you may guess without penalty on Parts 2, 4, and 5.

Did you visualize as you read? What should you do first? (Begin with Part 1.) What should you be aware of as you work? (Time limits; penalty for guessing.) Which two parts are the longest? (Parts 1 and 2—one page each.)

    Students often lose points on tests because they don't follow directions rather than because they don't know the answers. Test directions will usually give you information on time, scoring, and options. Try to understand the following directions. Then answer the questions that follow them.

      In the following test, circle the *T* if the statement is true. If the statement is false, circle the *F* and then correct the statement in the space provided. The odd-numbered questions count one point each and the even-numbered questions count two points each. (The one-point questions are considered to be easier than the two-point questions.) You should not answer all of the questions. Answer enough questions to give you a total of twenty points only. Answers beyond that will not be looked at. (You may answer any combination of one- and two-point questions to bring you to twenty points.) You will have fifteen minutes to complete this test.

1. Which of the following questions count two points? Put a circle around the correct answer(s).
   Questions: 1, 2, 3, 5, 6, 9, 10, 12, 13

2. Why do some of the questions count more than others?

   _____

3. How much time do you have to complete the test?

   _____

4. Why isn't it a good idea to answer all of the questions?

   _____

   _____

5. Would you be following the directions if you answered the following questions only? If not, why not?
   Questions: 1, 3, 4, 6, 8, 9, 11, 14, 15, 19, 20, 22, 26

   _____

6. Would you be following the directions if you answered the following questions only? If not, why not?
   Questions: 2, 4, 5, 7, 9, 10, 11, 12, 14, 18, 20, 21, 22, 23

   _____

Your answers should have been as follows: (1) circle 2, 6, 10, 12; (2) they are more difficult; (3) 15 minutes; (4) answers that total beyond 20 points will not be looked at; (5) yes; (6) no, you answered questions with a total of 22 possible points.

Most of the time, directions are not as complicated as the preceding set. Many students, however, still have difficulty with printed directions. The practice exercises can help you become more proficient in this skill than you are now. Do them carefully.

In Brief

▼

People have difficulty following directions when they read too lightly and get only a general idea of the procedure.

Suggestions for following directions:
  Decide to follow the directions.
  Be aware of the purpose of the directions.
  Read through the directions, noting:
    tools you'll need.
    materials you'll need.
    vocabulary you don't understand.
    procedures you don't understand.

As you follow the directions:
  Use the guide words.
  Understand the order of the steps.
  Visualize the process by:
    acting out the steps.
    drawing pictures.

Practice Exercises

Read the following sets of directions. Then answer the questions that follow them. Visualizing these directions will help you.

1. To ensure a smooth, even swing or a rhythmical, synchronized swing, it is imperative that a stable base be maintained throughout. Place the feet a comfortable distance apart with the weight pulled toward the inside of the ankles, slightly forward on the balls of the feet. This position is not to be exaggerated, but it should give a feeling of firmness with the ground.

   Flex the knees slightly to give a comfortable and relaxed feeling. This will also put the weight on the balls of the feet.

   Bend the trunk forward, as explained above, and hold the head stationary with the eyes focused on the ball.

   Let the arms hang comfortably from the shoulders. The right arm will extend a bit below the left, because the right hand is placed below with left hand on the grip.

   With a proper stance—the weight balanced over the feet, knees relaxed, trunk bent forward at the waist, head down, eyes focused on the ball—and the correct grip, the golfer is ready to hit the ball.

   Many golfers find that a preliminary waggle (lifting the club and replacing it while addressing the ball) helps to release tension, aids in securing a better footing, helps in seeing that the clubhead is in correct position, and aids in reminding them to use their wrists.

   a. How do you get the weight on the balls of the feet?

   _____

   b. Even though you have the proper stance, what might you do before you hit the ball?

   _____

   c. What should you do before you flex your knees?

   _____

2. **Tables.** Type each table double-spaced on a separate page. However, if your manuscript contains many tables, two or three to a page are acceptable, because it would not be efficient to give each table a separate page. Type every table with enough space between columns and around headings to indicate the divisions clearly, but leave to the editor the question of whether vertical or horizontal rules are needed. Table 2 illustrates a clearly typed table. For directions on numbering

table footnotes, see page 30. Place table footnotes directly beneath the table so that they will not be confused with text footnotes.

a. When is it acceptable to use two or three tables to a page?

_____

b. How do you prevent table footnotes from being confused with text footnotes?

_____

c. Why might the editor want to use vertical or horizontal rules?

_____

3. Several statements follow. Place either *1, 2, 3,* or *4* or any combination of *1, 2, 3,* or *4* in the space provided to the left of each statement. Place *1* if you strongly agree with the statement, *2* if you disagree strongly, *3* if you think the statement is incorrect (either wholly or partially), and *4* if you think the statement is correct but you don't have a strong feeling about it either way.

a. Which of the following combinations of answers would be reasonable according to the above directions? circle the number to the left of your answer.

(1) *1* and *3* (2) *2* and *3* (3) *3* and *4* (4) *1* and *2*

b. Which answer would you use if you had a strong favorable feeling about the

statement? _____

c. Why wouldn't the answer *1 and 4* be a reasonable choice?

_____

4. When you take notes from a class lecture about a topic that was assigned in advance, always try to gain as much knowledge are you can about the topic before the lecture begins. The laws of learning tell us that we learn faster and remember longer when we are even slightly familiar with the information given. When you enter the lecture room, take out your notebook immediately and have writing equipment ready so that you are prepared to take notes as soon as the lecturer begins. Getting ready after the lecture has begun may cause you to lose important information. Try to phrase the notes in your own words. This helps to ensure comprehension. Listen carefully for key words to main thoughts or lists of details or conclusions. Finally, be sure to look over the notes as soon as possible after the lecture and reorganize them if necessary.

a. What is the purpose of these directions? _____

_____

b. This paragraph mentions six different things to do. List them in your own words

_____

_____

_____

_____

_____

_____

c. The passage gives four reasons for following the directions given. List them in your own words.

_____

_____

_____

5. Writing a research paper requires several steps in order to go from an idea to a finished statement. First, you must select a topic. Your instructor may give you several areas from which you may choose. Before making a final decision, you should do a preliminary survey. Check each of the possible topics in the library and be sure there will be enough information about the one that you finally choose. Then research your topic completely. You should use note cards to put information on. Now develop an outline. To do this, you must think about an orderly way to present your material and you must think about the conclusions you will come to. The next step is to write the first draft. Follow your outline and use the material on your note cards. The next step is important. Put your work aside for at least a day, preferably two days, then reread it and be very critical of what you said and how you said it. Now you may be ready to write the final version or you may need to write one or two revisions. If you do, be sure to allow at least one day before rereading each one. When you do write your final paper, be sure that spelling, punctuation, and grammar are correct.

a. What are the steps in writing a research paper?

_____

_____

_____

b. What should you do before you finally select your topic?

_____

_____

c. There are at least six guide words that help you understand the order in which the directions should be followed. Circle at least four of them.

Each of the following paragraphs gives directions for a particular procedure. Following each paragraph is a list of some steps in the procedure. Number these steps in the order they should be followed. If two or more steps could be done at the same time, or if they mean the same thing, give them the same number.

6. In one example of the experimental method, the investigators wanted to learn whether having a pleasant, rewarding experience predisposed people to helping others. They planted dimes in the coin return of a telephone booth and, when a caller left the booth after finding a dime, they had a woman confederate hurry by and drop an armload of papers and notebooks. Of the eight men and eight women who found the dime, all except two of the men stopped to help the confederate pick up the papers. Of the sixteen women and nine men who did not find the dime, only one man attempted to help. The researchers felt they had made their point.

   _____ The woman confederate dropped papers and notebooks.

   _____ The caller left the booth.

   _____ The dime was planted.

   _____ The caller helped the confederate pick up the papers and notebooks.

   _____ The caller found the dime.

7. Place chicken, cut at joints, in water. Add vegetables, salt, and pepper and cook slowly, covered tightly, 2 to 3 hours. Then add sugar and citric acid (sour salt) and boil 3 minutes. Remove from flame and stir about 1 pint of this soup into the yolks gradually, so it will not curdle. Mix all together. Boiling water may be added if mixture is too thick.

   _____ Add sour salt.

   _____ Stir one pint of soup into yolks.

   _____ Cut the chicken at joints.

   _____ Place chicken in water.

   _____ Cover tightly.

8. If a stain is deeply imbedded, work the detergent thoroughly into the fabric. One way to do this is to rub detergent lightly into the stained area; then, holding the fabric with both hands, work the stained area back and forth between your thumbs. Bend the yarns sharply so that the individual fibers in the yarn rub against one another. It is this bending of yarns, rather than rubbing the surface of the fabric, that is effective in removing the stain. Go over the entire stained area in this way. Then rinse thoroughly.

_____ Rub the detergent lightly into the stained area.

_____ Rinse.

_____ Bend the yarns sharply.

_____ Determine if the stain is deeply imbedded.

_____ Grasp the fabric with both hands.

9. In reading the first card of a data group, the computer expects to match the name beginning at column 3 with the class name of the READ statement. If the match fails, the computer will skip over the remaining cards in this data group and try again on the next group. Repeated failure to find the desired class name will effectively exhaust the data and terminate execution of the program.

_____ The computer tries to match the name beginning at column 3 with the class name.

_____ The computer reads the first card of a data group.

_____ The computer tries a second group.

_____ The data are exhausted.

_____ The match fails.

10. Slice up tart, firm apples, leaving the skins on. To 3 or 4 tablespoons of sausage fat in the pan, add the apples, sprinkle with sugar, cover, and cook slowly until the apples are tender. Then remove the cover, turn the apples carefully so the pieces will hold their shape, and let them brown. Serve the fried apples on a hot platter with the fried sausage.

_____ Sprinkle apples with sugar.

_____ Let apples brown.

_____ Put fat in pan.

_____ Slice apples.

_____ Turn apples carefully.

11. There are various techniques for gathering random samples. For instance, in the situation described one might put the name of each of the students on a separate card. Then one might shuffle all the cards in a large container and draw at random the number of cards desired for the sample. The final step would be to consider only those students selected and ask them for their opinions, which would constitute the sample.

_____ Ask students for their opinions.

_____ Obtain a large container.

_____ Shuffle the cards.

_____ Draw the desired number of cards.

_____ Put students' names on cards.

12. To get MD we first fill in the D column with the deviations of the step midpoints (X) from the mean; in this case, from 52.00. We next fill in the FD column with the products of F and D for each step. Ignoring the minus signs, we get the arithmetic sum of this column, and substitute in the formula.

_____ Determine the products of F and D.

_____ Determine the deviations of the step midpoints from the mean.

_____ Fill in the FD column.

_____ Determine the arithmetic sum of the FD column.

_____ Ignore the minus signs.

13. A fractured arm or leg should be straightened out as much as possible, preferably by having two persons gently stretch it into a normal position. Then it should be "splinted"—that is, fastened to a board or something else to prevent motion and keep the ends of the broken bone together. As a splint, use a board, a trimmed branch from a tree, a broomstick, an umbrella, a roll of newspapers, or anything else rigid enough to keep the arm or leg straight. Fasten the arm or leg to the splint with bandages, strips of cloth, handkerchiefs, neckties, or belts. After splinting, keep the injured arm or leg a little higher than the rest of the patient's body. From time to time, make sure that the splint is not too tight, since the arm or leg may swell, and the blood circulation might be shut off. If the broken bone is sticking out through the skin but the exposed part of it is clean, allow it to slip back naturally under the skin (but don't push it in) when the limb is being straightened.

_____ Check to see that splint is not too tight.

_____ Fasten arm to splint.

_____ Allow bone that is sticking through skin to slip back under skin.

_____ Keep injured part higher than the rest of the body.

_____ Straighten out injured part.

14. To balance an equation, first count and then compare the number of atoms of each element on both sides of the equation to determine which ones are unbalanced. Then balance each element one at a time by placing small whole numbers in front of the formulas of the substances containing the unbalanced element so that the number of atoms of each element is the same on both sides of the equation. Next, check all elements after each individual element is balanced to make sure that in balancing one element, you haven't unbalanced others.

_____ Balance each element.

_____ Check all elements to see if any elements have become unbalanced.

_____ Count the number of atoms of each element on both sides of the equation.

_____ Place small whole numbers in front of the formulas of the substances containing the unbalanced element so that the number of atoms of each element is the same on both sides of the equation.

_____ Compare the number of atoms of each element on both sides of the equation.

15. Take the Jackson State Parkway into the Northern Parkway to the third exit after Exit 4. This will be Broker Avenue. Drive north one mile to Roper Road and turn left. Continue to Orange Street, turn right, and drive along Orange Street until you come to the Crown Shopping Center.

_____ Turn left onto Roper Road.

_____ Turn off the Northern Parkway onto the third exit after Exit 4.

_____ Get onto the Northern Parkway from the Jackson State Parkway.

_____ Drive along Orange Street.

_____ Turn off the Northern Parkway onto Broker Avenue.

16. If, while observing an experiment, a scientist has an idea concerning the general behavior of matter in the experiment, he or she may propose a *hypothesis*. This hypothesis is a tentative supposition to explain certain facts. To test the hypothesis, the scientist must conduct more experiments to obtain more supporting information, and then evaluate the results. If the results support his or her hypothesis, the scientist may advance a *theory* concerning the investigation. This theory is a verified hypothesis, a general principle that may be used to explain certain phenomena. Theories generally involve some speculation and are subject to change when more reliable facts are discovered. The atomic theory, for example, is still being refined today. If a hypothesis or a theory has withstood the test of further experiments, it may become a *scientific law*.

_____ The theory becomes a scientific law.

_____ The scientist evaluates the results of his or her experiments.

_____ The scientist advances a theory.

_____ The theory withstands the test of further experiments.

_____ The results of the experiments support the hypothesis.

17. To find out if a dial train combination is correct, divide the number of teeth in the minute wheel, which, in the following example, is 36, by the leaves of the cannon pinion, 12, and the number of teeth in the hour wheel, 48, by the number of leaves in the minute wheel pinion, 12. The quotients, 3 and 4, are multiplied and the result is 12, which is the correct combination for a dial train.

_____ Divide 48 by 12.

_____ Divide the number of teeth in the minute wheel by the leaves of the cannon pinion.

_____ Multiply 3 and 4.

_____ Divide 36 by 12.

_____ Divide the number of teeth in the hour wheel by the number of leaves in the minute wheel pinion.

18. The first step is to rank the measures of height, assigning rank 1 to the largest and rank *N* (in this case 10) to the smallest, and intermediate ranks to the other scores between these extremes. The tied scores are the only ones to cause any confusion, but these are handled in logical manner. For example, the two 71s, had they not been tied, would have filled rank positions 2 and 3; hence we split the points between them and assign the average rank, 2.5, to each. In the case of the triple tie between the 68s for ranks 6, 7, and 8, each is assigned the average rank again—in this case, 7. But we must be careful in ranking the next measure to skip rank 8, which has already been accounted for. In similar fashion we rank the other set of measures, the weights. Then, as the name of the method suggests, we fill in the *D* column with the differences in ranks, ignoring the minus signs. We finally square each *D* value, obtain ΣD^2, and substitute in the formula.

_____ Rank the measures of height.

_____ Rank the measures of weight.

_____ Fill in the D column.

_____ Ignore the minus signs.

_____ Square each D value.

19. The first step in giving a medicine is to check the physician's orders for dosage and timing. Read the label on the medicine container, and compare it with the orders. (It's a good idea to cover the label with transparent cellophane tape to protect the directions from stains.)

   Shake the container well if the label so directs. Remove the cap, cork, top of the box, etc., and read the label again.

   Pour the exact dose of liquid medicine into a spoon or medicine glass (a medicine glass with its accurate markings is preferable, since spoons vary greatly in size).

   If dosage is by the drop, count the number aloud and take care that the medicine does not go up into the rubber bulb of the dropper. Doses of nonliquid medicines—pills, capsules tablets, and powders—should be counted out carefully.

   Read the label on the container again as a final check on the accuracy of the dose and the kind of medicine. Then give the medicine to the patient according to the physician's instructions (plain, mixed with water, or followed by water or other liquid).

   Note on the patient's record that the medicine was given. Indicate kind of medicine, time, amount given, and any reaction to it.

   Wash the spoon or medicine glass and the drinking glass, and replace on the medicine tray. Keep this tray in a safe place, away from children.

_____ Check the label for directions.

_____ Check the label for directions a second time.

_____ Compare the label with the physician's orders.

_____ Pour the medicine out or count the pills.

_____ Wash the spoon.

20. **Prepare**

   Research in learning tells us that you learn new information best when you can relate or associate this new information with something that you already know. When you PREPARE your textbook for study, you reach back into the warehouse containing millions of bits and pieces of information you have stored in your mind during your lifetime up to the moment that you apply this technique. These connectors or associations are then lined up ready for use _before you actually read the chapter._ To prepare a chapter for study, _actively_ read five things. (_Actively_ means _read and think about,_ not just stare at.)

First, actively read the TITLE. What does it tell you about the content of the chapter? What do you *already* know about this topic? Don't be afraid to guess. Even if you guess incorrectly, you are reading actively and will correct your error as you proceed in the prepare steps. Thinking about the title helps to bring to the forefront of your mind any information you may have stored away on this topic. It helps commandeer and organize all of this information *before* you begin to actually read the chapter.

Next, read carefully the INTRODUCTION to the chapter. If there is no introduction, read the paragraph(s) before the first heading. Authors often give a brief outline of the chapter in their introduction. They tell you where they are going and how they are going to get there. Try to relate the introduction to the title. Doing this should either (1) reinforce your guess (after reading the title) as to what the chapter is about, or (2) help you to realize that your original thought was incorrect.

Third, turn to the end of the chapter and read actively the SUMMARY (if any) or questions about the chapter (if any). A summary will outline the important points made in the heart of the chapter, and questions at the end of a chapter will be geared to material that the author thinks is important. Again, try to relate the ideas in the summary and/or the questions to the information gathered in the title and the introduction. People who read murder mysteries are often told *not* to look at the last page or two of the book, because that will spoil it for them. They will discover who the murderer is, and this takes away all of the suspense and excitement of the book. In study, however, you *want* to be able to predict the author's ideas *before* you actually read the selection. The summary separates the fat from the meat. It gives you the highlights *before* you actually read the chapter.

Fourth, read (and think about) the first HEADING. How does it relate to the title and the introduction and the information at the end of the chapter? What will the subsection *probably* be about? Read actively, trying to correlate everything read so far.

Fifth, read actively the FIRST SENTENCE of each paragraph under the first heading. Although first sentences of paragraphs are not necessarily main-idea sentences, reading *all* first sentences will usually furnish you with all of the main points that the author makes. Don't be concerned, however, if even doing this does not seem to provide much information. The background it provides will be of help when you do the Q3R.

Now redo steps 4 and 5 for each subsection. In other words, read and think about the *second* heading and then read the first sentence of each paragraph in the *second* subsection. Then do the same for the *third* heading and *third* subsection and so on through the entire chapter. When going through the subsections and reading first sentences of paragraphs, you should also examine pictures, maps, charts, graphs, tables, and all other illustrative materials. Remember that these aids are not decorations but important aids to understanding the material. An author sometimes takes a page or more to explain verbally what is expressed in a table occupying perhaps a quarter of a page. When you prepare this table before reading the chapter, you are acquainting yourself with the highlights and can go through the verbal explanation much faster and with better understanding when you get to it. Also, people tend to remember best what they see first. When you look at illustrative material in advance, you are exposed to the important information *first* without the details interfering.

Also, while doing Step 5, look carefully at words that are underlined or printed in italics or boldface or capital letters. The author meant for these words to be given special attention, or they wouldn't have been given emphasis.

_____ Read the first heading.

_____ Think about the title.

_____ Read the first sentence of each paragraph under the first heading.

_____ Read the introduction.

_____ Relate the summary to the title.

_____ Relate the introduction to the title.

_____ Do steps 4 and 5 for each subsection.

Chapter 10

Understanding Figurative Language

In this chapter you will learn about figurative language. When you finish, you will know

- *how to recognize it*
- *how to understand it.*

Sometimes you can understand points that authors try to make or moods that they try to express when they compare that point or that mood to something that is familiar to you. That is, authors compare something they want their readers to understand with something already familiar to their readers. Figurative language is language that makes comparisons between things so that readers can understand these things better or visualize them more vividly.

It is important for you to be able to recognize figurative language when you read it. If you have difficulty in doing so, you may not understand what authors are really saying. It is also important for you to be able to understand figurative language. These two factors—recognizing figurative language and understanding it—are important if you are to fully comprehend reading material in which figurative language appears.

Read the following statements to discover their meanings.

1. *He hit a solid wall* in his attempt to solve the algebra problem.
2. The old man's face was a *raisin.*

What do these sentences really say? In sentence 1, the statement certainly doesn't mean that the person involved was so frustrated in trying to solve the algebra problem that he hit his head against a wall. What does a solid wall represent? One thing it suggests is separation. Things on one side of the wall are separated from things on the other side of the wall. Another quality is impenetrability. A solid wall stops you and prevents you from progressing any further. It is this quality of a solid wall that is being compared to the lack of progress being made in solving the algebra problem. In other words, you must discover the qualities of the figurative language that help you understand the comparison being made.

Look at sentence 2. What are some of the qualities of raisins? They are small, they are soft, and they are wrinkled. They are really dried-up grapes. Which of these qualities would help you to visualize the old man's face? The most appropriate one is the quality of being wrinkled.

How can you recognize figurative language when you read it? First of all, look for language that would not make good sense if taken literally. There is a good possibility that it is figurative language. Here are some of the common ways in which figurative language is used:

1. Sometimes authors make *direct* comparisons. When they do this, they often use the words *like* or *as*.
   The grass was like a green carpet.
   The room was as quiet as a graveyard.
2. Authors can also make *indirect* comparisons.
   a. Sometimes they say that one thing *is* something else.
      This car is a lemon.
      The harbor lights were diamonds set against the velvet of night.
   The author was really comparing the lights to diamonds, but instead of comparing them directly (The lights were *like* diamonds), he did it indirectly (The lights *were* diamonds), giving a little variety to the writing.
   b. Sometimes writers make an indirect comparison, but instead of mentioning both parts of the comparison (the car and the lemon), they mention only the figurative part: "I bought this lemon from a new car dealer." Read the next two examples.
      A hurricane whipped through the office and got all the work done in one day.
      The grapevine recommends that I take the course from Professor Jones.
   Everyone realizes that a *person* did the work, and that *people* recommended Professor Jones, but leaving out part of the comparison seems to give the reader a more vivid picture of what happened.
3. Sometimes authors *exaggerate* the comparison.
      She was a goddess of beauty.
      I was so thirsty that every time I moved my tongue, the dust flew.
      The factory was hotter than the hinges of Hell.
   No thinking person would accept these statements as fact, but the exaggerated language gives you the idea that the beauty, thirst and heat were extreme.

What should you do to understand figurative language? The following method will help:

1. Decide which things are being compared.
2. Think of the qualities of the figurative part of the comparison.
3. Decide which of these qualities is appropriate to the context in which the figurative language is used. This will help you to understand what the author is trying to say.

Consider the following statement: "John is lightning on the race track." If you were to follow the step-by-step sequence just mentioned, you would recognize that the statement does not make good sense if taken literally and that it is probably figurative language. Something that has to do with John on the race track is being compared to lightning. What are the qualities that are characteristic of lightning? It strikes suddenly. It is associated with thunder. It is fast. It is dangerous because it can kill a person or damage property. Which of these qualities is appropriate to the context? The only quality appropriate to this context is that lightning is fast. The meaning, then, is that John is fast on the race track (i.e., he is a very fast runner).

Sometimes authors do not limit the figurative language to an expression in a sentence but extend it to a number of sentences, a paragraph, or even a group of paragraphs. When this is done, the same step-by-step procedure for understanding would apply. Read the following passage carefully. Try to understand what the author is really saying.

No man is an island, entire of itself; every man is a piece of the continent, a part of the main. If a clod be washed away by the sea, Europe is the less . . . any man's death diminishes me because I am involved in Mankind. And, therefore, never send to know for whom the bell tolls. It tolls for thee.

In this example, the individual is likened to a piece of a continent, a part of the mainland—instead of an independent and isolated island. Humanity is compared to the total continent, to the mainland as a whole, and to Europe as a representative mainland. Death is compared to the sea. The qualities of the figurative language that are important here are that an island is separate and distinct from the mainland, that a clump of mainland is part of that mainland, that a continent or mainland is composed of many individual clumps, and that the sea can wash away individual clumps of the mainland so that they are gone forever. The author is saying, then, that no person is an entirely separate and isolated being; instead, each one is united to and a part of all humanity. Therefore, whenever any individual dies, all other individuals are "diminished."

The practice exercises that follow will provide an opportunity for you to become more skillful at understanding figurative language.

In Brief

Figurative language is language that compares unfamiliar things that the reader needs to understand or visualize with things the reader is familiar with. The reader must be able to recognize and understand figurative language.

To *recognize* figurative language:
 Look for language that doesn't make sense if taken literally.
To *understand* figurative language:
 Decide which things are being compared.
 Think of the qualities of the figurative part of the comparison.
 Decide which of these qualities fits the situation.

 Types of figurative language:

1. Direct comparison
 Mentions both things being compared.
 Uses words such as *like* or *as*. (*The grass was like a green carpet.*)
2. Indirect comparison
 Mentions both things being compared.
  Uses a verb such as *am, is, was*. (*The harbor lights were diamonds.*)
 Mentions only the figurative part of the comparison.
  (*A hurricane did the work in one day.*)
3. Exaggeration
 (*Every time I moved my tongue, the dust flew.*)

Practice Exercises

In each of the following statements there is a figurative expression. Answer the questions about that expression. The first one is done for you. (Be careful: more than one answer can be correct.)

1. Some people are like echoes. They always seem to have the last word.
   What things are being compared?
   a. some people and the last word
   (b.) some people and echoes
   c. some people and their habits
   d. echoes and the last word

   What likeness is being emphasized?
   (a.) Echoes are the last sound heard.
   b. Echoes are loud.
   c. Echoes seem to speak back to you.
   d. People's voices have a hollow sound.

In this expression, some people are being compared to echoes. The appropriate characteristic of an echo is that whenever one hears an echo it is the last sound to be heard. This, the expression suggests, is like some people who insist on making the final statement in a discussion or an argument. Thus (b) and (a) are the correct answers.

2. As a result of exposure to the extreme cold, her cheeks were like tomatoes.

   What things are being compared?
   a. her cheeks and tomatoes
   b. her cheeks and the extreme cold
   c. the extreme cold and tomatoes
   d. the extreme cold and her cheeks

   What likeness is being emphasized?
   a. Both were soft.
   b. Both were round.
   c. Both were red.
   d. Both were cold.

3. The girl had a peaches-and-cream complexion.

   What things are being compared?
   a. peaches and cream
   b. the girl and peaches and cream
   c. the girl's complexion and peaches and cream
   d. the girl and her complexion

What likeness is being emphasized?
a. Both are fuzzy and greasy and blotchy.
b. Both have a smooth texture and a healthy color.
c. Both are likable.
d. Both are delicate.

4. The winter landscape consisted of black leafless trees set against a background of gray sky and white crushed velvet.

What things are being compared?
a. trees and sky
b. winter and velvet
c. landscape and trees
d. snow and velvet

What likeness is being emphasized?
a. Both are soft and white.
b. Both are dark and lifeless.
c. Both are flat.
d. Both are shades rather than colors

5. The pile of papers on his desk was acting like rising bread dough.

What things are being compared?
a. papers and rising bread dough
b. papers and his desk
c. his desk and bread dough
d. his papers and bread

What likeness is being emphasized?
a. They are both getting higher.
b. They are both soft.
c. Both of them can be pressed down.
d. Both of them can be seen and watched.

6. The divorce left him with nothing but broken feathers and crushed dreams . . . and a profound unwillingness to trust.

What part of this statement is not literally true?
a. the divorce
b. the broken feathers
c. the crushed dreams
d. the unwillingness to trust

The figurative part of the passage describes:
a. his attitude
b. his financial success
c. his physical health
d. his marriage

7. The speech of the famous lecturer was Joe's sleeping pill.

What things are being compared?
a. the speech and the lecturer
b. the speech and Joe
c. the lecturer and Joe
d. the speech and a sleeping pill

What likeness is being emphasized?
a. Both can be boring (can put you to sleep).
b. Both can be interesting.
c. Both are informative.
d. Both have an effect on people.

8. The tree went to sleep for the winter.

What things are being compared?
a. the tree and sleep
b. the tree's condition and sleep
c. the tree's condition and winter
d. sleep and winter

What likeness is being emphasized?
a. Both are conditions of inactivity and rest.
b. Both are conditions of lowered temperature.
c. Both are susceptible to attack.
d. Both require little care.

9. John felt like a poor man who has inherited a large fortune.

What things are being compared?
a. John and a poor man
b. the feelings of two people
c. a poor man and a large fortune
d. John and a large fortune

What likeness is being emphasized?
a. happiness
b. poverty
c. wealth
d. inheritance

10. During vacation the school was a ghost town.

What things are being compared?
a. vacation and the school building
b. vacation and a ghost town
c. the school building and students
d. the school building and a ghost town

What likeness is being emphasized?
a. Both are learning situations.
b. Both need care and understanding.
c. Both are fun situations.
d. Both are quiet and deserted.

Each of the following statements contains a figurative expression. Decide for each one (a) what things are being compared; (b) which of the qualities of the figurative language is appropriate to the context in which the figurative language is being used; (c) the meaning of the figurative language. Write your answers in the space provided.

11. Questions about the cost of the project threw ice water on the proposal.

a. _____

b. _____

c. _____

This expression compares questions (about the cost) to ice water. The appropriate quality of ice water is that it cools things off quickly. The figurative expression means that people suddenly became less in favor of the proposal. Appropriate answers would be:
a. questions and ice water
b. Ice water cools things off.
c. People suddenly became cool toward (felt less in favor of) the proposal.

12. After a hard day's work, Joe was a *burned-out candle*.

a. _____

b. _____

c. _____

13. Her money was the *medicine that brought the failing business back to health.*

a. _____

b. _____

c. _____

14. After the case was settled, the two girls left the courtroom *like a pair of doves.*

a. _____

b. _____

c. _____

15. His life was an open book.

a. _____

b. _____

c. _____

16. He knew that they were after him. He tried to run, but his feet *felt like lead.*

a. _____

b. _____

c. _____

17. The grade for a course is just *the tip of the iceberg;* the greater value is found *beneath the water.*

a. _____

b. _____

c. _____

18. The politician's speech was a *broom that swept the facts under the rug.*

a. _____

b. _____

c. _____

19. Harry was smart, but he was like putty in Mary's hands.

a. _____

b. _____

c. _____

20. To a thirsty person lost on the desert, a pint of water is a *gallon of champagne.*

_____

_____

_____

Explain the meaning of the following paragraph in your own words.

21. Life is an open sea and I am on an air-filled raft on that sea. Sometimes the sea is rough and pounds at me, hurling me and rocking me until my very survival is threatened. Sometimes the sea is calm and beautiful and its waves softly caress me. Even then, however, as at all times, its salt and its pressures slowly wear me down. I must make my way through the sea, and the sea must provide sustenance for me. If I work hard, the sea may provide me with plenty of food. A moment later, however, the sea may sweep the food away.

_____

_____

_____

_____

Chapter 11

Understanding Graphics

In this chapter you will learn about graphic material. When you finish it, you will know how to

- *read graphs, tables, and charts*
- *read maps and diagrams.*

Graphics are pictures that give information. Graphics include maps, charts, diagrams, graphs, and tables. *Maps* and *diagrams* are pictures in the traditional sense that usually show shapes, distance, location, and how things fit together. Tables, charts, and graphs usually use bars, lines, or other shapes to give a picture of how things compare or how they change. Sometimes, however, instead of lines or bars, numbers or words are used, as in television schedules. If you want to be able to get the most from your college textbooks, or even newspapers and TV news, you must be able to deal with graphics.

WHY DO GRAPHICS EXIST?

Graphics have some real advantages over ordinary written text:

1. Tables, graphs, and charts deliver information more quickly than ordinary text can. In a TV schedule you can find almost immediately what is playing on Channel 8 at noon. Reading through several paragraphs for the information would take much longer.
2. Maps and diagrams can show information impossible to put in print. Just imagine trying to use words to describe the shape of Texas and the relative locations of Fort Worth and Amarillo.
3. Graphics have another advantage. For most people, pictures are easier to remember than words. And textbooks want you to remember the information.

HOW TO READ GRAPHICS

Skilled readers follow these steps in dealing with graphics:

1. Read around the edge of the graphic to get a general idea of its purpose. The title will probably be at the top, sometimes at the bottom. Scales usually appear down the sides or across the bottom. These scales can show money, distance, time, calories, percentages, power, or a host of other measurements. By checking these scales, you see what information is being presented, or what comparisons are being made. This gets you ready for the next step.

2. Set your purpose. If the graphic has nothing that you need, skip it. If there is one bit of information you need, decide what it is. Sometimes you need just a general idea of the information. Other times you need to dig deeply and understand all the pieces of the graphic. Once you've decided on your purpose, the next step is automatic.

3. Read to achieve your purpose. Read as little or as much as necessary to find out what you need to know.

READING GRAPHS, TABLES, OR CHARTS

Now let us apply these steps to Figure 11.1.

Figure 11.1 *Occupational Employment Trend*

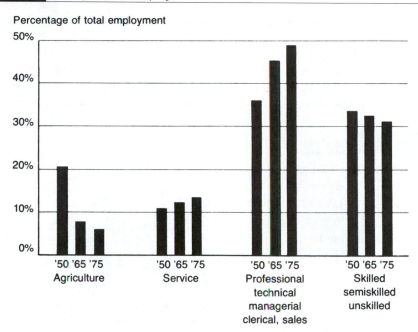

Start with the title. (This one appears at the top of the graph.) The words *Occupational* and *Employment* let you know that the chart deals with jobs. *Trend* is a change, over a period of time, so the title means that the chart will trace changes in jobs. The percentage scale on the left tells you that these changes will involve the percentage of people employed. The information along the bottom tells you that the changes will be in four categories of workers and will cover the time from 1950 through 1975.

When you've finished step 1, you know that the chart divides the workforce into four categories and lets you see the relative size of each category as well as to what extent the category was increasing or decreasing from 1950 through 1975.

Now answer these questions.

1. Which group of workers shows a small but steady increase?

   _____

2. Which group shows the greatest change from 1950 to 1965?

   _____

3. Which group has a steady decrease from 1950 to 1975?

   _____

4. In which two groups is the rate of change slowing down?

   _____

The answers are (1) service, (2) agriculture (21% to 8%), (3) skilled, (4) agriculture and professional (large change 1950 to 1965, smaller change 1965 to 1975).

Answer the following questions by referring to the table in Figure 11.2.

1. What is the title? What industry groups are being considered?
2. In what two ways does the table show employment changes from 1965 to 1975?
3. Which industry shows the greatest amount of change?
4. Which group shows a loss in employment?

Figure 11.2 *Employment Changes by Industry Group*

Industry	1965	1975	Numerical Change	% Change
Manufacturing	64,900	125,000	+ 60,100	+92.6%
Mining	15,800	18,000	+ 2,200	+13.9
Contract construction	23,000	40,000	+ 17,000	+73.9
Transp., public utilities	25,000	32,000	+ 7,000	+28.0
Wholesale and retail	94,500	140,000	+ 45,500	+48.1
Finance, Insurance & Real Estate	21,900	35,000	+ 13,100	+59.8
Services	66,400	110,000	+ 43,600	+65.7
Government	92,200	132,000	+ 39,800	+43.2
Agriculture	36,300	33,000	− 3,300	− 9.1
All other (*)	61,800	85,000	+ 23,200	+37.5
Total	501,800	750,000	+248,200	+49.5%

(*) *Includes self-employed, domestic and unpaid family workers.*

In answer to question 1, the title tells us that the table shows employment changes by industry groups; and the column headed "Industry" lists the industry groups being considered. In answer to question 2, two of the column headings indicate that the table shows both *numerical change* and *percentage change*. How would you answer questions 3 and 4, which provide specific purposes for reading? For these questions, you will need to use the columns that show numerical changes and percentage changes. When you look under percentage changes, for example, do you see that manufacturing shows a change of +92.6 percent, the greatest amount of change, and that agriculture shows a loss of employment, a change of –9.1 percent?

READING MAPS

Now let us apply these steps to the map in Figure 11.3.

Figure 11.3

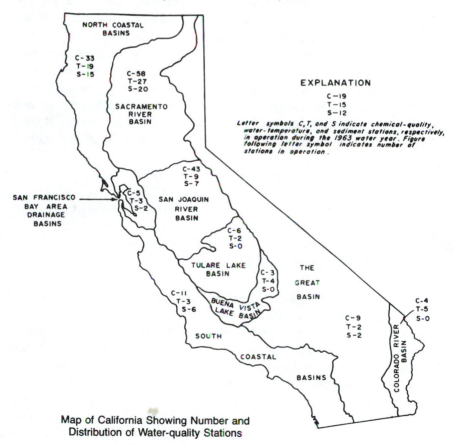

Quality of Waters in California, 1963

Map of California Showing Number and
Distribution of Water-quality Stations

The first step asks you to read the material around the edges of the graphic. The title of this map tells you that it is a map of California and that it shows the number and distribution of water-quality stations in 1963. In other words, reading this map will tell you where in California these water-quality stations were, and how many of them there were in each place.

This map does not have a scale of miles. (This is unusual—most maps do.) However, it does have a key and a legend (explanation). The key contains the letters C, T, and S, each followed by a number. The legend explains that the letters stand for chemical-quality, water-temperature, and sediment stations, respectively, that were operating in 1963. The legend also points out that the number following each letter represents the number of stations in operation.

You should always notice how the different parts of the map are related to each other. Notice that in this map, California is divided into various river basins and that C, T, and S information is provided for each one. (On other maps you should notice such items as divisions into states or territories, or the location of such things as the equator, the poles, mountains, valleys, cities, transportation facilities, or longitude and latitude.)

Next, you should determine your purpose and then read for your purpose. The title suggests that your general purpose is to discover the number and location of water-quality stations in California in 1963. As in reading graphs, charts, or maps, your purpose may be more specific. When that is so, read for that specific purpose. For example, read the map to discover the number of sediment stations in the Sacramento River Basin. In order to do this, you should notice that the Sacramento River Basin is in the upper portion of the map. The number of sediment stations is indicated by the letter S, and the number following it (as indicated in the legend). Within the area of the Sacramento River Basin the letter S is followed by the number 20, indicating that there were 20 sediment stations in the Sacramento River Basin.

Answer the following questions by referring to the map.

1. Which basin has the most chemical-quality stations? How many does it have?
2. What is the total number of stations in the Great Basin?
3. In which basins are there no sediment stations?
4. How many basin areas are there?

The answer to the first question can be found by locating the largest number next to the letter C. The Sacramento River Basin has 58 chemical-quality stations, more than any other. The answer to question 2 can be found by first locating the Great Basin and then adding the numbers following the C, T, and S. If you do this you will find that the answer is 13. A zero follows the S in the Tulare Lake Basin, the Buena Vista Lake Basin, and the Colorado River Basin. These stations, then, are the answer to question 3. Question 4 can be answered by counting the number of basin areas indicated on the map. There are nine.

Practice reading maps, charts, graphs, and tables in the exercises that follow. These exercises should provide the opportunity for you to become skillful at reading graphic material.

In Brief

▼

Graphics: pictures that give information
Trend: a change over a period of time
Types of graphics: maps, charts, graphs, diagrams, tables
Advantages of Graphics:
> They give information more quickly than print can.
> They give information impossible to give by print.
> People remember pictures better than they do words.

Steps in Reading Graphics:

1. Read around the edge of the graphic.
2. Set your purpose.
3. Read for your purpose.

Practice Exercises

1. Questions for Figure 11.4

1. What is the purpose of this map?

_____

2. What is the latest date that any area became associated with the United States?

_____

3. Other than the original thirteen states, what was the largest land acquisition of the United States?

_____

4. Which parts of the United States were acquired by purchase? Name them.

_____

Figure 11.4 *Map: The United States of America*

2. Questions for Figure 11.5

1. Which city has the least amount of sunshine in May?

_____

2. Which city has the most amount of sunshine in January?

_____

3. Does this table tell you average monthly temperatures for the cities mentioned?

_____

Figure 11.5 *Climate Comparison*

Average Percentage of Possible Sunshine for Representative Cities

	Jan.	Feb.	Mar.	Apr.	May	Jun.	Jul.	Aug.	Sep.	Oct.	Nov.	Dec.	Avg.
Phoenix, AZ	77	79	83	88	93	94	84	85	89	88	84	77	86
Tucson, AZ	80	84	85	91	93	93	76	79	88	90	87	82	86
Boston, MA	52	57	58	55	58	63	65	66	64	61	52	54	59
Chicago, IL	43	47	51	54	61	67	69	68	65	63	44	43	58
Los Angeles, CA	72	73	75	68	68	68	82	82	80	74	78	72	74
Miami, FL	67	73	73	72	68	62	63	64	58	59	66	65	66
New York, NY	50	55	57	59	62	65	66	64	63	61	53	50	60
St. Louis, MO	53	45	52	53	62	69	70	70	66	63	53	45	58

3. Questions for Figure 11.6

1. How many hours of TV watching are scheduled per week?

_____

2. Which two subjects are worked on (don't count class time) for more than five hours per week?

_____

3. How many hours of recreation are scheduled per week?

_____

4. According to this schedule, could this student attend an earlier or later church service if he wanted to?_____

How do you know?_____

Figure 11.6   *Time Schedule**

Hour	Mon.	Tues.	Wed.	Thurs.	Fri.	Sat.	Sun.
7:00	Breakfast	～	～	～	～	Sleep	Sleep
8:00	Psychology	Study Accounting	Psychology	Study Accounting	Psychology	Breakfast	}
9:00	Study Psychology	Accounting	Study Psychology	Accounting	Study Psychology	Accounting	Breakfast
10:00	Philosophy	Chemistry	Philosophy	Chemistry	Philosophy	Chemistry	Church
11:00	Speech	Study Chemistry	Speech	Study Chemistry	Prepare speech	Study Chemistry	}
12:00	Lunch	～	～	～	～	～	→
1:00	Sociology	Chemistry Lab	Sociology	Work on Chem Lab report	Sociology	Recreation	Recreation
2:00	Physical Education	}	Physical Education	}	Do Accounting Problems	}	}
3:00	Study Philosophy	Softball	Study Philosophy	Softball		}	}
4:00	Study Psychology	}	Study Accounting	}	}	}	}
5:00	Relax	～	～	～	～	→	Dinner
6:00	Dinner	～	～	～	～	→	Review
7:00	Work	～	～	～	～	Relax	}
8:00	Study Philosophy	Study Psychology	Study Philosophy	Study Philosophy	Recreation	Recreation	Look over speech
9:00	Study Sociology	Watch Television	Study Sociology	Study Sociology	}	}	Study Sociology
10:00	Study Chemistry	}	Study Accounting	Study Chemistry	}	}	Make-up
11:00	Sleep	～	～	→	}	}	Sleep

Name _____

*The hours for recreation are underlined with dots; they are flexible and can easily be changed. The hours for study are underlined with dashes; they are flexible and can be exchanged with other flexible hours. The hours that cannot be altered are underlined with a solid line; they are fixed hours. The hours not underlined may be exchanged, but exchange would cause considerable inconvenience.

4. Questions for Figure 11.7

1. Which city has the smallest fluctuation in temperature throughout the year?

_____

2. Which city has the greatest fluctuation in temperature throughout the year?

_____

3. During which two months of the year do all three cities have approximately the same temperature?

_____

4. Which city is the coolest during the summertime?

_____

Figure 11.7   *Annual Temperature Fluctuation*

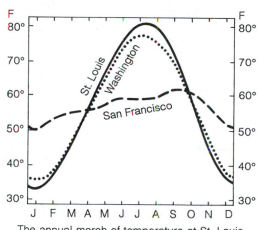

The annual march of temperature at St. Louis,
at San Francisco, and at Washington, D.C.

5. Questions for Figure 11.8

1. What should you do if someone other than Pat answers the phone?

_____

2. What should you do if you may not speak to Pat?

_____

3. What two things might you do once Pat gets on the phone?

_____

4. Under which two circumstances should you put the receiver down?

_____

Figure 11.8 *A Flow Diagram for Calling a Friend*

From Sielaff and Aberle, *Introduction to Business* (Wadsworth, 5th Ed., 1977; p. 119).

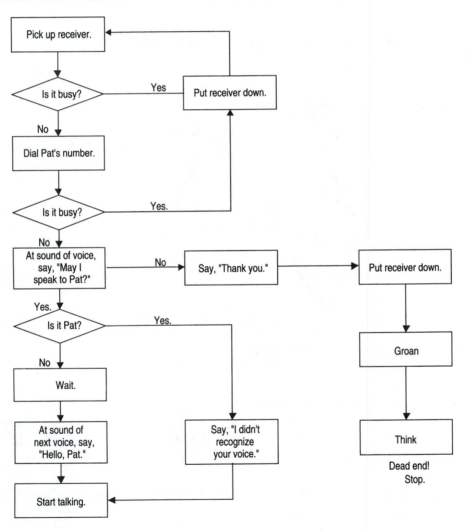

6. Questions for Figure 11.9

1. How far is it from Dallas to Chicago?_____

2. How far is it from Portland, Maine, to Los Angeles if you go through Chicago?

_____

3. How far would you travel if you went from Chicago to Miami, then back to Chicago, and then to Dallas? _____

4. Does this map tell you how far it is if you travel directly from Miami to Los Angeles? _____

Figure 11.9 *Distances from Chicago to Selected Cities*

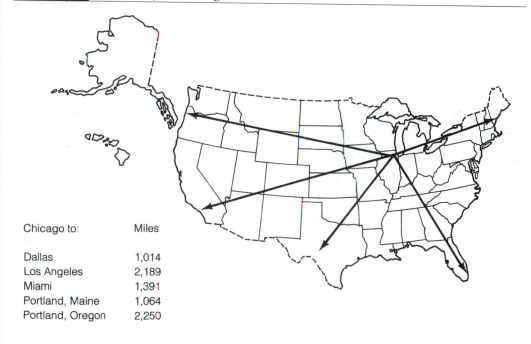

Chicago to:	Miles
Dallas	1,014
Los Angeles	2,189
Miami	1,391
Portland, Maine	1,064
Portland, Oregon	2,250

7. Questions for Figure 11.10

1. If it took you 180 seconds to read Selection 3, what would your rate be?

_____

2. If your WPM was 368 for Selection 9, how long did it take you to read it?

_____

3. If your WPM was 349 for Selection 3 and 408 for Selection 10, which selection took longer to read?

_____

4. If you took 4 minutes and 50 seconds to read Selection 11, how long would it take you to read Selection 3 if you read it at the same WPM?

_____

Figure 11.10 _Reading Rate Table (words per minute)_

Time (min. + sec.)	Selection Number											
	1	2	3	4	5	6	7	8	9	10	11	12
1:00	2160	2545	1630	1860	1665	1711	1938	1845	1780	1702	1971	1866
1:15	1728	2036	1304	1488	1332	1369	1550	1476	1424	1362	1577	1494
1:30	1440	1697	1087	1240	1110	1140	1292	1230	1187	1134	1314	1244
1:40	1296	1527	978	1116	999	1027	1163	1107	1021	1021	1183	1120
1:50	1178	1388	889	1014	908	933	1057	1006	971	928	1075	1018
2:00	1080	1273	815	930	832	855	969	923	890	851	986	933
2:10	997	1175	752	858	768	790	894	852	822	786	910	861
2:20	926	1091	699	797	714	733	831	791	763	729	845	800
2:30	864	1018	652	744	666	684	775	738	712	681	788	746
2:40	810	954	611	698	624	642	726	692	668	638	677	700
2:50	762	898	575	656	588	604	684	651	628	601	696	659
3:00	720	848	543	620	555	570	646	615	593	567	657	622
3:10	682	804	515	587	526	540	612	583	562	537	622	589
3:20	648	786	489	558	500	514	581	554	534	511	591	560
3:30	617	727	466	531	476	489	554	527	509	486	563	533
3:40	589	694	445	507	454	467	529	503	485	464	538	509
3:50	563	664	425	485	434	446	506	481	464	444	514	487
4:00	540	636	408	465	416	428	485	461	445	426	493	466
4:10	518	611	391	446	400	411	465	443	427	408	473	448
4:20	498	587	376	429	384	395	447	426	411	393	455	431
4:30	480	566	362	414	370	380	431	410	396	378	438	415
4:40	463	545	349	399	357	367	415	395	381	365	422	400
4:50	447	527	337	385	344	354	400	382	368	352	408	386
5:00	432	509	326	372	333	342	388	369	356	340	394	373

8. Questions for Figure 11.11

1. In which of the three systems would you use up the smallest number of the items over a period of a year?

_____

2. Which of the three systems is probably the most wasteful?

_____

3. In which of the three systems is the material making up the items used in a different form? _____

4. *a.* What is the purpose of this table? _____

_____

   b. What conclusions(s) does the author probably want you to reach after studying it? _____

_____

Figure 11.11 *Comparison of Three Programs for Handling Solid Wastes*

Item	Throwaway System	Recycling System	Ecologically Based System
Glass bottles	Dump or bury	Grind, remelt; remanufacture; convert to building materials	Ban all nonreturnable bottles and reuse (not remelt and recycle) bottles
Bimetallic "tin" cans	Dump or bury	Sort with magnets; remelt	Limit or ban production; use returnable bottles
Metal objects	Dump or bury	Sort; remelt	Sort, remelt; but tax items lasting less than ten years
Aluminum cans	Dump or bury	Sort; remelt	Limit or ban production, use returnable bottles
Paper	Dump, burn, or bury	Incinerate to generate heat	Compost or recycle; tax all throwaway items; establish national standards to eliminate overpacking
Plastics	Dump, burn, or bury	Incinerate to generate heat or electricity	Limit production; use returnable glass bottles, tax frivolous throwaway items and packaging
Garden and food wastes	Dump, burn, or bury	Incinerate to generate heat or electricity	Compost, return to soil as fertilizer or use as animal feed

9. Questions for Figure 11.12

Figure 11.12 explains the operation of a switch that allows an automobile starter to operate only when the gear selector lever is in certain positions. The starter will operate when the gear selector is in the "Park" position.

1. Does "continuity" between C and D terminals mean that the starter will or will not operate?

2. What other position of the gear selector lever will allow the starter to operate?

3. What does *R* stand for in this guide?

Figure 11.12 *Continuity Guide for Neutral Safety Switch*

Position of Gear Selector Lever	Switch Terminal			
	A	B	C	D
P			o—o	
R	o—o			
N			o—o	
D				

o———o indicates continuity

10. Questions for Figure 11.13

1. What should be done if the class wanted is not open?

2. What should be done once the schedule is completed?

3. What should be done if no substitute class is available?

4. Under which two circumstances should you add the name to the class list and reduce the list by one seat?

Figure 11.13 Simplified Flowchart of Class Registration

From Swindle. _Fundamentals of Modern Business_ (Wadsworth, 1977, p. 438).

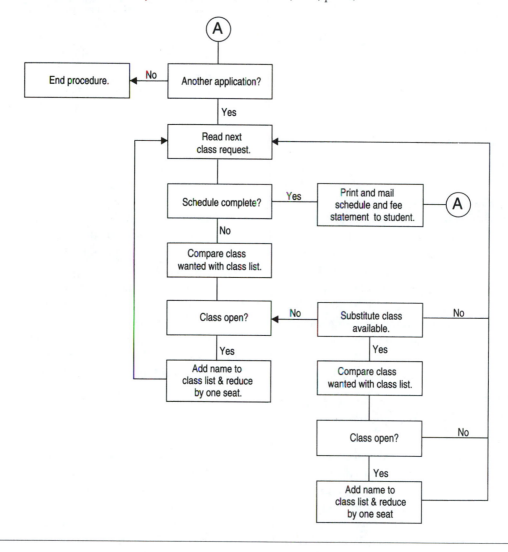

Chapter 12

Developing Critical Comprehension

This chapter deals with the critical comprehension of reading material. When you finish it, you will know how to

- *infer tone*
- *infer purpose*
- *recognize bias or opinion*
- *distinguish between fact and opinion*

People are active, thinking beings. And because we're people, we like to tell others about our activities and thoughts. Also because we're people, we're curious. We want to know where a celebrity goes for her favorite food, what our friends did last weekend, why that married couple won't speak to each other. For these reasons people talk and listen, read and write.

Writers, being human, have opinions, prejudices, and other feelings, all of which appear in their writing. Readers need to be able to read and evaluate material without being overly influenced by the writer's opinions and feelings. They also need to guard against being influenced by their own opinions and feelings. That's what critical comprehension is about—how to keep from being influenced too much by the author's opinions and feelings or your own.

INFERENCE

Much of this chapter is based on *inference:* using your knowledge or experience to understand what hasn't been directly stated. Making inferences is a common thought process. "If you see a well-dressed man get out of a chauffeur-driven car, you use your knowledge about the way people live to *infer* that the man is wealthy. If you see a man with a small satchel entering a medical office, you *infer* that he is a doctor. If three police cars converge upon a building and police get out of the cars with guns drawn, you *infer* that the police are after someone in that building and that the person is considered dangerous.

PURPOSE

When you read critically, you use inference to decide two important things: First, what is the author trying to cause you to do or think? Second, should you go along with it? When you think about the first thing—what the author is trying to accomplish—you're thinking about his *purpose*. His purpose is his reason for writing. One way to determine the purpose is to think about the author's background. If you are about to read a speech on labor unions made by an executive at a meeting of business people, you can infer that a certain purpose will probably be pursued. If, on the other hand, a speech on the same topic is made by a union leader at a labor rally, you can infer that the speech will have a completely different purpose. Knowing the probable purposes of these speeches will enable you to think more clearly about them: which elements of them to accept and which to investigate before accepting. But you must be cautious about yourself, too. You have prejudices and biases—we all do. If your background of experiences has caused you to have feelings about executives, big business, or labor unions, that bias can cause you to misunderstand some of the information in these speeches.

BIAS

Bias is a tendency to have your mind made up before you hear the facts. Bias causes us to accept the ideas that fit our belief, and reject the ideas that oppose it, without really thinking about the merits of the ideas.

Check your own biases by answering yes or no to the following statements.

1. When a person is 70 years of age or older, insurance should not pay for very expensive medical treatment.
2. Lotteries and other forms of gaming should be used to raise money for public expenditure.
3. There should be daily prayer in all schools.
4. Cigarette smoking should be banned from all public places.

Did you have any immediate reaction to the previous statements? Strong or quick reactions to ideas are signals that you have convictions about those things, a bias, and that you need to be very careful to evaluate the ideas before accepting or rejecting them.

TONE

Tone, in writing, is just like tone of voice: it adds meaning to the words. A person may listen to your list of all the things that went wrong for you today, then say, "Oh, you poor thing." Spoken in one tone of voice, it shows sympathy; spoken in another tone of voice, it shows ridicule. Readers need to be aware of tone to evaluate what they read completely. Sometimes authors will be very straightforward about their purpose—the manufacturer wants you to buy his product; the politician wants you to vote a certain way—but sometimes they will be vague or even deceptive. In those cases you can infer purpose by identifying the tone of the article.

Following is a list of some of the tones that writers use. It's not complete, but it gives you an idea of the range of tones possible in writing.

admiring	formal
amused	matter-of-fact
angry	resentful
disbelieving	sad
excited	scornful

Remember, as you read, that tone indicates an author's attitude toward something, but it is also quietly influencing you, the reader. It's difficult, for instance, to be in favor of something you are reading about when the author has an amused and scornful attitude toward it.

Notice the tone in the following paragraph:

> To be buried alive is the most terrible thing that can happen to a person. A woman had presumably died and was deposited in the family vault, which for three years was left undisturbed. At the end of that time it was opened in order to place another coffin in it. How fearful a shock awaited the husband, who personally opened the door. As the door swung outwardly back, some white clothed object fell rattling into his arms. It was the skeleton of his wife in her white shroud.

The purpose of this paragraph was to horrify the reader. Mentioning "buried alive" in the first sentence set the tone of dread and anticipation, which was realized in the final sentence.

Now read this paragraph to discover its tone:

> The rites of preparing for bed were elaborate and unchanging. The blankets had to be tucked in at the foot of his cot. The rag rug was adjusted so that his bare feet would strike it when he arose in the morning. The alarm clock was wound, the hot-water bottle was filled and placed precisely two feet from the bottom of the cot.

Does your knowledge and experience, as well as your understanding of the author's slightly humorous tone, help you to see that the person described is fussy to the point of being ridiculous?

What is the tone of the following paragraph?

> He was lulled to dreaming by the caressing warmth. The light fell on the inner surface of the tub in a pattern of delicate wrinkled lines which slipped with a green sparkle over the curving porcelain as the clear water trembled. Babbitt lazily watched it; noted that along the silhouette of his legs against the radiance on the bottom of the tub, the shadows of the air-bubbles clinging to the hairs were reproduced as strange jungle mosses. He patted the water, and the reflected light capsized and leaped and volleyed.

Can you feel the contentment and relaxation in this paragraph?

DEALING WITH PURPOSE, BIAS, AND TONE

If readers are to correctly determine the tone and purpose of a selection, they must read deliberately, considering what is being said and how it is being said. What are some things to look for?

Look at Titles   Too often, the title is taken for granted, and the reader pays very little, if any, attention to it. Yet no other part of a selection can give the reader so much information for so little expenditure of time. Although some titles are mere attention getters and will not help you to understand purpose or point of view, this kind of title is rarely found in serious articles or in textbook material. In such material, titles often reveal the authors' purpose in writing. What can we learn from the following title?

The Hydrogen Bomb—We Don't Have to Die

First, we have an opinion. The author feels that we don't necessarily have to be killed as a result of a nuclear explosion. Second, we have a *purpose.* After this title the author is duty bound to support his or her contention that we don't have to die. The author's purpose in writing, then, is to convince readers that what he or she suggests in the title really is so.

Read Introductory Material   Authors often state their purpose, and even reveal their biases, in the first few paragraphs of a chapter or in the introduction and preface to a book. Read this Preamble to the Declaration of Independence:

> When, in the course of human events, it becomes necessary for one people to dissolve the political bonds which have connected them with another, and to assume, among the powers of the earth, the separate and equal station to which the laws of nature and of nature's God entitle them, a decent respect to the opinions of mankind requires that they should declare the causes which impel them to the separation.

Clearly, Jefferson is using the Preamble to indicate his purpose in writing the Declaration of Independence. Out of respect for people's opinions worldwide, the author feels that he must justify the colonies' break with England.

Notice the Setting   The setting may indicate the tone. What tone can you infer from the following?

> The sky was dark and cloudy and the atmosphere damp as they stepped into the graveyard. She looked around carefully and then whispered to him . . .

The tone suggested here is one of mystery and fear. The author enhances this tone through setting.

Notice Words that Suggest Irony or Humor   Try to discover the tone of the following paragraph. Does the author really consider this pie "an *excellent* breakfast dish"?

Recipe for New England Pie

To make this excellent breakfast dish, proceed as follows: Take a sufficiency of water and a sufficiency of flour and construct a bullet-proof dough. Work this into the form of a disk, with the edges turned up some three-fourths of an inch. Toughen and kiln-dry it a couple of days in a mild but unvarying temperature. Construct a cover for this redoubt in the same way and of the same material. Fill with stewed dried apples; aggravate with cloves, lemon-peel, and slabs of citron; add two portions of New Orleans sugar, then solder on the lid and set in a safe place till it petrifies. Serve cold at breakfast and invite your enemy.

Did you see how words such as "bullet-proof," "toughen and kiln-dry," "aggravate," "petrifies," and "invite your enemy" help you to understand that the author is making fun of (satirizing) New England cooking?

FACT VS. OPINION

No discussion of critical comprehension would be complete without touching on fact and opinion. As you know, a *fact* is a piece of information that has been tested and found true. Everyone who knows about this piece of information can agree upon it. An *opinion*, on the other hand, has not been proved. It is a judgment, based on feeling. Problems separating fact from opinion arise because writers sometimes state an opinion as if it were fact. The situation is complicated by the tendency of readers to accept everything that backs up, and reject everything that opposes, their beliefs.

The statement, "It is better to live in Phoenix, Arizona, than to live in Los Angeles, California," expresses an opinion. It is based on feeling or attitude.

"Medical doctors treat ill people" is a fact, however. It can be proven. It is not based on attitude or feeling. For the following statements, write *F* if the statement is fact and *O* if it is opinion.

_____ **1.** More people live in Chicago, Illinois, than in Akron, Ohio.

_____ **2.** Math is an easier subject to learn than biology.

_____ **3.** People in Mexico speak Spanish.

_____ **4.** Grapes are smaller than apples.

_____ **5.** Mustard tastes good on a sandwich with Swiss cheese.

Do you realize that sentences 1, 3, and 4 are facts while sentences 2 and 5 are opinions?

In the exercises that follow, think carefully about the question before you decide on an answer. Try to understand any errors you make and apply this understanding to your future reading.

In Brief

Good readers must be able to understand what a piece of writing means, and then decide whether or not to accept its ideas. To do this, they must make inferences about the author and be sensitive to the unstated elements in the writing itself.

Bias: a preference or prejudice. The reader accepts or rejects ideas without examining them.

Inference: a guess. The reader uses his or her existing knowledge and experience to understand what hasn't been directly stated.

Tone: similar to a speaker's tone of voice. It indicates the attitude the author wants to create in the reader.

Inferences a reader should make about the author:

    Author's purpose: reason for writing the piece

    Author's bias: prejudice; tendency to favor or oppose something

Dealing with the author's purpose, bias, and tone:

1. Realize that everyone, including authors and readers, has bias.
2. Realize that an author's bias will sometimes determine his or her purpose.
3. Read to determine the author's bias.
    Knowing the author's background is helpful.
    Title, preface, and/or introduction often reveal bias and purpose.
4. Factor out bias as you read.
    If the author's bias is similar to yours:
        Be careful—the bias will be difficult to detect.
        Be careful—you'll accept ideas without testing them.
    If the author's bias is different from yours:
        Be careful—you'll reject ideas without testing them.

Fact vs. Opinion

Fact: something that can be proved
Opinion: a judgment; not amenable to proof

Readers must be careful not to accept opinion as fact.

Practice Exercises

A. Decide whether each of the following statements is fact or opinion. Then, in the space provided, write *F* if it is fact and *O* if it is opinion.

_____ 1. Food tastes better when you are hungry.

_____ 2. Children should be seen and not heard.

_____ 3. The President of the United States is elected for four years.

_____ 4. Blue and red are a pleasing color combination.

_____ 5. Abortion is wrong.

_____ 6. My religion is better than yours.

_____ 7. Rich people are more intelligent than poor people.

_____ 8. Women are more capable than men in the work world.

_____ 9. Blind people cannot enjoy life.

_____ 10. Smoking cigarettes is harmful to your health.

_____ 11. Everyone should have eight hours of sleep each day.

_____ 12. Most college graduates earn more money in their lifetime than do noncollege graduates.

_____ 13. Homosexuals are inferior people.

_____ 14. Ten pounds of feathers weigh as much as ten pounds of lead.

_____ 15. A college degree can be earned in four years.

_____ 16. Gambling is sinful.

_____ 17. Some people live to be over one hundred years old.

_____ 18. All college students learn mostly by reading books.

_____ 19. You must eat three meals a day in order to be healthy.

_____ 20. All college students need automobiles in order to get around.

Practice Exercises

B. What is the tone of the following paragraph? Circle the letter preceding the word you choose.

1. Imagine that you are bobbing around ever so gently on a forty-foot fishing yacht. After having been out to sea all day, you are now anchored in a beautiful little cove on the Gulf of Mexico. The cool blue water looks especially inviting because the weather is hot and sticky. Then someone says, "Let's go swimming" and slips over the side.

   a. excitement

   b. relaxation

   c. humor

   d. selfishness

The tone here is one of relaxation. The setting that the author paints and the words he uses help us to understand this. Cool inviting water, gentle bobbing at anchor after being away all day— all help to set the tone. This person is relaxing after a day out at sea. Slipping into the cool water to get out of the hot, sticky weather intensifies this feeling.

2. Read this paragraph from an introduction to a biology textbook. What is the author's purpose? What is his bias?

   We should also note that productive, rewarding careers can be built on a knowledge of biology. University laboratories are always in need of men and women to make the new discoveries that soon will make this book obsolete. Men and women are also needed to apply their knowledge of biology in such practical fields as medicine and agricultural research. Teachers of biology will continue to be needed to pass the knowledge acquired by earlier generations on to the generations to come.

The author's purpose is to show the various ways in which a career can be made of biology. His bias is stated in the first sentence: " . . . productive, rewarding careers" can be made in biology.

3. Which of the words following this paragraph best expresses its tone? Circle the letter preceding the word you choose.

   It is now dark, a little after eight o'clock on a winter evening. The downstairs light is on, the blinds are drawn. A man comes to the front door, raps lightly, and is admitted. Soon another man, walking at a leisurely pace, rounds the corner and enters. He has parked his car on another street.

   a. hatred

   b. mystery

   c. friendship

   d. fear

4. Which of the choices following the paragraph would best express the tone of this example? Circle the letter preceding your choice.

Martha and Vivian live in Ventura, California. As neighbors, they had treated each other and their respective families to a variety of homemade soft drinks. This practice had, in fact, become a contest between the two women to see who could create the most refreshing drink, using different combinations of citrus fruits and flavorings.

One day Vivian served members of the two families a beverage that had been squeezed from limes, lemons, and grapes, flavored with mint, and mixed at very high speed in a blender. The resulting mixture was tart, but not too tart; foamy, but not too foamy. It was delightfully refreshing and an instant success with all members of both families.

a. competitive and resentful
b. competitive and friendly
c. loving and neighborly
d. rewarding but tiring

5. Which of the descriptions following paragraph 5 best expresses the change in tone in this example? Circle the letter preceding the description you choose.

In boyish enthusiasm he had jumped on his bicycle and headed out, at the crack of dawn, for the closest hunting ground. The boy's heart beat with excitement as he reached his destination, dropped his bike and, with gun in hand, climbed over the barbed wire fence. . . . Then it happened! One of the barbs caught in his jacket and, as he tried to free himself, he dropped the gun. It fired, and he crumpled to the ground.

a. from suspense to relief
b. from tension to relaxation
c. from happiness to tragedy
d. from excitement to boredom

6. Which of the statements following paragraph 6 best expresses the author's purpose in this paragraph? Circle the letter preceding the statement you choose.

He drew his pay in dollars. He learned the value of American clothing and the variety of purchases that could be made in drugstores. He learned to buy, cook, and enjoy American food. He absorbed American poker, and discovered gin rummy and craps. He acquired a taste for bourbon. He studied the history and geography of the United States until he was, unknowingly, better informed on these subjects than most American high school graduates. He could even name the members of the president's cabinet.

a. to show the nature of American culture
b. to show how well informed the person was about American culture
c. to show how poorly informed American high school graduates are
d. to show the effect of careful training

7. Which of the descriptions following the paragraph best describes the author's purpose? Circle the letter preceding the statement you choose.

This series meets the need to individualize instruction. Each book provides a method for achieving success in a particular skill, and also provides a great many practice exercises in that skill. When an instructor (or a student) determines that help in a skill is needed, he or she can read the rationale and then do as many practice exercises as are necessary to become proficient. Although a group of students may meet in the same place at the same hour (be it classroom or lab), each student can work on the particular skill that meets *his or her* need. Thus, we have tailor-made, individualized instruction without the prohibitive cost of a one-to-one teaching situation.

a. to explain why this series is better than any other
b. to explain how the book is organized
c. to tell the purpose of this series and its advantages and to tell how students should use it
d. to tell why this series was written and to tell the advantage of a one-to-one teaching situation

8. Which of the choices following the example best describes the feelings of the people in this paragraph? Circle the letter preceding your choice.

A recent incident may be used to illustrate this point. Chuck Frazer, the office manager, asked Louise Townsend to compute and type customer invoices. When Louise revealed that she had never done such work before, Chuck assured her that she would be able to handle the job once she had been taught the fundamentals.

Two weeks after she had been on the job, however, the vice-president of sales stormed into the office waving some papers and demanded, "Who screwed up these invoices?" Chuck studied the invoices briefly and agreed that they were inaccurate, but he did not place the blame on Louise. When the vice-president insisted that he be told who had made the mistakes, Chuck again refused to identify Louise. Instead, he replied: "Since it is my responsibility to make certain that invoices are computed accurately, I am to blame for the errors; and I can assure you that the problem will be resolved immediately."

a. anxiety and responsibility
b. fear and disapproval
c. anxiety and revenge
d. fear and irresponsibility

9. Which of the words following the example best describes the tone of the paragraph? Circle the letter preceding the word you choose.

Brig. Gen. Warren A. Black came starkly awake: his eyes wide open, his toes spread and digging into the sheet beneath him, his fingers forming into fists, his stomach flat and tight. His skin was covered with a sweat that was really a slime of fear. He knew that in a few more minutes his wristwatch alarm would go off. Aware of a thin scratchiness behind his eyeballs, he wanted to go back to sleep. But he jerked awake. Sleep was dangerous.

a. fear
b. anger
c. fatigue
d. mystery

10. Which of the words following the paragraph best expresses the tone? Circle the letter preceding the word you choose.

As I listened to the words and realized what they meant, a great shadow seemed to pass from my soul. I did not know how this treasure had weighed me down until now that it was finally removed. It was selfish, no doubt, disloyal, wrong, but I could realize nothing except that the golden barrier was gone from between us.

a. disappointment
b. relief
c. guilt
d. selfishness

11. Which of the words following the paragraph best expresses the tone? Circle the letter preceding the word you choose.

One such place was the War Room at Omaha. Every man and instrument in the War Room was at readiness. The place glowed. The lights from thousands of little dials, the merged loom from scores of scopes, and the light from the big world map on the wall had wiped out the pools of shadow.

a. humility
b. disapproval
c. preparedness
d. humor

12. What is the author's purpose in these paragraphs? Write your answer in the space provided.

We hope you will be happy in your new home. It represents the finest in workmanship and design. It's built to last, and complies with the rigid building standards of our community.

However, like a new automobile, your home will require careful "breaking in" by you, the owner. A few continuing obligations are the builder's, but in general it's up to you now to take over and care for this assembly of many materials and mechanical devices.

_____

_____

13. Which of the descriptions following paragraph 13 best expresses the author's purpose? Circle the letter preceding the answer you choose.

When the Thirty Years' War was ended, no corner of the European Continent was left without its foci of infection. And although the dreadful period of this war overshadows all other events of the century, the subsequent years were by no means peaceful ones. The campaigns of Turenne, the wars in the Netherlands and in Russia, and continued warfare with the Turks—especially the siege of Vienna in 1683— offered typhus all the opportunities it needed for continuous activity. And in Italy— especially Sicily—famines gave the disease a free hand in some of the most severe epidemics of its history. Meanwhile France itself was not spared, and 1651 and 1666 were calamitous typhus years for Poitou and Burgundy.

a. to compare war with disease
b. to compare the results of the wars in the Netherlands, Russia, Italy, and France
c. to show how terrible war is
d. to show how typhus spread after the Thirty Years' War

14. What is the tone of this paragraph?

The petition must state specific course names and numbers and is to be submitted with the doctoral program of study, which will designate the language to be passed and the language for which course work is to be substituted. These courses shall be in one field, must be external to the major and minor areas of interest and must form a coherent group. There must be evidence the courses will contribute more to the candidate's program than would a second language.

_____

_____

15. What is the author's purpose in writing the following paragraph?

Final preparation for presentation. Your paper should be on standard-sized paper, it should be neat, and it should be typewritten. It should carry such identifying data as the course for which it is written, the date, and—most important of all—your name and any other information requested by your instructor. If the instructor should indicate that a typewritten page is optional, then of course you can present it in longhand. Make sure your paper is readable and that it makes sense. This is the time to make sure your paper is grammatically acceptable and your spelling is correct. A final note of caution—reread the final copy with a critical eye, for typographical errors, spelling, punctuation, and total appearance—and make necessary corrections.

_____

_____

16. What was the author's purpose in writing this paragraph? Write your answer in the space provided.

We have tried, in this text, to focus upon techniques of reading that will help students understand better and hence enjoy more what they read. The primary emphases of this book—all departures from the conventional book of essays or basic rhetoric—are these: strong emphasis on motivation growing out of student interest, strong emphasis on techniques showing how to read, and strong emphasis on practical methods for learning vocabulary.

_____

_____

17. Which of the words following this paragraph best expresses what the author is asking for? Circle the letter preceding the word you choose.

With malice toward none, with charity for all, with firmness in the right as God gives us to see the right, let us strive on to finish the work we are in, to bind up the nation's wounds, to care for him who shall have borne the battle and for his widow and his orphan, to do all which may achieve and cherish a just and lasting peace among ourselves and with all nations.

a. responsibility
b. charity
c. unity
d. malice

18. What is the tone of the following paragraph? Circle the letter preceding your choice.

Darkness all about him now, entire and fathomless night. No single ray threaded it, no flake of light drifted through. There was no silence here, but if he dared to listen, he could hear tappings and creakings, patterings and whispers, all furtive, all malign. It was horrible, the dark. The rats lived there, the hordes of nightmare, the wobbly faces, the crawling and misshapen things.

   a. fear and anxiety
   b. disappointment and worry
   c. anger and frustration
   d. anger and disappointment

19. Read this section of the introductory statement in a biology textbook to discover the author's purpose. Write your answer in the space provided.

Just as a scientist builds upon the work of the past, so students can better understand the significance of the recent discoveries in biology if they first learn the classical statements of the problems. Furthermore, the earlier interpretations are more closely related to what the student can see about him with the aid of the relatively simple tools and techniques of the elementary laboratory. Therefore, the older knowledge is examined first in the chapters. Only then are the discoveries of electron microscopy, biochemistry, and modern physiological techniques discussed.

_____

_____

20. Which of the words following the paragraph best describes the author's purpose or position? Circle the letter preceding the word you choose.

While this drama of assault and counterassault was being enacted, a dramatic struggle between Truman and MacArthur reached its climax. Recalling Lincoln's difficulties with the temperamental McClellan, it was a struggle between a chief of state who had to think of many broad considerations, and a general who thought only of military objectives; between a president determined to keep control of the situation, and a commander using political pressure to force the government's hand.

   a. pro-Truman
   b. pro-MacArthur
   c. objective
   d. pro-McClellan

Quizzes

Vocabulary Quiz 1

For each of the following passages, determine the meaning of the words in italics from among the choices given. Circle the letter to the left of your choice. In each case the choices are actual dictionary meanings for the word.

1. She enjoyed watching the *float* go down the street.
   a. a tool for smoothing a surface
   b. a hollow ball that regulates liquid level
   c. an exhibit in a parade
   d. a platform anchored near a shoreline

2. He liked to *pick* the apples from the tree.
   a. to pierce with a pointed instrument
   b. to rob
   c. the best or choicest one
   d. to pluck

3. He *turned* to his doctor for help when his condition took a *turn* for the worse. After he took some new medication, his condition *turned* around.
   When *turned* appears the first time, it means
   a. faced in the direction of
   b. inverted
   c. sought aid or support
   d. converted
   The word *turn* means
   a. rotate
   b. set in another direction
   c. twist out of shape
   d. change into
   When *turned* appears the second time, it means
   a. rotated
   b. twisted out of shape
   c. changed appearance
   d. changed direction

In the following passages, decide the meaning of each italicized word (some may be nonsense words) by using context and/or structure. Write the meaning in the space provided.

4. Which details are important to the story line and which are *superfluous*?

   Superfluous _____

5. When a person doesn't have a meaningful role to play in life, he is apt to *disengage*. Disengagement refers to the mutual withdrawal of a person from the community around him.

   Disengage _____

6. Why do printed directions cause so much difficulty? Mainly because students get only a general idea of what is wanted and do not *attend* to each step in the directions.

   Attend _____

7. In the twentieth century, humans had made more progress in medicine than in all previous history. *Kaddors* such as yellow fever, smallpox, typhoid fever, and diphtheria were under control or eliminated.

   Kaddors _____

8. During its first few days of life, the *neonate* will spend most of its time in the fetal position.

   Neonate _____

9. The human eye is roughly spherical in shape. It is bounded by three distinct layers of tissue. The outer layer, the *sclerotic* coat, is extremely tough.

   Sclerotic _____

10. There is another kind of knowledge of nature called *a priori* knowledge. *A priori* knowledge is knowledge that does not rely on observation, knowledge to which we cannot imagine an exception.

    A priori _____

    _____

11. Religions are undergoing *secularization*—that is, becoming too worldly.

    Secularization _____

12. Privacy refers to being left alone, but there are different kinds such as solitude, intimacy, and anonymity. Which of these different kinds of *borluk* can you identify with?

    Borluk _____

13. He was *obsilted* about his promotion. This was one of the best days of his life.

    Obsilted _____

Vocabulary Quiz 2

For each of the following passages, determine the meaning of the words in italics from among the choices given. Circle the letter to the left of your choice. In each case the choices are actual dictionary meanings for the word.

1. Give an *account* of yourself during the last few days.
   a. a record of credit and debit entries
   b. an explanation of one's conduct
   c. value of importance
   d. a sum of money in a bank

2. Please *conduct* yourself properly at the meeting.
   a. to lead
   b. to transmit sound or electricity
   c. to behave
   d. to act as leader

3. We will have to go to the *pool* for more materials to build the house.
   a. an available supply
   b. a small body of water
   c. all the money bet on an event
   d. the game of billiards

4. His new *crown* made him feel and look and chew his food better.
   a. a royal headdress
   b. the highest part of something
   c. a tooth substitute
   d. a type of gold coin

5. She had a beautiful *crystal* fruit bowl.
   a. clear, colorless glass of superior quality
   b. the cover of a watch dial
   c. a type of radio receiver
   d. very clear quartz

In the following passages, decide the meaning of each of the italicized words (some may be nonsense words) by using context and/or structure. Write the meaning in the space provided.

6. Although the animal looked friendly and playful, it was really very *siboncure*.

   Siboncure _____

7. He was *exonerated* by the jury and was free to return home to his family.

Exonerated _____

8. The North American continent has four principal geographic regions: the central plains; the Canadian Shield, on the north; the Appalachian Highlands, on the east; and a broad system of mountain ranges, in the west, which are called collectively the *Cordillera*.

Cordillera _____

9. To find your own identity, you must face the real world and explore it. You must discover what you can do and how well you do it. You must build things—cars, boats, racers, stereos. You must *pit* your physical strength against your peers in football, swimming, and mountain climbing.

Pit _____

10. Frequently this exploration *manifests* itself by a period of negativism. Every parental suggestion is greeted by "No."

Manifests _____

11. The cowboy was a board-whacker. Each time he held superior cards, he *whanged* them, one by one, with exceeding force, down upon the improvised table, and took the tricks with a glowing air of prowess and pride that sent thrills of indignation into the hearts of his opponents.

Whanged _____

12. Despite the popular notion that we are becoming a nation of couch potatoes, *berns* such as tennis, swimming, and running are becoming more and more popular.

Berns _____

13. I absolutely *harbet* seafood and refuse to eat it.

Harbet _____

14. She is very *amenable* to your suggestion and is certain to follow up on it.

Amenable _____

15. Don't deal with him! He is a *charlatan*—an imposter, a fraud.

Charlatan _____

Vocabulary Quiz 3

For each of the following passages, determine the meaning of the words in italics from among the choices given. Circle the letter to the left of your choice. In each case the choices are actual dictionary definitions of the word.

1. He said that he will *back* the candidate, but he expects to be paid *back*.
   When *back* is used the first time, it means
   a. toward the rear
   b. to give financial support
   c. to go in reverse
   d. in return
   When *back* is used the second time, it means
   a. in reverse
   b. in return
   c. toward the rear
   d. to give financial support

2. The place is really *jumping* tonight.
   a. full of activity
   b. increasing sharply
   c. springing into the air
   d. leaving in violation of

3. The young man finally came out of his *shell* when he attended college.
   a. a shy manner
   b. exterior framework
   c. a bullet casing
   d. an outer covering

4. The job had to be redone because he used *green* lumber to build the shelves.
   a. inexperienced
   b. not in condition for a particular use
   c. a color
   d. sickly

In the following passages, decide the meaning of each italicized word (some may be nonsense words) by using context and/or structure. Write the meaning in the space provided.

5. Because she was very *sagacious*, people came to her for advice all the time.

   Sagacious _____

6. The glue had a *tenacious* grip. Nothing could pull the two items apart.

   Tenacious _____

7. Most present-day cosmetologists are able to perform many different kinds of jobs. They are truly *versatile*.

   Versatile _____

8. Throughout human history, *farlets*, whether they be caves, tents, houses, or apartments, have been carefully chosen and vigorously defended.

   Farlets _____

9. The *insurgence* was the result of the unjust treatment and the anger of the people. They finally rose up and overthrew the government.

   Insurgence _____

10. Tell the truth openly and honestly. Don't let your friendship for him stop you from being *candid*.

    Candid _____

11. She was a very *amiable* person. Everybody liked her.

    Amiable _____

12. How fast you read depends upon the difficulty of the material and your purpose in reading it. If the material is very *sepulant*, such as in a physiology or philosophy book, you should read the material more *gronally*. Easier material, however, should be read more rapidly.

    Sepulant _____

    Gronally _____

13. A builder constructing a row of houses according to the same plan wishes them to have the same size and shape, that is, to be *congruent*.

    Congruent _____

14. To replace the seat washer, shut off the water to the faucet. Unscrew the cap nut with a monkey wrench, placing cloth or thick paper between the jaws of the wrench to prevent *marring* the cap nut.

    Marring _____

Main Idea Quiz 1

Paragraphs 1, 2, and 3 are followed by four statements (labeled a, b, c, d). Read each paragraph and determine the main idea. Then circle the letter (a, b, c, or d) of the statement you choose.

1. The reasons for migration are many. Demographers often speak of "push" and "pull" factors. People can be "pushed" out of an area because of unsatisfactory conditions there. Wars, unemployment, persecution, famine, blight, and pollution are but a few of the many reasons people may choose to pack up and leave the place where they are living. Correspondingly, people may be "pulled" to areas because of good economic opportunities, good climate, congenial political and social conditions, and a countless variety of other reasons. Very often, migration reflects both push and pull factors, as in the migration of many people from Ireland to the United States in the 1840s. Ireland was suffering a devastating potato famine, while the United States was regarded as the land of golden opportunity.

   a. People are "pulled" to areas because of good economic opportunities.
   b. There are many reasons for the migration of people.
   c. People moved from Ireland because of the potato famine.
   d. Wars, unemployment, and persecution cause people to move.

2. Before any federal agency can spend or commit funds, the Congress must grant it the authority to do so. The budget is the president's request to Congress for the authority to spend the money necessary to carry out the existing and proposed programs of the federal government. It is submitted to the Congress in January of each year, nearly 6 months before the start of the fiscal year. The Congress considers the president's requests and may accept some of them, modify or reject others, and add new proposals of its own.

   a. Congress must authorize all money that is spent by the federal government.
   b. Congress may reject some or even all of the president's requests.
   c. The fiscal year is from January to December.
   d. Congress raises money by taxing the people.

3. People usually refer to taxes in terms of their being much too high. In reality, they are probably even higher than you imagine, because in addition to the federal income tax we are studying here, there are many other federal, state, and local taxes, such as sales tax, inheritance tax, state and sometimes local income tax, personal property tax, real estate tax, taxes on furs and jewels, just to mention a few. These are the most obvious ones.

   a. We pay too many taxes.
   b. We pay more taxes than we realize.
   c. We should not have to pay real estate tax or inheritance tax.
   d. Some taxes are hidden.

Read paragraphs 4 and 5 and then, in the space provided, state the main idea of each in your own words.

4. What we get from federal taxes is a little harder to see, but nonetheless important. They also provide protection, but on a national basis. They support our army, navy, and air force with the newest weapons systems possible to give the strength we need to our nation's defense. They provide the necessary materials and equipment for such flights as those made by astronauts and other explorers into outer space. They help ensure that our foods and drugs meet the high standards we have set for them. They finance research projects that find the cause of man's diseases and continue to improve our agricultural products. They finance our relations with other countries.

_____

_____

_____

5. In the twentieth century, humans had made more progress in medicine than in all previous history. Scourges such as yellow fever, smallpox, typhoid fever, and diphtheria were under control or eliminated. World War II revealed how rapidly medicine was advancing. In the Spanish-American War, more men died of disease than of wounds; in World War II the fighting men were generally as healthy as they would have been at home. The problem of dealing with malaria in Pacific islands and Burmese jungles was met by the development of a synthetic drug, atabrine, to replace quinine. Penicillin and sulfa drugs greatly reduced infection of wounds.

_____

_____

Main Idea Quiz 2

Paragraphs 1, 2, and 3 are followed by four general statements (labeled a, b, c, d). *Read each paragraph and determine the main idea. Then circle the letter (*a, b, c, *or* d) *of the statement you choose.*

1. Perhaps even more important than their role as transmitters of disease is the competition that insects give us for food. Every plant crop that man raises for his own use also feeds a multitude of insects. Some insects suck the juices of plants, stunting their growth and making them easy prey for disease organisms. Other insects actually chew and devour plant parts. A swarm of grasshoppers can consume every green leaf in a field of corn in a remarkably brief period. The larvae of many moths, butterflies, and beetles are also destructive crop pests. In those parts of the world where the human population barely has enough to eat, competition with the insects often results in serious famine. Even where there is enough food, we must depend on the untiring efforts of agricultural scientists and farmers in their war on insect enemies.

   a. Insects cause famine.
   b. Insects compete with us for food.
   c. Insects are to be feared as enemies who eat our food and transmit diseases to us.
   d. Our agricultural scientists are at war with our insect enemies.

2. The business community today is getting to be a world of computers. The executive or manager who has no knowledge of electronic data processing is at a severe disadvantage. One does not have to be an expert or specialist, since one can hire experts, but one must be able to evaluate the performance of the people one hires and the new systems that are proposed. As computer capabilities are increased, the manager must update his or her knowledge to include the latest technology.

   a. The business community today is getting to be a world of computers.
   b. It is important for the business manager or executive to know about electronic data processing.
   c. The business manager or executive does not have to be an expert in electronic data processing.
   d. The business manager or executive must keep up with the latest developments.

3. The living organism, from birth to death, is in a constant state of change—growing and degenerating, sustaining injury and repairing the damage, reproducing, transforming ingested foods into different kinds of energy, adapting

itself to its environment, or failing to find an adjustment. All of this activity in man involves the death and orderly replacement of thousands of cells every day.

    a. There are millions of cells in the living organism.

    b. The living organism is in a constant state of change.

    c. Without change the organism would die.

    d. The living organism is constantly growing.

Read paragraphs 4 and 5 and then, in the space provided, state the main idea of each in your own words.

4. Many regard the automobile as a necessity rather than a luxury, especially given the extent to which interactions are organized around it. As serious efforts are being made to create more reliance on public mass transit, we are learning of more and more functions cars have for us. Cars give us status. We eat meals and watch movies in them. They give us freedom, opportunities to escape parents and crowded cities. Cars made suburbs possible. People get engaged in cars, and some start families there. Imagine robbing a bank and then jumping aboard a bus for your getaway.

_____

_____

5. Humans have always depended on wood. It is one substance, which we grow, that can provide us with shelter, fuel, and clothing. It is a substance which gives us materials ranging from the softest tissues to hard, metal-like plastics. Look around you! How many things can you see right now that are made of wood? A few years ago, it was found that humans use wood and wood products in at least 4,000 ways. Probably by now, hundreds of new uses have been developed.

_____

Main Idea Quiz 3

Paragraphs 1, 2, and 3 are followed by four general statements (labeled a, b, c, d). Read each paragraph and determine the statement that best expresses the main idea. Then circle the letter (a, b, c, or d) of the statement you choose.

1. What troubled people especially was not just the tragedy—or even its needlessness—but the element of fate in it all. If the *Titanic* had heeded any of the six ice messages on Sunday . . . if ice conditions had been normal . . . if the night had been rough or moonlit . . . if she had seen the berg 15 seconds sooner—or 15 seconds later . . . if she had hit the ice any other way . . . if her watertight bulkheads had been one deck higher . . . if she had carried enough boats . . . if the Californian had only come. Had any one of these "ifs" turned out right, every life might have been saved. But they all went against her—a classic Greek tragedy.

   a. There were so many ways that the sinking of the *Titanic* could have been avoided that it seemed almost fated to occur.

   b. People were especially troubled by the *Titanic* disaster.

   c. If only ice conditions had been normal, the tragedy would not have occurred.

   d. One of the causes of the tragedy was the negligence of the captain in not heeding the six ice messages on Sunday.

2. The fact that electronic computers are used for data processing has led the general public to believe that it is a mysterious, complicated science and that the computers are giant brains. Both notions are false. Basically, a computer is a high-speed adding machine which does what it is told to do. If the input data are varied even slightly, the computer cannot operate until it is programmed to accept the variations. The business operations it performs are impressive only because of the extremely high speed of manipulation, but most of these operations have been in use for decades. Unlike humans, the computer performs repetitive calculations without getting tired or bored.

   a. A computer is a high-speed adding machine that cannot think.

   b. A computer is a mysterious giant brain.

   c. A computer is impressive because of its high speed.

   d. A computer is superior to humans in many ways.

3. A business uses as many accounts as it needs for keeping track of its operations. A small firm with few pieces of equipment, for instance, may have only one account for all its equipment. A larger business will probably need an account

for each type of equipment or even, in some cases, for a single piece of equipment. A business with only one owner will need only one capital account; a partnership will need a capital account for each partner.

a. Large businesses need more accounts than small businesses.
b. One-owner businesses need fewer accounts than partnerships.
c. Businesses use as many accounts as they require in order to operate efficiently.
d. The number of accounts is a clue to the size of the business.

Read paragraphs 4 and 5 and then, in the space provided, state the main idea of each paragraph in your own words.

4. The physical origin of the basic figures of geometry is evident. Not only the common figures of geometry but the simple relationships, such as perpendicularity, parallelism, congruence, and similarity, derive from ordinary experiences. A tree grows perpendicular to the ground, and the walls of a house are deliberately set upright so that there will be no tendency to fall. The banks of a river are parallel. A builder constructing a row of houses according to the same plan wishes them to have the same size and shape, that is, to be congruent. A worker or machine producing many pieces of a particular item makes them congruent. Models of real objects are often similar to the object represented, especially if the model is to be used as a guide to the construction of the object.

_____

_____

5. Rights of property are of several kinds. There is the property that one has in things that one has made oneself. There is property in what one has received as a recompense for making something for somebody else; or for doing any service to somebody else; among which services must be reckoned that of lending to that person what one has made, or honestly come by. There is property in what has been freely given to one, during life or at death, by the person who made it, or honestly came by it.

_____

_____

Details Quiz 1

1. What does this paragraph mention as a disadvantage of a time-limit test? (Circle the letter preceding the statement you choose.)
   a. There may not be enough time to reach top performance.
   b. Poor reading speed may prevent getting an accurate score.
   c. It is a group test rather than an individual test.
   d. One cannot find the student's individual performance.

   Is the group test a time-limit test in which reading speed is an important factor in determining a student's score? Or is the group test a work-limit test in which a student has all the time he needs to reach his top performance? Unless the test is the latter, the factor of speed may be so important that the score will not as adequately reflect mental ability as will the mental age revealed by the Stanford-Binet or another individual test.

Answer the following questions in the spaces provided.

2. What seemed to be Captain Ahab's purpose in studying the sea charts and the log books?

   Had you followed Captain Ahab down into his cabin after the squall that took place on the night succeeding that wild ratification of purpose with his crew, you would have seen him go to a locker in the transom, and bringing out a large wrinkled roll of yellowish sea charts, spread them before him on his screwed-down table. Then, seating himself before it, you would have seen him intently study the various lines and shadings which there met his eye; and with slow but steady pencil trace additional courses over spaces that before were blank. At intervals, he would refer to piles of old log-books beside him, wherein were set down the seasons and places in which, on various former voyages of various ships, Sperm Whales had been captured or seen.

   _____

   _____

3. Why is it important that Nature laid out the geographical regions in a north-south direction?

   The North American continent has four principal geographic regions: the central plains; the Canadian Shield, on the north; the Appalachian Highlands, on the east; and a broad system of mountain ranges, on the west, which are called collectively the Cordillera. In building the continent Nature laid out these geographic regions in a general north-south direction. Thus we find that the plains and the mountain systems of Canada extend into the United States. Later, we will see how this north-south trend in the continent's geography affected Canada's relationship with our own country and how it influenced the course of Canada's history.

   _____

   _____

4. Under what circumstances may you be entitled to a refund? How do you obtain a refund?

There are other cases where you may be entitled to refunds. A later audit of the return may be made by the Internal Revenue Service and an overpayment disclosed. The Service will inform you in a case of this kind. You may later discover that you have overpaid your tax, in which case you must file a claim for refund on an amended return or on Form 843. Such claim must be filed within 3 days from the date the return was due or the date it was filed, or within 2 years from the date the tax was paid, whichever is later.

_____

_____

5. What problem is created as a result of people's continuing dependence on wood?

Humans have always depended on wood. It is one substance, which we grow, that can provide us with shelter, fuel, and clothing. It is a substance that gives us materials ranging from the softest tissues to hard, metal-like plastics. Look around you! How many things can you see right now that are made of wood? A few years ago, it was found that humans use wood and wood products in at least 4,000 ways. Probably by now, hundreds of new uses have been developed. Since trees are the sole source of wood, it is only natural for us to ask, "What about the forests of the United States? Can they supply us with enough wood to meet our present needs? Is there any way we can be sure our forests will continue supplying us with wood year after year?"

_____

_____

Details Quiz 2

1. Why won't the bee sting you if you try to paint it? (Circle the letter preceding the statement you choose.)
   a. It wants to be allowed to return for the rest of the honey.
   b. It doesn't see you because it flies backwards.
   c. It is too busy devouring the honey.
   d. It wants to get back to the hive as quickly as possible.

If you desire a more definite proof, you have but to watch a bee that shall just have discovered a few drops of honey on your windowsill or the corner of your table. She will immediately gorge herself with it; and so eagerly, that you will have time, without fear of disturbing her, to mark her tiny belt with a touch of paint. But this gluttony of hers is all on the surface; the honey will not pass into the stomach proper, into what we might call her personal stomach, but remains in the sac, the first stomach—that of the community, if one may so express it. This reservoir full, the bee will depart, but not with the free and thoughtless motion of the fly or butterfly; she, on the contrary, will for some moments fly backwards, hovering eagerly about the table or window, with her head turned toward the room.

Answer the following questions in the spaces provided.

2. Why was *The Rite of Spring* conceived?

The third ballet by Stravinsky was *Le Sacre du Printemps (The Rite of Spring)*. The production was conceived by Diaghilev, partly as a means of holding the interest of the Paris audience. He had in past years presented classical ballets and Russian legends, and so, with his keen artistic judgment and calculated showmanship, he decided to capitalize on the Parisians' interest in primitive art. African sculpture and masks had attracted the attention of artists such as the German painters Kirchner and Marc, as well as Picasso in Paris. Diaghilev chose to depict prehistoric rites culminating in the sacrifice of a human being—hardly typical of the stories usually associated with classical ballet.

_____

_____

_____

3. What will happen to someone who fails to account for money entrusted to him or her?

In taking "care that the laws be faithfully executed," a strict performance of duty will be exacted from all public officers. From those officers, especially, who are charged with the collection and disbursement of the public revenue, will prompt and rigid accountability be required. Any culpable failure or delay on their part to account for the moneys entrusted to them at the times and in the manner required by law will in every instance terminate the official connection of such defaulting officer with the government.

_____

_____

4. Who may we have to count on to protect us from the destruction that insects cause?

Perhaps even more important than their role as transmitters of disease is the competition that insects give us for food. Every plant crop that humans raise for our own use also feeds a multitude of insects. Some insects suck the juices of plants, stunting their growth and making them easy prey for disease organisms. Other insects actually chew and devour plant parts. A swarm of grasshoppers can consume every green leaf in a field of corn in a remarkably brief period. The larvae of many moths, butterflies, and beetles are also destructive crop pests. In those parts of the world where the human population barely has enough to eat, competition with the insects often results in serious famine. Even where there is enough food, we must depend on the untiring efforts of agricultural scientists and farmers in their war on insect enemies.

_____

_____

5. What is the difference between the content of the regular issue and the content of the mid-monthly issue? How can you distinguish between the appearance of the regular issue and the mid-monthly issue?

The _Reader's Guide_ is published twice a month, except July and August, when the mid-monthly issue is omitted. The regular monthly issues are dated the 10th; the mid-monthly, the 25th. The mid-monthly issues supplement the preceding issue and are to be discarded as soon as the next regular monthly issue appears. These supplementary or mid-monthly issues are easy to distinguish from the others, as they are bound in white paper, while the regular monthly issues are bound in green paper.

_____

_____

_____

Details Quiz 3

1. How did Army basic training prepare a WAC for her job?
   (Circle the letter preceding the statement you choose.)
   a. It gave her supplies, checkups, and training.
   b. It taught her to march, make a bed, and care for uniforms.
   c. It taught her discipline, leadership, and *esprit de corps.*
   d. It taught her military subjects such as map reading, military history, and chemical warfare.

   The object of basic training was to prepare a WAC for her responsibilities as a member of the army and to develop her best potentials for a satisfying career in the service. During the first week, called "processing week," she received her uniforms and equipment, medical and dental checks, and was given additional tests. During the ensuing 8 weeks, the trainee learned to march, to make her bed in true army style, and to care for her uniforms properly. She learned the true meaning of such words as discipline, self-discipline, leadership, and esprit de corps. She attended classes in military subjects to include military justice, map reading, first aid, intelligence, personnel, military history, chemical, biological and nuclear warfare, and military customs and courtesies.

Answer the following questions in the spaces provided.

2. What are the three conflicting views mentioned and to whom are they ascribed?

   Most modern psychologists agree with Watson that the evidence on which psychological theories are based must be publicly observable. However, they also agree with the introspectionists that the processes of the mind are of psychological interest and that a person's report of his private experience may be of value. And they recognize, as Freud did, that a person is not aware of all the factors that are affecting his thinking and his behavior. How can these apparently conflicting points of view be reconciled?

   _____

   _____

   _____

3. Why does the decimal system use the number 10 as a base?

   When humans first had to keep track of our possessions, we had to invent numbers so that we could count. Presumably, because we had ten fingers and it was easy to perform simple calculations by counting on fingers, we developed a numbering system (or counting system) based on the number 10. This is called the decimal system. Several different numbering systems with other bases have also been tried, but the decimal system became universal and survived.

_____

_____

4. What causes the "Adam's apple"?

    The larynx, or voice box, is an enlarged portion of the trachea. Like the rest of the trachea, it is protected by cartilage. Associated with the deepening of the voice, which occurs during adolescence in boys, is an enlargement of the larynx. As a result of this enlargement, the cartilage covering protrudes at the front of the neck, forming the "Adam's apple.'

_____

_____

5. Why did it become necessary to keep records?

    It used to be possible for people to operate a business without keeping any records. They could buy and sell strictly for cash, and whether they made a profit was of no concern to the government or anyone else. Thus, a furniture maker could run a one-person independent business. He would buy his supplies and materials at the lumber yard and hardware store and pay cash. In his shop he would build a desk or table and chairs, for example, and then sell the articles to local customers, who in turn paid cash as they received the furniture. However, if business improved, our furniture maker found it necessary to keep track of facts concerned with the business. If he had several orders, he found it cheaper to buy supplies in larger quantities. He may have lacked the funds to pay for everything at once, but on the strength of his orders he could easily have bought on credit. His customers, also, may have preferred to pay their bills at some later date, so that our furniture maker had to keep track of what was owed him and by whom.

_____

_____

Relationships I, Quiz 1

For each of the following sentences or group of sentences, decide whether the relationship is EXAMPLE, EXPLANATION, or COMPARISON-CONTRAST. Then write your answer in the space provided.

1. Good notetakers usually develop their own systems of abbreviations and symbols. They may, for example, use boxes, circles, or arrows for emphasis.

   _____

2. Unlike rabbits, which are born naked, blind, and helpless, hares are born with fur, open eyes, and the ability to move about.

   _____

3. Work, paid employment, may someday cease to be important and proper for most people. Automation will produce all of the goods and most of the services that man needs.

   _____

The following sentence is followed by four statements. For each statement, mark E if it is an EXAMPLE, XP if it is EXPLANATION, or CC if it is COMPARISON-CONTRAST. If it is none of these, mark O.

4. An outstanding quality of the European peasant was love and respect for the soil.

   _____ The American, however, rarely loved the soil.

   _____ The French peasant loved the soil.

   _____ The German peasant loved the soil.

   _____ This was because the soil provided food and shelter.

The letters following paragraphs 5 and 6 correspond to a sentence in the paragraphs. Decide the function of each indicated sentence—that is, decide how it relates to the other sentences in the paragraph. Determine if it is explanation, example, or comparison-contrast. Then write your choice in the space provided.

5. (a) It is sometimes difficult for children to sit quietly and concentrate on the music they hear. (b) Today's society is so permeated with "background music" that children have become accustomed to engaging in some form of physical activity during the performance of music. (c) Thus, they have not learned to

focus attention upon the music itself. (d) In addition, the pressures of contemporary living create an almost constant tension, even in small children, so that complete relaxation—which is so necessary for the purposes of the listening lesson—seems to be extremely difficult to achieve.

b. _____

d. _____

6. (a) The talents, training, and interests that Alexander Graham Bell took with him when he sailed from England seem to have been combined especially to help him succeed in inventing the telephone. (b) His mind was instinctively inventive. (c) He had a sensitive ear and an excellent training in music. (d) He was second to none in his understanding of the organs of speech and the production of speech sounds. (e) His interest in electricity was growing day by day. (f) And his intense desire to help the deaf led him directly to friendship with men who gave him financial backing for his electrical experiments.

b. _____

c. _____

d. _____

Relationships I, Quiz 2

For each of the following sentences or group of sentences, decide whether the relationship is EXAMPLE, EXPLANATION, or COMPARISON-CONTRAST. Then write your answer in the space provided.

1. Most interviewers are honest and want applicants to know all the details of their jobs before they are hired. But a few interviewers may deliberately or inadvertently slur over details that are important to the applicant.

   _____

2. Talk to people who are already working in the field you wish to enter. They can give you information that can be obtained in no other way.

   _____

3. The golf swing is influenced by the individual's build and his or her rhythm of movement. For instance, a tall, slender person may have a longer swing than a short, stocky person, whose swing may be more compact.

   _____

The following sentence is followed by four statements. For each statement, mark E if it is an example, XP if it is explanation, or CC if it is comparison-contrast. If it is none of these, mark O.

4. Interest in physical fitness and positive health is not new.

   _____ The ancient Greeks were interested in it.

   _____ An understanding of the relationship between physical fitness and positive health is relatively new, however.

   _____ The Romans were very interested in physical fitness and positive health.

   _____ Interest in calorie counting is relatively new, though.

The letters following paragraphs 5 and 6 correspond to a sentence in the paragraph. For paragraph 5: Decide how each of the indicated sentences relates to the first sentence in the paragraph. For paragraph 6: Decide how each of the indicated sentences relates to the last sentence in the paragraph. Remember that sentences can be related by EXPLANATION, EXAMPLE, or COMPARISON-CONTRAST. Mark your choice on the line following the sentence letter.

5. (a) The harpsichord looks somewhat like the grand piano. (b) The case or body is much the same; there are black and white keys in the same arrangement, and

both instruments have a few pedals. (c) But there the similarity ends. (d) Unlike the piano, in which the strings are struck by a hammer, the harpsichord's strings are *plucked* by a quill, which looks something like the point of a tack. (e) When a key is depressed, a wooden jack with a quill in it moves up by the string, catches it, and makes the typical brittle sound as it is released.

b. _____

d. _____

6. (a) For more than 45 years after inventing the telephone, Bell lived a vigorous and creative life, most of it in Washington and at his summer home, Beinn Bhreagh, on Cape Breton Island in Nova Scotia. (b) He gave years of unselfish service in behalf of the deaf. (c) He became tremendously interested in aviation, foresaw its importance, and did much to foster its progress. (d) He produced other communication devices, though none as significant as the telephone, and carried on constructive studies in eugenics. (e) His mind was ever inquiring and his range of interests wide.

b. _____

c. _____

d. _____

Relationships I, Quiz 3

For each of the following sentences or group of sentences decide whether the relationship is EXAMPLE, EXPLANATION, or COMPARISON-CONTRAST. Then write your answer in the space provided.

1. Some students find final-exam week the easiest time of the year (not the most relaxed, but the easiest). They have turned their papers in on time, have kept up to date with their reading, and have discharged their other responsibilities in a reasonably orderly way.

   _____

2. Our purpose in work is to change something or to create or produce something. Our purpose in play, however, is to relax, exercise, entertain, amuse, or refresh ourselves.

   _____

3. Visiting the location of your potential job and observing what happens there is one way to find out about the working pattern of the job. If you are interested in being a newspaper reporter, visit the newspaper office or plant, not for one fifteen-minute period, but for half a day. Do this on two or three different days.

   _____

The following sentence is followed by four statements. For each statement, mark E *if it is an example,* XP *if it is explanation, or* CC *if it is comparison-contrast. If it is none of these, mark* O.

4. From time immemorial, autobiographies have been a rich and unique source of information about people's lives.

   _____ On the other hand, biographies aren't nearly as helpful.

   _____ This is because it is assumed that autobiographers give accurate information about themselves.

   _____ One reason for this is that an autobiographer knows more about himself or herself than anyone else does.

   _____ The autobiography of Benjamin Franklin provides a wealth of information about him.

The letters following paragraphs 5 and 6 correspond to a sentence in the paragraph. Decide the function of each indicated sentence (that is, decide how it relates to the other sentences in the paragraph). Determine whether it is EXPLANATION, EXAMPLE, or COMPARISON-CONTRAST. Then write your choice in the space provided.

5. (a) A number of terms have emerged that help describe aspects of family structure. (b) The family one is born into is called the family of orientation. (c) The family of which one is a parent is called the family of procreation. (d) The nuclear family, a much-used term today, refers to the married couple and their children. (e) The conjugal family is one related by marital ties; the consanguine family is one related by blood ties.

   b. _____

   d. _____

6. (a) There are a number of suggestions that may help you prepare a good set of notes. (b) First, obtain a good looseleaf notebook, one that will last, with tabular index. (c) By having a looseleaf notebook, all of your notes for all of your subjects are together in one place, and there is only one notebook to keep track of. (d) Also, you can take out and replace or rewrite any given page without disturbing other material.

   b. _____

   c. _____

   d. _____

Relationships II, Quiz 1

The following two sentences are followed by four statements. For each statement, mark D *if it is* DEFINITION, R *if it is* REPETITION, CE *if it is* CAUSE- EFFECT, *or* CN *if it is* CONCLUSION. *If it is none of these, mark* O.

1. Thomas Edison once remarked that invention is 1 percent inspiration and 99 percent perspiration.

    _____ By invention we mean turning an engineering design into a usable product.

    _____ According to Edison, invention is hard work.

    _____ Because of this, Edison had to work many long hours.

    _____ There might be more inventions if less work and more "inspiration" were involved.

2. There was continuous heavy rainfall in the area.

    _____ As a result there was a considerable amount of flooding.

    _____ Many businesses may have to close down because of water damage.

    _____ By continuous heavy rainfall we mean four inches per day for several days.

    _____ The stores were soon sold out of raincoats and umbrellas.

The letters following paragraph 3 correspond to a sentence in the paragraph. Decide how each indicated sentence relates to other sentences in the paragraph. Determine whether it is DEFINITION, REPETITION, CAUSE-EFFECT, *or* CONCLUSION. *Then write your choice in the space provided.*

3. (a) An increase in blood pressure in the capillaries or a decrease in plasma proteins (such as may follow prolonged malnutrition) will result in the production of abnormally great quantities of lymph. (b) If the lymphatic system is unable to handle the increased lymph production successfully, the lymph will begin to accumulate in the tissues and to distend them. (c) This condition is known as edema. (d) Another cause of edema is blockage of the lymph vessels. (e) In the tropics this may occur as a result of infection with a parasitic roundworm, the filarial worm. (f) The resulting edema causes portions of the body, such as the legs or arms, to become grossly enlarged. (g) This condition is known as elephantiasis.

    b. _____

    c. _____

    e. _____

    g. _____

Relationships II, Quiz 2

The following two sentences are followed by four statements. For each statement, mark D if it is DEFINITION, R if it is REPETITION, CE if it is CAUSE-EFFECT, or CN if it is CONCLUSION. If it is none of these, mark O.

1. On the average, college graduates make more in their first year on the job than untrained workers make in a year at the height of their earning powers.

   _____ College graduates make more money than untrained people.

   _____ Many people go to college for this reason.

   _____ Making more money will also make you happier.

   _____ An untrained person is one who has never gone to college.

2. There are more clerical workers than almost any other kind of worker.

   _____ It is expected that this trend will continue.

   _____ Clerical workers make up one of the largest segments of the working class.

   _____ A clerical worker is one who does paperwork in an office.

   _____ As a result there are more training programs for clerical workers than for any other kind of worker.

The letters following paragraphs 3 and 4 correspond to a sentence in the paragraph. Decide how each indicated sentence relates to other sentences in the paragraph. Determine whether it is DEFINITION, REPETITION, CAUSE-EFFECT, or CONCLUSION. Then write your choice in the space provided.

3. (a) We are now working out with a number of countries a joint agreement designed to strengthen the security of the North Atlantic area. (b) Such an agreement would take the form of a collective defense arrangement within the terms of the United Nations Charter. (c) The primary purpose of these agreements is to provide unmistakable proof of the joint determination of the free countries to resist armed attack from any quarter. (d) If we can make it sufficiently clear, in advance, that any armed attack affecting our national security would be met with overwhelming force, the armed attack might never occur.

   b. _____

   d. _____

4. (a) The explosive growth of technical knowledge has greatly increased the sophistication and complexity of a multitude of jobs. (b) There is now a labor gap—shown by a shortage of professional, semiprofessional, and technical personnel and by the many unskilled workers who cannot find jobs. (c) Consequently, in this age of automation and competition, it is no longer sufficient just "to want" to be a policeman or an electronic technician. (d) Jobs that traditionally required a period of apprenticeship now require a program of formal training coupled with a program of sound general education.

b. _____

d. _____

Wrap-up Quiz: Relationships I & II

This quiz combines elements of Relationships I and Relationships II. Sentences 1, 2, and 3 are followed by four statements. For each statement, mark E if it is EXAMPLE, XP if it is EXPLANATION, D if it is DEFINITION, CC if it is COMPARISON-CONTRAST, CN if it is CONCLUSION, CE if it is CAUSE-EFFECT, and R if it is REPETITION.

1. The majority of present-day cosmetologists are able to perform many different kinds of jobs.

   _____ This means they are more likely to get hired.

   _____ The same person may dye hair, manicure nails, give permanent waves, or wash and set hair.

   _____ Some, however, specialize in a single operation.

   _____ Most cosmetologists today are truly versatile.

2. Teenagers are taking an increasingly active part in organizations that advance public welfare.

   _____ They are realizing their power as citizens.

   _____ Because of this, there is hardly an organization devoted to the public welfare that doesn't include teens.

   _____ They feel a responsibility to help others.

   _____ Some teens, though, are too involved in their jobs and other obligations to join these organizations.

3. Some students seem to study at times and in places where they are visible and available to social traffic.

   _____ Because of this, they don't get much studying done.

   _____ They don't want to study.

   _____ They'll be sorry when the test comes along.

   _____ As a result their concentration is not very intense.

The letters following paragraphs 4 and 5 correspond to a sentence in the paragraph. Decide how each indicated sentence relates to other sentences in the paragraph. Determine whether it is EXAMPLE, EXPLANATION, COMPARISON-CONTRAST, DEFINITION, REPETITION, CAUSE-EFFECT, or CONCLUSION. Then write your choice in the space provided.

4. (a) Students have always been somewhat more interested in reforming academic life than are their professors or college administrators. (b) The U.S. National Student Association, for example, discovered the need for academic freedom for students shortly after it was founded two decades ago. (c) The American Association of University Professors began to get interested in 1960 and by 1965 had produced a statement of its own. (d) In retrospect, it seems unpardonable that the AAUP should have waited forty-five years to turn the coin of academic freedom to its other face.

    b. _____

    d. _____

5. (a) Typically, the community college is a commuter institution where the majority of students live at home and commute to school. (b) Consequently, the "closeness" and identification with the school that students often feel at a resident college may not be as strong at the junior college. (c) At a resident college, the student's whole life revolves around the campus. (d) Such things as bull sessions in the residence halls and interfraternity and intramural sports competitions focus attention on and help cement loyalty for the resident college.

    b. _____

    c. _____

Outlining and Mapping, Quiz 1

1. This map is wrong. Draw it correctly in the box provided.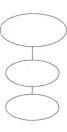

2. Use the material from the following paragraph to fill in the blanks in the partial outline after it.

The human eye is roughly spherical in shape. It is bounded by three distinct layers of tissue. The outer layer, the sclerotic coat, is extremely tough. It is white in color (the "white of the eye") except in front. Here it forms the transparent cornea that admits light into the interior of the eye and bends the light rays so that they can be brought to a focus. The surface of the cornea is kept moist and dust-free by the secretion of the tear glands.

Title: _____

I. Spherical shape
II. Outer layer (sclerotic coat)

    A. _____

    B. _____
    C. Cornea
       1. Transparent

       2. _____

       3. _____

3. Use the material from the following two paragraphs to fill in the second level of the outline under it.

There is no doubt that flying from New York to California has many advantages over driving. For one, you will get there faster. Flying takes only a fraction of the time that driving does. Your trip will probably be more comfortable, especially considering the service on airplanes today. And you will arrive feeling less tired than if you drove.

Driving, on the other hand, offers opportunities and advantages that flying cannot provide. You can enjoy scenery not visible from the air and visit places that you have never been to before. Also, it is considerably less expensive if there are three or four people going.

I. Advantages of flying

_____

_____

_____

II. Advantages of driving

_____

_____

_____

4. Make a two-level outline from the following paragraph. Use the space under the outline's title.

Carpet is being installed with greater and greater frequency in schools and colleges throughout the country. Schools with carpeting have found maintenance costs lower than they were for bare floors. Carpets are an added safety factor because they eliminate the hazards of spills on slippery, newly waxed floors. Acoustics are greatly improved because of the carpet's ability to absorb significant amounts of impact and airborne noise, making classrooms quieter places for study. Another psychological plus is that carpeting duplicates a homelike atmosphere that is more conducive to study.

Title: Why the Use of School Carpeting is Increasing

_____

_____

_____

_____

_____

_____

_____

_____

Outlining and Mapping, Quiz 2

1. This map is wrong. Draw it correctly in the box provided.

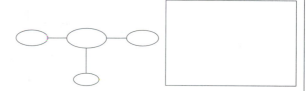

2. Use the material from the following paragraph to fill in the blanks in the outline after it.

When done properly, group sessions have many advantages. First, students are motivated to study before coming to the meeting because they do not like to appear uninformed in front of their friends. Second, group sessions require the students to express themselves aloud to others, a situation that often points up a lack of understanding where they thought they had adequate understanding. Third, having to explain something to others is not only an excellent reinforcement of learning, but utilizes the Recall step of PQ3R in a somewhat different guise; many people have said that they never really understood something until they were forced to explain it to someone else. Fourth, such participation corrects misconceptions and fills in gaps of knowledge. Fifth, hearing what others have to say offers a new slant on the material.

Title: _____

  I. Students study before the meeting

     A. _____

 II. _____

     A. _____

III. Reinforces learning

     A. Explaining to others improves learning

 IV. _____

  V. _____

3. Make a one-level outline from the following paragraph. Use the space under the outline's title.

How can you learn to concentrate better? Visualizing will help. Visualizing forces attention to one thing only. If you try to see specific pictures as you read, it will help you to concentrate. Not looking back will also help you to concentrate. When you do not allow yourself to look back, you force yourself to concentrate in order to get the meaning the first time. Making sure of your purpose is a third way to force concentration. When you read for a particular purpose, you will concentrate on what you read because, as you read, you ask yourself, "Does this satisfy my purpose?"

Title: How to Concentrate Better

_____

_____

_____

_____

4. Make a two-level outline from the following four paragraphs. Use the space under the outline's title.

The first step in becoming a good listener is very simple. Sit up straight in your chair! This first step sets the stage for your *active* listening.

A second step for making classroom listening an active process is to develop the habit of using questions to analyze what the speaker is saying. Ask yourself questions that will help capture the essential meaning in the lecturer's flow of words: "Why is he saying that?" "What does he mean by that?" "What is the main point of what he is saying?"

A third step that will help you develop into an active listener is to take notes on what the lecturer is saying. The act of writing will make you physically as well as mentally active as you try to determine the important ideas and facts that should be captured in your notes.

A fourth step involved in becoming an active listener is to familiarize yourself with the lecturer's topic before the lecture through assigned reading. If you have prior knowledge of the lecturer's subject, you can develop a keener interest in what he is saying and the time you spend in class will be more valuable for you. By contrast, if the subject is "foreign," then what the lecturer is saying will mean little and the hour will be lost.

Title: Becoming a Better Listener

_____

_____

_____

_____

_____

_____

_____

_____

_____

Outlining and Mapping, Quiz 3

1. This map is wrong. Draw it correctly in the box provided.

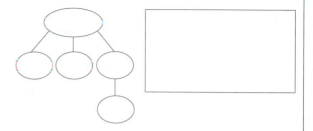

2. Use the material from the following paragraph to fill in the blanks in the partial outline after it.

   A number of bodily changes accompany the psychological state called emotion. Violent emotion, for example, produces changes in the distribution and composition of the blood. The blood pressure may rise or fall; the blood vessels in the skin may dilate or contract—so that blood rushes to the surface of the body or is routed to the interior of the body. These changes in blood distribution are sometimes visible to the casual observer. The red face of embarrassment, the flushed face of anger, and the ashen face of fright are all indications that the blood vessels have dilated or contracted. There is also a substantial chemistry of emotion, since the endocrine glands are active and tend to pour hormones into the bloodstream during powerful emotional states. In addition, changes may occur in the blood-sugar level, in the adrenaline content of the blood, and in its acid-base balance. Furthermore, in states of intense excitement the heart rate increases violently, the rate and depth of breathing increase, and the muscles become tense or trembling.

Title: Bodily Changes Caused by Violent Emotions
I. Blood distribution
   A. _____
   B. _____
II. Blood composition
   A. Hormones
   B. _____
   C. _____
   D. _____

3. Make a one-level outline from the following paragraph. Use the space under the outline's title.

   Several unique advantages arise from publishing individual chapters as separate volumes rather than under a single cover. Each book or chapter can be written by an author identified with the subject matter of the area. New chapters can be added, individual chapters can be revised independently, and, possibly, competitive chapters can be provided for controversial areas. Finally, to a degree, an instructor of the beginning course in psychology can choose a particular set of chapters to meet the needs of his or her students.

Title: Advantages of Publishing Each Chapter as a Separate Booklet

_____

_____

_____

_____

4. Make a two-level outline from the following paragraph. Use the space under the outline's title.

The community college attempts to meet the varied educational needs of local communities at a post-high-school level. The community college has three broad curricula: (1) preprofessional, which prepares you to transfer to a senior college or university in order to pursue a bachelor's degree; (2) vocational, technical, and semiprofessional, which is terminal and prepares you for immediate employment but not for transfer to a senior college; (3) continuing education, or adult education, which is generally noncredit and is aimed at personal development.

Title: Curricula Available at Community Colleges

_____

_____

_____

_____

_____

_____

_____

_____

_____

PQ3R, Quiz 1

Directions: Answer the following questions by writing the answer in the blank or drawing a circle around the letter of your choice.

1. What does the *Q* in PQ3R represent?

   _____

2. PQ3R has a three-part guarantee: (1) you save time, (2) you understand the material better. What is the third part?

   _____

3. When you are following the steps in PQ3R, which item from the following pair should you do first?
   (a) first sentences (b) headings

4. When using PQ3R, you change chapter titles into questions. What other part of the chapter do you change into a question?

   _____

5. A good time to review is just before you go to sleep. Name another good time to review.

   _____

   An article has a one-word title: "GLASS." Its two headings are

   Through the Ages
   Today's Frontiers

6. What will the first heading cover?

   _____

7, 8. Which *two* of the following topics will probably be covered under the second heading?
   a. new types of glass
   b. locations of the largest glass manufacturers
   c. how glass is formed into bottles
   d. new uses for glass

The first two paragraphs under the heading *Through the Ages* begin with these sentences:

Glass was discovered long ago.
The Egyptians were another culture that knew how to make glass thousands of years ago.

9. You need more information from the first paragraph. What question do you need to ask yourself to get that information?

_____

Another paragraph under *Through the Ages* begins with this sentence:

Unlike the Greeks, the Romans used glass for practical, everyday uses.

10. Name one way that the Romans probably used glass.

_____

11. Name one way that the Greeks probably used glass.

_____

A paragraph under *Today's Frontiers* begins with this sentence:

With the exception of two important characteristics, foam glass is similar to the foam plastic found in today's furniture.

12. Will this paragraph focus on the similarities or differences between foam glass and foam plastic?

_____

PQ3R, Quiz 2

Directions: Answer the following questions by writing the answer in the blank, or drawing a circle around the letter of your choice.

1. What does the second *R* in PQ3R represent?

_____

2. PQ3R has a three-part guarantee: (1) you save time, (2) you remember the material better.

What is the third part? _____

3. When you are following the steps in PQ3R, which item from the following pair should you do first?
(a) summary (b) headings

4. When using PQ3R, you change headings into questions. What other part of the chapter do you change into a question?

_____

5. One way to do the RECITE step is to write the material. What is the other way to recite?

_____

An article has the title: "HOME SWEET HOUSE." Its first heading is *Prehistoric Shelter*. The first sentence under this heading is:

Because early humans had to follow game, they had no houses. Instead, they found shelter in trees, overhanging rocks, or caves.

The only other paragraph under the first heading begins with this sentence:

Later, when humankind's mode of living changed, houses became appropriate.

6. What occupation will probably be mentioned in this second paragraph?
a. healer
b. hunter
c. farmer
d. priest

7. What characteristic of this change would cause housing to become appropriate?
    a. its time in history
    b. the intelligence required
    c. its permanence
    d. the development of tribal units
    The article's second heading is *Housing Design*. The first sentence under this heading is:

Housing design, whether from thousands of years ago in Egypt or across the street today, is driven by three major forces.

The second paragraph begins with this sentence:

But in other places wood was plentiful, so wood became the material of choice.

8. What did the *first* paragraph probably say about wood?

_____

The next paragraph begins with this sentence:

The second force affecting design is weather.

9. Name a type of weather and the necessary housing designed to cope with it.

_____

10. What was the first major force affecting housing design?

_____

After the paragraph stating that housing was designed to deal with weather, another paragraph begins:

Weather wasn't the only thing that man needed protection from.

The next paragraph begins:

While it's true that floods are weather *related*, the same cannot be said of the various predators that man had to protect himself from.

And the next paragraph begins

But humans' most serious predator was not the four-footed variety.

11. What was the third major force in housing design?

_____

12. What will probably be mentioned as humans' most serious predator?

_____

PQ3R, Quiz 3

Directions: Answer the following questions by writing the answer in the blank, or drawing a circle around the letter of your choice.

1. What does the third *R* in PQ3R represent?

_____

2. PQ3R has a three-part guarantee: (1) you understand the material better, (2) you remember the material better. What is the third part?

_____

3. When following the steps in PQ3R, which item from the following pair should you do first?
(a) summary (b) first sentences

4. When using PQ3R, you treat chapter titles and headings the same way. What do you do with them before you look at the material under them?

_____

5. One way to do the RECITE step is to say the material aloud. What is the other way to recite?

_____

A chapter in an introductory business textbook has this title: "DATA PROCESS-ING." The introductory paragraph defines and explains data processing. The two headings following that paragraph are

Data Processing Systems
Computers in Business

6, 7. Which *two* of the following questions will probably be answered in the first heading?
a. What are the various types of data processing systems?
b. Who developed each system?
c. What are the major uses for each system?
d. When was each system developed?

The first two paragraphs under *Data Processing Systems* begin with these sentences:

Basically, there are two different data processing systems.
    The second type of data processing system is the computerized system.

8. You need more information from the first paragraph. What question do you need to ask yourself?

_____

The heading *Computers in Business* has three subheadings:

Computers in Banking
Computers in Manufacturing
Computers in Insurance

9. The same question will be answered under each heading. What is that question?

_____

Another heading in this chapter is *Data Processing Centers*. The first paragraph under this heading begins with this sentence:

Many firms have a need for automatic data processing, but hold back because of cost factors, chiefly the cost of the equipment necessary.

10, 11. What two other cost factors will probably be significant?
    a. Cost of electricity
    b. Cost of training employees
    c. Cost of transporting the information
    d. Cost of maintaining the equipment

Another heading in the article is *Programming a Computer*. It is followed by a half page of text.

12. After reading this material, would the reader be able to program a computer?
    a. No. Business people don't need to be able to program a computer.
    b. Yes. Programming a computer is very important.
    c. No. Programming a computer is too complex to be covered in a half page.

Locating Specific Information, Quiz 1

Read each of the following paragraphs and, in the space provided, answer the questions preceding them.

1. Which words define spontaneous combustion?

Store explosive or flammable fluids carefully, outside the home if possible. Never use gasoline, benzine, naphtha, and similar fluids indoors—if their vapors mix with air in a closed space, they will ignite readily from any kind of a spark. Rags soaked with oil or turpentine sometimes catch fire by themselves (this is called spontaneous combustion), and therefore should never be left lying around.

_____

_____

2. Which words tell why one should learn the chemical symbols?

It is important that the student begin to learn the symbols immediately. Since they represent the basic building blocks of matter, they will be used extensively in the remainder of this book and in future chemistry courses the student may take. To write chemical equations, one must know the chemical symbols. One way to learn the symbols is to practice writing them a few minutes every day, by first making a list of the names and the symbols side by side and then alternately writing the names and the symbols.

_____

_____

3. Which words tell why golf offers an opportunity for sportsmanship?

Golf can be as strenuous as you want to make it. Since the golfer sets his or her own pace, golf can be stimulating or relaxing. Endurance and strength may be improved by increasing the number of holes played and the distance of balls hit. Golf offers the opportunity to be out-of-doors, to walk or ride while enjoying nature and fellowship. It can be challenging, satisfying, and relaxing, even if played during a short period of leisure time. Because it is challenging, golf offers opportunity for sportsmanship, whether alone or with a group.

_____

_____

4. Which words indicate the result of not giving adolescents much responsibility?

In years past, and in many parts of the world today, adolescents received a great deal of responsibility, ranging from household chores to working side by side with adults in the field and the factory. This was not just busy work, but work essential to keep the family going. In our country today, we do not need adolescents to take these responsibilities, but—simultaneously—we have deprived them of the feeling that they are making a real contribution.

_____

_____

5. Which words tell the first use of automatic data processing?

Businesses large and small use computers in data processing. Each week sees new equipment and software introduced, and new uses developed for existing technology. Initially, automatic data processing was confined to accounting operations; however, the field has burgeoned so that now the equipment does such diverse tasks as handling airline reservations, maintaining personnel records, and teaching reading and arithmetic to elementary school and preschool children. Automatic data processing has started a revolution that affects almost every aspect of our lives.

_____

_____

6. Which words tell how a key punch machine operates?

An older type of data processing method was the punched-card system, in which information was recorded by punching small holes on a card. Printed information was placed in punched-card form by an operator at a machine called a key punch. The machine had a keyboard resembling that of a typewriter. When the operator struck a key on the keyboard, a positioned hole was punched in the card. Many colleges and universities used punch cards: course numbers, units of credit, grades, and student names easily fit the punched-card format.

_____

_____

7. Which words tell the amount of decline in the number of bookkeepers?

8. Which words tell why checks are coated with magnetic ink?

In banking, computers have had their greatest influence on demand deposits, or checking accounts. One major bank in the United States reports that computers have led to an 80-percent decline in the number of bookkeepers in demand deposit activity despite a 10-percent rise in the number of checking accounts. Virtually all checks used in this country are coated with magnetic ink symbols so that they can be processed by computer systems.

7. _____

_____

8. _____

_____

Locating Specific Information, Quiz 2

Read each of the following paragraphs and, in the space provided, answer the questions preceding them.

1. Which words tell where our commerce suffered most?

   The ships of the new navy were soon at sea. In December they numbered fourteen men-of-war properly armed, and eight converted merchantmen. Some of them were small, but most of them were fast and well manned. They were well able to deal with the French privateers; and the frigates, the pride of the fleet, showed that they could meet successfully ships of equal size from the French navy. Squadrons were stationed in the West Indies, where our commerce suffered most, with orders to seize privateers wherever found.

   _____

   _____

2. Which words tell the three conditions necessary for germination?

   Germination is the resumption of growth of the embryo plant inside the seed. Proper temperature, proper amounts of moisture, and an adequate supply of oxygen are all necessary for it to occur. What is proper or adequate for one species may not be for another, but for each species these three conditions must be met to some degree.

   _____

   _____

3. Which words tell why a pilot cannot fly too many hours at one time?

   There are many things which a pilot must be aware of at one time: the feel of the plane under him, the noise of the motors, the messages from the ground which his earphones are bringing in, the indicators on his instrument panels, and meteorological events in the surroundings of the plane. This constant use of all his senses may be very tiring and because of this nerve strain, a pilot cannot fly too many hours at a time. Pilots are put in unprecedented situations in which they actually have no standards by which to judge what constitutes minimum performance. They are subject to strain not characteristic of most occupations because they are periodically subject to checks and the flight surgeon can "ground" them at the first indication of a physical defect. Moreover, unpredictable crisis situations may arise which crucially affect the career progress of the pilot.

4. Which words tell how the Bobbie Brooks company increased its turnover in clothing?

Large retailing firms are finding computers invaluable in handling accounts payable, payrolls, sales, audits, and accounts receivable. Computers are also being used for inventory control and market analysis. The apparel firm of Bobbie Brooks, for example, was able to increase its turnover in clothing 30 to 40 percent by using a computer to control its inventory.

5. Which words tell why firms need a larger volume of work to justify the installation of automatic data processing equipment?

Many firms have a need for automatic data processing equipment but do not have a large enough volume of work to justify its installation, which is costly. To fill this need, many data processing centers have been established throughout the United States that operate on a shop basis. Business firms can bring their technical problems to the centers and have specialists handle the complicated work for them.

6. Which words tell why executives need to see the broad implications of data processing?

Data processing equipment will continue to grow in importance. However, the machinery is of no value unless it can be integrated into the total organization. Only top executives can make decisions that will reorganize departments so they can make the most efficient use of these tools. Hence, there is a need for executives who see the broad implications, ramifications, and applications of data processing. A fertile field for recruiting future executives may be among data processing specialists.

7. Which words tell how much the cost of computation has decreased with the use of computers?

8. Which words tell what type of managers will take over the more responsible business positions?

In the opinion of many who have studied management science, we are still only on the threshold of really significant use of computers. An important reason for this slow progress is a basic mismatch between computers and managers. Over the last 25 years, computers have changed unbelievably. Speed has increased by a factor of 1000. Costs of computation have gone down by a factor of over 100. Memory capacity is up by a factor of 1000. However, the managers in responsible positions have changed very little. Many of them grew into their present positions in the precomputer era; hence they are heavily entrenched in precomputer thinking, organization, and methods. As a new breed of managers trained in computer technology takes over the more responsible business positions, we can look forward to great innovations in the use of computers.

7. _____

_____

8. _____

_____

Locating Specific Information, Quiz 3

Read each of the following paragraphs and, in the space provided, answer the questions preceding them.

1. Which words tell what time of day to ventilate a house?

Ventilate the house when outside air is drier than that inside. As the air comes in, it takes moisture from the damp interior walls and furnishings. Then the moisture vapor is carried outdoors. Since cool air holds less moisture than warm air, take advantage of cool nights to freshen the air in the entire house.

Run an electric fan in places that cannot be exposed to outdoor breezes. Special-purpose fans, such as adjustable window fans, can be used to help remove moisture and keep the house well ventilated.

_____

_____

2. Which words tell how often peas and okra should be gathered?

When to gather vegetables is a very important part of good gardening. Many people let vegetables get too ripe before harvesting them. Vegetables should be eaten while they are young and tender. They taste better, and many of them have more protective food value then than they do when they get too mature.

Vegetables like beans, peas, okra, and lettuce should be gathered every day or two. Vegetables should not be allowed to stand after gathering. When they become wilted or dried out, they are not as good. All vegetables should be cooked, eaten, or preserved in some way as soon after harvesting as possible.

_____

_____

3. Which words tell the relative positions of the sun, earth, and moon at the time of neap tides?

Twice each month, when the moon is a mere thread of silver in the sky, and again when it is full, we have the strong tidal movements—the highest flood tides and the lowest ebb tides of the lunar month. These are called the spring tides. At these times, sun, moon and earth are directly in line and the pull of the two heavenly bodies is added together to bring the water high on the beaches, and send its surf leaping upward against the sea cliffs, and draw a brimming tide into the harbors so that the boats float high beside their wharfs. And twice each month, at the quarters of the moon, when sun, moon and earth lie at the apexes of a triangle, and the pull of the sun and moon are opposed, we have the moderate tidal movements called neap tides. Then the difference between high and low water is less than at any other time during the month.

_____

_____

4. Which words tell the age at which negativism reaches its peak?

Frequently this exploration manifests itself by a period of negativism. Every parental suggestion is greeted by "No." While this is frustrating to the parents, it probably is an important step in the development of self-awareness and independence. Such negativism typically reaches its peak between the ages of two and a half and three and a half and then normally declines. Although negativism is annoying, parents who know that such a stage is common can tolerate it with some amusement. For other parents, however, negativism represents a severe threat to parental authority and the parent may act vigorously and forcefully.

_____

_____

5. Which words tell why two hoppers and a stacker are necessary?

Suppose we are given two decks of cards, each arranged alphabetically or numerically. We wish to interleave the two into one deck and still preserve the original sort. This process is called collating or merging, and a machine which can perform this function is called a collator. Such a machine must have two hoppers for the two decks of cards, and a stacker to receive the collated deck. Obviously, the collator must sense the information on each card and direct the cards in turn. This permits the collator to be used for other tasks as well as collating.

_____

_____

6. Which words tell why da Vinci felt that a painter should know mathematics?

Leonardo da Vinci's work provides excellent examples of paintings embodying mathematical perspective. Leonardo prepared for painting by deep and extensive studies in anatomy, perspective, geometry, physics, and chemistry. In his *Treatise on Painting*, a scientific treatise on painting and perspective, Leonardo gives his views. He opens with the statement "Let no one who is not a mathematician read my works." Painting, he says, is a science which should be founded on the study of nature and, like all sciences, must also be based on mathematics. He scorns those who think they can ignore theory and by mere practice produce art: "Practice must be founded on sound theory."

_____

_____

7. Which words tell how much money the Nationwide Insurance Company saved each year?

No large insurance company could operate competitively today without an electronic data processing installation. The Nationwide Insurance Company is a good example of the effect computers have had on the insurance business. This company installed data processing equipment to calculate renewal billings and through this one application produced annual savings of $200,000 as a result of clerical staff reductions. Mutual of Omaha has designed its computer system to process benefit claims overnight, with next-day payment authorizations at the local level. Computers are also being used increasingly to provide marketing analyses and financial forecasts.

_____

_____

8. Which words tell what computers do with machine tools?

Manufacturing companies are using computers for production control in such applications as shop scheduling and assembly line balancing, as well as in scheduling labor requirements and numerically controlling machine tools. Advanced management sciences, like operations research, are finding computers increasingly helpful in making skillful decisions on inventory policy, long-range market strategies, plant and warehouse locations, and capital investment programs. Power companies are making extensive use of computers to achieve maximum effectiveness from their facilities.

_____

_____

Following Printed Directions, Quiz 1

Each of the following selections gives directions for a specific procedure. After each selection is a list of some steps in the procedure. Number these steps in the order they should be followed. If two or more steps should be done at the same time, or if they mean the same thing, give them the same number.

1. Remove the entrails after cutting the entire length of the belly from the vent to the head. Cut around the pelvic fins and remove them. Remove the head, including the pectoral fins, by cutting above the collarbone. If the backbone is large, cut down to it on each side of the fish, and then snap the backbone by bending it over the edge of the cutting board or table. Cut any remaining flesh which holds the head attached to the body. Cut off the tail.

   _____ Remove the pelvic fins.

   _____ Cut the length of the belly from the vent to the head.

   _____ Remove the pectoral fins.

   _____ Remove the entrails.

   _____ Remove the head.

2. If after carefully removing a portion of the waterproof shell (by dissolving it away in dilute acid), one places the egg in pure water, water will diffuse into the egg. As osmosis continues, more and more water accumulates within the egg and this crowding in of additional molecules results in a buildup of pressure.

   _____ There is a buildup of pressure.

   _____ Obtain dilute acid.

   _____ The water diffuses into the egg.

   _____ Remove the waterproof shell.

   _____ Place the egg in water.

3. The pollen combs collect pollen from the pollen brushes of the other legs. Then with the stiff spines (the pectin) of the pollen packer of one leg, the bee removes the pollen from the pollen combs of the opposite leg. Straightening of the leg then forces the anvil-shaped auricle up against the pollen caught under the pectin. The pollen is squeezed through the joint and up into the pollen basket on the outside of the tibia.

   _____ The bee straightens its leg.

_____ The pollen is squeezed through the joint.

_____ The auricle is forced up against the pollen.

_____ Pollen is collected.

_____ Pollen is removed from the pollen combs of the opposite leg.

4. By marking the scout bees with paint and watching them upon their return to an observation hive, von Frisch discovered that the scouts perform a little dance on the vertical surface of the combs after depositing their load of nectar or pollen. This dance seems to stimulate the foragers and soon they begin to leave the hive and fly to the food source.

_____ The bees dance.

_____ The foragers leave.

_____ The bees are painted.

_____ The foragers are stimulated.

_____ The bees deposit their nectar.

Following Printed Directions, Quiz 2

Each of the following selections gives directions for a specific procedure. After each selection is a list of some steps in the procedure. Number these steps in the order they should be followed. If two or more steps should be done at the same time, or if they mean the same thing, give them the same number.

1. The cards are inserted face forward with the nine-edge down. This may vary in other machines, but instructions are usually attached at the hopper. At the touch of a button, cards are fed down to the card bed and move across it from right to left. As the card moves, it passes under a punching station and then—about a card's length away—under a reading station. When it reaches the left-hand end of the bed, it is lifted and placed in the stacker, and at the same time a new card is fed from the hopper to the right-hand end of the bed. At the end of the run, all the cards will be in the stacker in the same order in which they were placed in the hopper.

   _____ The card passes under a reading station.

   _____ Make sure that the instructions at the hopper are understood.

   _____ The card is lifted and placed in the stacker.

   _____ A button is pressed.

   _____ A new card is fed from the hopper to the right-hand end of the bed.

2. The injured area on the tree is prepared by cutting away all torn and dead bark to live, healthy tissues. If there is danger of any disease being present the wood should be disinfected with corrosive sublimate, potassium permanganate, or Bordeaux paste.

   The cions selected should be long enough to reach over the injured area to healthy bark on either side. Extra length should be allowed so that the cions will be slightly arched at the middle when they are in place. Water sprouts growing from below the injured area may be grafted in above the wound.

   Both the upper and lower ends of the cion should be cut wedge-shaped, but the cut on one side should be about twice as long as on the opposite side. A "T" cut should be made in the bark above and below the injured area. Then the wedge-shaped ends should be slipped under the bark with the longest cut surface next to the wood of the tree.

   _____ Cut away torn and dead bark.

   _____ Select the cions.

_____ Cut the upper and lower ends of the cion wedge-shaped.

_____ Make a "T" cut in the bark.

_____ Slip the wedge-shaped ends under the bark.

3. Fit the guide and die over the end of the pipe and turn the stock to the right (for a right-hand thread) until the die teeth just catch on the end of the pipe. Then apply a liberal amount of thread cutting oil or lard oil on the end of the pipe and the die teeth. Continue to turn the stock and die until the end of the pipe projects about one-half thread through the front end of the die. This gives a full thread. Additional turning of the stock will make a loose thread. Do not use oil on brass or copper IPS pipe. Instead use soapy water or else no lubricant at all. When the thread is finished, the stock is turned to the left until the die comes off the pipe. The die and stock, as well as the end of the pipe, should be cleaned of all chips and oil. If a thread is imperfectly cut or is crooked, it seldom can be corrected with the die. The imperfect thread should be cut off the pipe and a new thread formed.

_____ Clean the pipe of chips and oil.

_____ Turn the stock to the left.

_____ Turn the stock to the right.

_____ Check to see how far the end of the pipe projects through the front end of the die.

_____ Check for imperfect threads.

4. Fill the joint with molten lead at one pouring. Melt enough lead for all joints to be run, and dip enough molten lead with the ladle to make one complete joint at one pouring. Wipe the hub and spigot ends of the pipe dry and free from foreign matter before pouring the lead. Moisture will cause molten lead to fly out of the joint. Wear goggles and gloves while pouring, and keep clear of the range of flying lead even though the parts may appear dry.

_____ Wipe hub and spigot ends of the pipe dry and free of foreign matter.

_____ Melt lead.

_____ Keep clear of the range of flying lead.

_____ Put on goggles and gloves.

_____ Fill the joint with lead.

Following Printed Directions, Quiz 3

Each of the following selections gives directions for a specific procedure. After each selection is a list of some steps in the procedure. Number these steps in the order they should be followed. If two or more steps should be done at the same time, or if they mean the same thing, give them the same number.

1. To prepare a hot water bottle: Fill the rubber bag about half full of hot but not boiling water—the water must not be so hot as to hurt the patient if the bottle should leak or break. Screw the stopper about halfway in, being sure the washer is correctly in place; then gently squeeze the bag until water can be seen at the top. This forces air out, and makes the bag softer and more comfortable in use. While holding the bag in this position, screw the stopper tight. Finally, turn the bag upside down to check for leaks, test its temperature by holding it against your skin, wrap it in a towel or regular cover, and apply it to the affected area. Remove it when it gets cool, refill, and reapply for as long as directed by the physician.

   _____ Squeeze the bag.

   _____ Screw the stopper about halfway in.

   _____ Make sure the stopper is screwed in tightly.

   _____ Heat water.

   _____ Hold the bag against your skin.

2. After the baby is born, wrap a fold of towel around her ankles to prevent slipping and hold her up by the heels with one hand, taking care that the cord is slack. To get a good safe grip, insert one finger between the baby's ankles. Do not swing or spank the baby. Hold her over the bed so that she cannot fall far if she should slip from your grasp. The baby's body will be very slippery. Place your other hand under the baby's forehead and bend its head back slightly so that the fluid and mucus can run out of its mouth. When the baby begins to cry, lay her on her side on the bed close enough to the mother to keep the cord slack.

   _____ Let fluid and mucus run out of the baby's mouth.

   _____ Insert one finger between the baby's ankles.

   _____ Place your hand under the baby's forehead.

   _____ Hold her up by the heels.

   _____ Bend the baby's head back.

3. To dress the faucet seat, unscrew the stem from the body, as already explained. Screw the adjustable threaded cone of the dressing tool down into the body of the faucet, thus centering it over the seat. Then gently rotate the wheel or bar handle on top of the tool several times while the cutter on the bottom trims the seat to a new, true surface. Now it is necessary to remove all cuttings that have lodged inside the faucet body, otherwise they will quickly damage a new seat washer when the faucet is shut off. It usually is necessary to turn on the water to allow enough flow to flush out these cuttings.

_____ Rotate the wheel or bar handle.

_____ Flush out cuttings.

_____ Unscrew the stem from the body.

_____ Screw the cone of the dressing tool down into the body of the faucet.

_____ Turn on the water.

4. The solution, such as a sugar solution, is placed in the porous cup, in the pores of which has been deposited the semipermeable membrane. The cup is immersed in pure water. Water flows through the membrane and the solution rises in the tube until the hydrostatic pressure prevents further osmosis. The hydrostatic pressure is then equal to the osmotic pressure of the resulting solution in the cup.

_____ A semipermeable membrane is put in the pores of the cup.

_____ The solution is placed in the cup.

_____ The solution is prepared.

_____ Water flows through the membrane.

_____ The hydrostatic pressure prevents further osmosis.

Understanding Figurative Language, Quiz 1

Each of the following statements contains a figurative expression. Answer the questions about that expression by circling the letter of the correct response.

1. Gray hair is the light of the moon casting a silver-white hue in the evening of life.
   What things are being compared?
   a. gray hair and evening
   b. gray hair and old age
   c. gray hair and the moon
   d. gray hair and moonlight
   What likeness is being emphasized?
   a. Both appear at the end (of a day or of a life).
   b. Both are pleasant.
   c. Both are relatively high (on the head or in the sky).
   d. Both are peaceful.

2. Marrying to find happiness is like gambling to become rich.
   What things are being compared?
   a. marriage and wealth
   b. gambling and wealth
   c. marrying and gambling
   d. happiness and wealth.
   What likeness is being emphasized?
   a. Both are fun.
   b. In both situations you may become wealthy.
   c. In both situations the odds are against you.
   d. In both situations you are taking a chance.

3. To a determined person, competition is like adding fuel to a fire.
   What things are being compared?
   a. a determined person and a fire
   b. a determined person and fuel
   c. a determined person and competition
   d. competition and adding fuel to a fire
   What likeness is being emphasized?
   a. Things get hotter.
   b. There is more vigorous action.
   c. Things get brighter.
   d. Energy is wasted.

In the following statements some figurative expressions have been italicized. Decide for each one (a) what things are being compared; (b) which quality of the figurative language fits the context; and (c) the meaning of the figurative language. Write your answers in the spaces provided.

Example: He entered jail *a lamb*; he emerged a wolf.
a. a man and a lamb
b. A lamb is innocent and harmless.
c. The man was not dangerous when he entered jail.

4. The counselor became a *storage cabinet* for the student's worries.

   a. _____

   b. _____

   c. _____

5. Her *razor-sharp tongue* cut her neighbor's reputation to pieces.

   a. _____

   b. _____

   c. _____

6. Doing business without advertising is like waving your arms in the dark.

   a. _____

   b. _____

   c. _____

What do the following statements mean? Write your answers in the space provided.

7. Summer's free-flowing river was clutched in the icy hand of winter.

   _____

8. He looked like a puppy watching his master go off to school.

   _____

*U*nderstanding *F*igurative *L*anguage, *Q*uiz 2

Each of the following statements contains a figurative expression. Answer the questions about that expression by circling the letter of the correct response.

1. The brighter the torch of love burns, the less likely it is to be put out by the storm of jealousy.
     What things are being compared?
   a. love and a storm
   b. love and jealousy
   c. a burning torch and a storm
   d. love and a burning torch
     What likeness is being emphasized?
   a. Both are liable to be extinguished.
   b. Both are fuel.
   c. Both eventually burn out.
   d. Both lead the way.

2. A person's reputation is a delicate piece of hand-carved glass and must be carefully treated.
     What things are being compared?
   a. a person's reputation and delicate glass
   b. a person and his reputation
   c. a person and glass
   d. a person's reputation and good workmanship
     What likeness is being emphasized?
   a. Both can be seen through.
   b. Both are unattractive when dirty.
   c. Both are easily shattered.
   d. Both are very revealing.

3. Her memory is like a sieve that lets the little details pass through but retains the bigger ideas.
     What things are being compared?
   a. her memory and little details
   b. her memory and a sieve
   c. a sieve and little details
   d. a sieve and bigger ideas

What likeness is being emphasized?
a. Both are selective.
b. Both are faulty.
c. Both retain only part of the material.
d. Both are incomplete.

In the following statements some figurative expressions have been italicized. Decide for each one (a) what things are being compared; (b) which quality of the figurative language fits the context; and (c) the meaning of the figurative language. Write your answers in the spaces provided.

Example: He entered jail *a lamb*; he emerged a wolf.
a. a man and a lamb
b. A lamb is innocent and harmless.
c. The man was not dangerous when he entered jail.

4. The pillow fight created *a snowstorm* in the room.

a. _____

b. _____

c. _____

5. He was gone like *a snowflake on the water.*

a. _____

b. _____

c. _____

6. Freedom is a *campfire* that, if not tended, will be extinguished.

a. _____

b. _____

c. _____

What do the following statements mean? Write your answers in the space provided.

7. Their kids were the glue that held their marriage together.

_____

8. The teacher nailed him to his chair with one glance.

_____

Understanding Figurative Language, Quiz 3

Each of the following statements contains a figurative expression. Answer the questions about that expression by circling the letter of the correct response.

1. Because we are social creatures, people are like the workings of a watch—we have to work together or not at all.
   What things are being compared?
   a. people and social creatures
   b. people and work
   c. people and watch workings
   d. watches and social creatures
   What likeness is being emphasized?
   a. Both are social creatures.
   b. Both have to work together.
   c. Both need to work.
   d. Neither has time to work.

2. Shopping malls are locusts that eat up the grass and the trees.
   What things are being compared?
   a. shopping malls and trees
   b. city and country
   c. eating and land use
   d. shopping malls and locusts
   What likeness is being emphasized?
   a. Both grow.
   b. Both consume things.
   c. Both occupy space.
   d. Both are places where people live.

3. To a propagandist, telling both sides of the story is like putting a cockroach in the soup.
   What things are being compared?
   a. telling only one side of the story and eating soup
   b. telling both sides of the story and putting a cockroach in the soup
   c. a propagandist and a cockroach
   d. a propagandist and soup
   What likeness is being emphasized?
   a. Both add something necessary.
   b. Both spoil things.

    c. Both make people curious.

    d. Both add things that people don't want.

In the following statements some figurative expressions have been italicized. Decide for each one (a) what things are being compared; (b) which quality of the figurative language fits the context; and (c) the meaning of the figurative language. Write your answers in the spaces provided.

    Example: He entered jail *a lamb;* he emerged a wolf.

    a. a man and a lamb

    b. A lamb is innocent and harmless.

    c. The man was not dangerous when he entered jail.

4. The people of the village scattered like *dry leaves* in the path of the oncoming soldiers.

    a. _____

    b. _____

    c. _____

5. The death of his parents was *the thief* that robbed him of his childhood.

    a. _____

    b. _____

    c. _____

6. His promises are *clouds without rain.*

    a. _____

    b. _____

    c. _____

What do the following statements mean? Write your answers in the space provided.

7. The angry sunset was finally calmed by the sea.

    _____

8. The book had all the excitement of *a soggy cigarette butt.*

    _____

Understanding Graphics, Quiz 1

Directions: Use the map on this page to answer questions 1–4.

1. What is the capital of Nebraska?

_____

2. Is it farther (a) from Dallas to San Antonio, or (b) from Pittsburgh to Detroit?

_____

3. In what state is Kansas City located?

_____

4. Which city is located farther north, Jacksonville or New Orleans?

_____

⊙ INDICATES CAPITAL OF STATE
● INDICATES OTHER IMPORTANT CITIES

The United States of America

Directions: Use the table on this page to answer questions 5–8.

5. How does Bayer Plus differ from Bayer?

_____

6. What brand contains caffeine?

_____

7. Which two types of pain relievers are most similar?

_____

8. Is Anacin–3 enteric coated?

_____

OTC Pain Relief Primer

Type/Dosage	Common Brands	What It Does
aspirin 325 mg 500 mg	Anacin[1] Ascriptin[2] Bayer Bayer Plus[2] Bufferin[2] Ecotrin[3]	Relieves mild to moderate pain from headaches, sore muscles, menstrual cramps, and arthritis; reduces fever.
acetaminophen 325 mg 500 mg	Anacin–3 Excedrin[1] Pamprin[4] Midol[4] Tylenol	Relieves mild to moderate pain from headaches and sore muscles; reduces fever.
ibuprofen 200 mg	Advil Motrin–IB Nuprin Pamprin–IB	Relieves mild to moderate pain from headaches, backaches, and sore muscles; relieves minor pain of arthritis; provides good relief of menstrual cramps and toothaches; reduces fever.
naproxen sodium 200 mg	Aleve	Relieves mild to moderate pain from headaches, backaches, and sore muscles; relieves minor pain of arthritis; provides good relief of menstrual cramps and toothaches; reduces fever.

1. Contains caffeine.
2. Contains buffers.
3. Enteric coated.
4. Contains ingredients other than analgesics.

Directions: Use the diagram on this page to answer questions 9–12.

9. In all three diagrams illustrating malocclusions, should the insets showing the teeth be moved in order to line them up with the other part of the diagram showing the lips?
   a. No, don't move them; they are correctly aligned.
   b. Yes, move them down and to the right.
   c. Yes, move them down and to the left.

10. Which type of malocclusion makes the chin appear larger?

_____

11. Which type of malocclusion gives the best appearance to the lips and jaw?

_____

12. Which type of malocclusion occurs when the lower teeth protrude?

_____

Types of Malocclusions

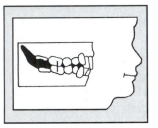

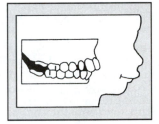

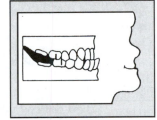

Class I
Teeth line up correctly, but they are crooked, crowded, turned, or spaced too far apart.

Class II
Upper teeth protrude and lower teeth are too far back. Also called an "overbite."

Class III
Lower teeth are too far in front, or upper teeth are too far back. Also called an "underbite."

Directions: Use the chart on page 295 to answer questions 13–16.

13. What type of food does this chart examine?

_____

14. How many grams are in a normal serving?

_____

15. How many grams are in this container?

_____

16. How much Vitamin A, B6, and C are added when one-half cup of skim milk is added?

_____

Nutrition Facts

Serving Size 1 cup (35g)
Servings Per Container 10

Amount Per Serving	Cereal	Cereal with 1/2 cup Skim Milk
Calories	130	170
Calories from Fat	0	0

	% Daily Value**	
Total Fat 0g*	**0%**	**0%**
Saturated Fat 0g	**0%**	**0%**
Cholesterol 0mg	**0%**	**0%**
Sodium 200mg	**8%**	**11%**
Total Carbohydrate 30g	**10%**	**12%**
Dietary Fiber 4g	**16%**	**16%**
Sugars 18g		
Protein 3g		

Vitamin A	25%	25%
Vitamin C	25%	25%
Calcium	10%	25%
Iron	10%	10%
Thiamin	25%	30%
Riboflavin	25%	35%
Niacin	25%	25%
Vitamin B6	25%	25%

* Amount in Cereal. One half cup skim milk contributes an additional 40 calories, 65 mg sodium, 6g total carbohydrate (6 g sugars), and 4g protein.

** Percent Daily Values are based on a 2,000 calorie diet. Your daily values may be higher or lower depending on your calorie needs:

	Calories:	2,000	2,500
Total Fat	Less than	65g	80g
Sat Fat	Less than	20g	25g
Cholesterol	Less than	300mg	300mg
Sodium	Less than	2,400mg	2,400mg
Total Carbohydrate		300g	375g
Dietary Fiber		25g	30g

Calories per gram:
Fat 9 • Carbohydrate 4 • Protein 4

INGREDIENTS: WHOLE WHEAT, SUGAR, MALT EXTRACT, CORN SYRUP, TRISODIUM PHOSPHATE, VITAMIN C (SODIUM ASCORBATE), IRON, NIACINAMIDE, VITAMIN A (PALMITATE), CALCIUM CARBONATE, VITAMIN B6 (PYRIDOXINE HYDROCHLORIDE), RIBOFLAVIN, THIAMIN, BHT TO PRESERVE FRESHNESS.

Understanding Graphics, Quiz 2

Directions: Use the map on this page to answer questions 1–4.

1. In what state is Fort Smith National Historic Site located?

_____

2. In what states do you find Route 59?

_____

3. What is the main highway from Little Rock to Fort Smith?

_____

4. Does the river in Oklahoma generally run (a) north/south, or (b) east/west?

_____

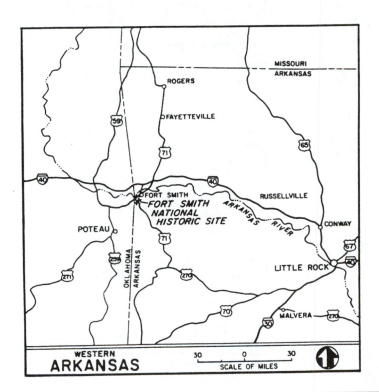

WESTERN
ARKANSAS

SCALE OF MILES

Directions: Use the table on this page to answer questions 5–8.

5. The purpose of this table is to show _____ in large worksites and in small worksites.

6. What size is a worksite with 78 employees?

   _____

7. How many worksites were surveyed?

   _____

8. What length interview was usually conducted in a small worksite?

   _____

Table 2 *Completed Interviews*

Length of Interview	Large Worksites 100 or more employees		Small Worksites 50 to 99 employees		Total Worksites	
	Number	**%**	**Number**	**%**	**Number**	**%**
Short	247	23.8	137	42.8	384	28.3
Medium	155	14.9	69	21.6	224	16.5
Long	636	61.3	114	35.6	750	55.2
Total	1038	100.0	320	100.0	1358	100.0

Directions: Use the diagram on page 298 to answer questions 9–12.

9. Where is the solarium? (a) to the right (b) to the left (c) at the top (d) at the bottom

   _____

10. When would the rock bin's stored heat be used? (a) day (b) night _____

11. The broken lines from the sun that appear inside the house indicate that the walls on the left are made of what material?

    _____

12. Because the summer sun is almost directly overhead, how much summer sun would strike the walls on the left of the house? (a) less (b) more (c) the same amount _____

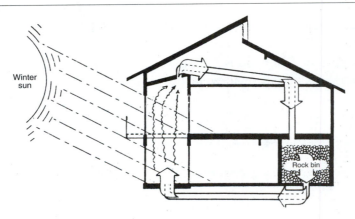

Excess heat collected in solarium stored in rock bin for later use.

Directions: Use the graph on page 298 to answer questions 13–16.

13. Does this graph show the *number* of worksites offering physical fitness testing?

_____

14. What does the number 19.9 above Cancer Screening represent?

_____

15. Does this chart show the percentage of employees who passed the cholesterol test?

_____

16. What is the most commonly given test?

_____

Types of Exams Offered by Worksites Reporting Physical Exams (%)

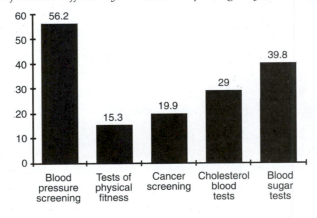

Understanding Graphics, Quiz 3

Directions: Use the map on page 299 to answer questions 1–4.

1. What is the purpose of this map?

   _____

   _____

2. Is gold found in the dense forest area? _____

3. In which area is cotton found? (a) north (b) south (c) east (d) west

4. How many miles is it from Bouake to Abidjan?

   _____

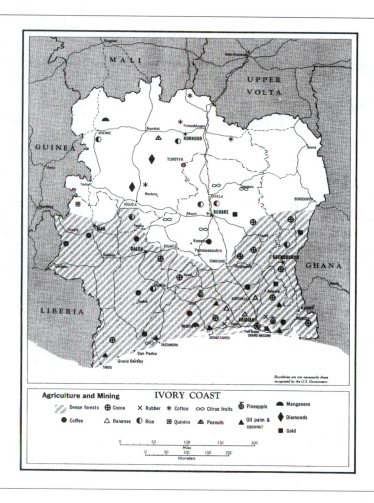

Directions: Use the table on page 300 to answer questions 5–8.

5. How much will $1.00 invested now at 6 percent grow to in thirty years?

_____

6. For how long must you invest $1.00 and at what percentage for it to be worth $17.00?

_____

7. How much more will $1.00 invested at 15 percent be worth at the end of fifteen years than $1.00 invested at 8 percent for the same amount of time?

_____

8. If you invested $1.00 at 8 percent for nine years and then invested the proceeds at 10 percent for five more years, how much would you then have?
   a. $1.61
   b. $4.17
   c. $3.45
   d. $3.22

Compound Amount of $1

Amount to Which $1 Will Grow by End of Specified Year at Compounded Interest

Year	3%	4%	5%	6%	7%	8%	10%	12%	15%	20%	Year
1	1.03	1.04	1.05	1.06	1.07	1.08	1.10	1.12	1.15	1.20	1
2	1.06	1.08	1.10	1.12	1.14	1.17	1.21	1.25	1.32	1.44	2
3	1.09	1.12	1.16	1.19	1.23	1.26	1.33	1.40	1.52	1.73	3
4	1.13	1.17	1.22	1.26	1.31	1.36	1.46	1.57	1.74	2.07	4
5	1.16	1.22	1.28	1.34	1.40	1.47	1.61	1.76	2.01	2.49	5
6	1.19	1.27	1.34	1.41	1.50	1.59	1.77	1.97	2.31	2.99	6
7	1.23	1.32	1.41	1.50	1.61	1.71	1.94	2.21	2.66	3.58	7
8	1.27	1.37	1.48	1.59	1.72	1.85	2.14	2.48	3.05	4.30	8
9	1.30	1.42	1.55	1.68	1.84	2.00	2.35	2.77	3.52	5.16	9
10	1.34	1.48	1.63	1.79	1.97	2.16	2.59	3.11	4.05	6.19	10
11	1.38	1.54	1.71	1.89	2.10	2.33	2.85	3.48	4.66	7.43	11
12	1.43	1.60	1.80	2.01	2.25	2.52	3.13	3.90	5.30	8.92	12
13	1.47	1.67	1.89	2.13	2.41	2.72	3.45	4.36	6.10	10.7	13
14	1.51	1.73	1.98	2.26	2.58	2.94	3.79	4.89	7.00	12.8	14
15	1.56	1.80	2.08	2.39	2.76	3.17	4.17	5.47	8.13	15.4	15
16	1.60	1.87	2.18	2.54	2.95	3.43	4.59	6.13	9.40	18.5	16
17	1.65	1.95	2.29	2.69	3.16	3.70	5.05	6.87	10.6	22.2	17
18	1.70	2.03	2.41	2.85	3.38	4.00	5.55	7.70	12.5	26.6	18
19	1.75	2.11	2.53	3.02	3.62	4.32	6.11	8.61	14.0	31.9	19
20	1.81	2.19	2.65	3.20	3.87	4.66	6.72	9.65	16.1	38.3	20
25	2.09	2.67	3.39	4.29	5.43	6.85	10.8	17.0	32.9	95.4	25
30	2.43	3.24	4.32	5.74	7.61	10.0	17.4	30.0	66.2	237	30
40	3.62	4.80	7.04	10.3	15.0	21.7	45.3	93.1	267.0	1470	40
50	4.38	7.11	11.5	18.4	29.5	46.9	117	289	1080	9100	50

This table shows to what amounts $1.00 invested now will grow at the end of various years, at different rates of growth compounded annually. For example, $1.00 invested now will grow in thirty years to $5.74 at 6 percent. In other words, $5.74 due thirty years hence is worth now exactly $1.00 at a 6 percent rate of interest per year. If you invest $100 now at 10 percent, you will have $1,740 in thirty years. Isn't that worth it?

Directions: Use the diagram on page 301 to answer questions 9–12.

9. In this diagram is the house being heated or cooled?

_____

10. Is well water being circulated through the heat pump?

_____

11. Which is made of one-inch pipe?   *a.* the well casing   *b.* the closed loop

12. Where does the fluid in the loop pick up heat?
   a. from the well water
   b. from the heat pump

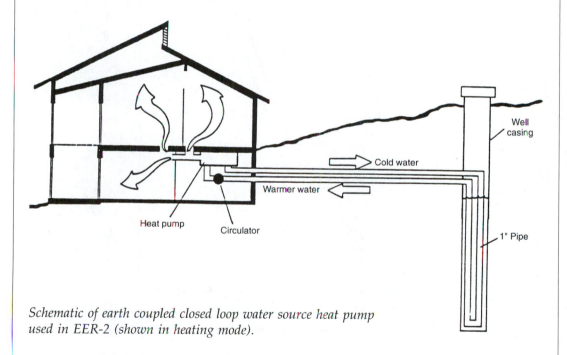

Schematic of earth coupled closed loop water source heat pump used in EER-2 (shown in heating mode).

Directions: Use the chart on page 302 to answer questions 13–16.

13. At all ages, is the percentage of people using corrective lenses higher for males or for females?

_____

14. For both males and females, during which *two* age spans is there a leveling off of use of corrective lenses?

_____

15. At which age are half of the females using corrective lenses?

_____

16. What percentage of the males twenty years old use corrective lenses?

_____

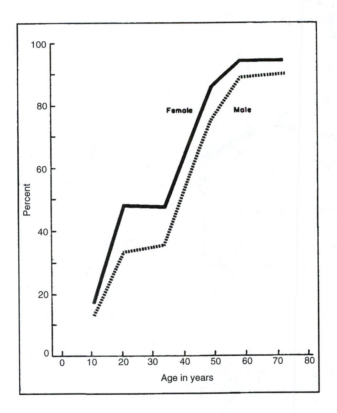

Percent of persons with corrective lenses by sex and age at the time of interview.

Developing Critical Comprehension, Quiz 1

Directions: Indicate whether the numbered sentences are fact—F, opinion—O, or a mixture of fact and opinion—F&O. Answer in the blank provided.

_____ **1.** The best way to prepare for a career in business is to major in business.

_____ **2.** People are not as healthy as they used to be. Studies show that the number of people diagnosed with cancer increases every year.

_____ **3.** An Oldsmobile is the best car in the world.

_____ **4.** This week I'll review my favorite restaurant—Pancho Pickwick's Chinese Cuisine.

_____ **5.** Although Pickwick's is located in the upscale part of town—Broadway and Third Avenue—its prices are moderate to low.

_____ **6.** The decor is rough plank tables, benches, and sawdust on the floor.

_____ **7.** The six-gun-totin' servers seat you on a first-come basis, so unless your group fills the table, you'll be seated with whoever shows up at that time.

_____ **8.** You'll meet some interesting people, but if you're looking for a romantic dinner for two, you'll be happier elsewhere.

Directions: Which statement best describes the purpose of the following selections?

So you've avoided taking penicillin and other wonder drugs to get rid of minor infections because you know that the germs will become immune to the drugs? Don't look now, but it didn't do you any good. The other people who took those drugs indiscriminately have created superpowerful germs that are immune to our medicines. And those germs are now ready to attack *you*.

Choose *two* purposes. To inform   To compare   To alarm   To present a solution

9. _____

10. _____

Americans spend more time watching TV than reading. And studies show that TV can influence their lives, sometimes tragically. Yet in the course of their education, most American children receive numerous lessons in how to read, but none in how to watch TV.

Choose one purpose. To inform To compare To offer a solution To persuade

11. _____

Directions: Read the following selection to detect bias.

The federal government is too big and too dangerous to be run by the average person on the street. We need intelligent people who are specifically educated for careers in public service.

12. Circle the person most likely to be biased *in favor of* the idea presented above.

A political activist A U.S. Army general A university professor A labor union member

Developing Critical Comprehension, Quiz 2

Directions: Indicate whether the numbered sentences are fact—F, opinion—O, or a mixture of fact and opinion—F&O. Answer in the blank provided.

_____ **1.** English food is bland and overcooked.

_____ **2.** A circle has 360 degrees.

_____ **3.** Job sharing—two employees who each work twenty hours per week, instead of one employee working forty hours—has increased productivity while reducing absenteeism. Despite this, only 4 percent of the nation's employers offer this option.

_____ **4.** This film is set in some unnamed Arab country.

_____ **5.** The villain, with the usual large organization of weird and dangerous types, is trying to take over the world. The hero, master of every combat skill and vehicle known to humanity, tries to stop him.

_____ **6.** The writing and acting aren't too bad: people do what people would do in those situations. Even when they don't, the action is fast enough to let you accept it.

_____ **7.** But the real star, of course, is the special effects team.

_____ **8.** Oh, and the car. The car has to be the costar. It is built from American parts and is the fastest, baddest, everythingest car there ever was.

_____ **9.** If you want 123 minutes of mindless comic book action, this is your movie.

Directions: Which statement best describes the purpose of the following selections?

Should our tax money be spent on a kids' after-school basketball league? Of course not! It's just one more activity where parents are somewhere watching their kids, instead of being at home where they belong, watching TV. It's just one more activity where kids, exhausted after a hard day of sitting around in school, are running around getting tired instead of resting in front of a video game at home. It's just one more attempt to undermine our country's values by stressing team spirit and sacrifice instead of the all-American idea of "Me first." Unless we defeat ideas like this, who knows what the horrible results may be?

Choose *one* purpose. To persuade To compare To describe To analyze

10. _____

One appeal of the Nazi youth movement was that it was clearcut. Everything was black and white, good or bad. The rituals and uniforms fostered a sense of unity and identity clearly different from that of the general population.

Choose *one* purpose. To alarm To entertain To compare To analyze

11. _____

Directions: Read the following selection to detect bias.

Well, the wizards in Washington have simplified the income tax. Again. Last year's simplified version took over eight hundred pages to explain. This year's new, even more simplified version takes over a thousand pages to explain. If that seems a little strange to you, it just shows that you don't understand how things work in Washington.

12. Circle the person most likely to be biased *against* the idea presented.

A Democrat A Republican A member of Congress A member of a labor union

Developing Critical Comprehension, Quiz 3

Directions: Indicate whether the numbered sentences are fact—F, opinion—O, or a mixture of fact and opinion—F&O. Answer in the blank provided.

_____ **1.** Forty-eight percent of the students in Mesa College major in business administration.

_____ **2.** Lentils are more nutritious than pinto beans, but pinto beans taste better.

_____ **3.** The percentage of females in higher level math classes is increasing.

_____ **4.** Crystal Springs is a perfectly located weekend retreat for people in the tri-city area.

_____ **5.** It's close enough to reach in a half-day's drive, but far enough that most people don't attempt a one-day outing.

_____ **6.** That keeps away the "Trash it and leave it" crowd who make life miserable for the rest of us.

_____ **7.** A privately owned camping area is located within 500 yards of the actual springs, with facilities for 34 tents and 57 campers.

_____ **8.** The showers and bathrooms are clean, your fellow campers are friendly, and there's a store that stocks groceries and camping supplies.

_____ **9.** Activities include horseback riding (theirs or yours), nonpowered boating (theirs or yours), hiking, or just sitting around.

Directions: Which statement best describes the purpose of the following selections?

A culture is shaped by its mythology. Greeks were taught to be heroic by the tales of Odysseus. Englishmen were taught to be chivalrous by the King Arthur stories. Americans are taught mainly by the mythology of cartoons, but what are they taught? Bugs Bunny teaches that it's okay to cheat, lie, and take advantage of people, just so you win. The Road Runner teaches that violence is fine; it's even funny!

Choose *two* purposes. To inform To present a solution To alarm To compare

10. _____

Alcohol consumption by Americans is not something new. The Puritans set sail for America with fourteen tons of water, but three times that tonnage of beer.

Choose *one* purpose. To compare To persuade To inform To entertain

11. _____

Directions: Read the following selection to detect bias.

No restrictions should be placed on lobbyists at the national level. Lawmakers need to hear all sides, and lobbyists can present those ideas. To assume that law-makers can be swayed by lobbyists is not only erroneous, it's insulting.

12. Circle the person most likely to be biased *toward* the idea presented.

An owner of a small business A member of Congress A lobbyist A professor

PQ3R Practice Selection

Now that you have had practice in applying the skills presented so far, try using them to study and understand this selection taken from a college science textbook. Do a PREPARE on the selection and try to understand the content by being sensitive (1) to how the information is presented and (2) to the vocabulary used. Use your knowledge of paragraph structure and the other comprehension skills to understand and remember the material.

Two sets of questions follow the section: (1) a series of questions based on the PREPARE, which you should answer immediately after doing the PREPARE, and (2) general questions based on the material presented. To answer the questions, read actively and try to see how ideas are related. Good luck!

From *Foundations of College Chemistry*

By Morris Hein

MATTER DEFINED

Perhaps few people have ever stopped to realize how many different types of material things there are in the world. Every day we come into contact with countless kinds of matter. Air, food, water, rocks, soil, glass, this book—all are different types of matter. Broadly defined, **matter** is anything that has mass and occupies space.

When an apparently empty tube, mouth downward, is submerged into a beaker of water, the water rises slightly into the tube but does not completely fill it. The space in the tube not occupied by water contains air. This simple experiment proves that air, which is matter, occupies space, even though air is invisible.

Matter exists in three physical states: solid, liquid, and gas. A **solid** has the characteristic of definite shape, with its particles closely compact and firmly cohering to each other. A solid does not necessarily have to fill or take the shape of its container. For example, a crystal of sulfur will retain the same shape and size whether it is placed in a beaker, on a watch glass, or just laid on a table. A solid tends to resist deformation of its structure.

Most commonly occurring solids, such as salt, sugar, quartz, and metals, are crystalline. Crystalline materials exist in regular, recurring geometric patterns. Solids such as plastics, glass, and gels, because they do not have any particular regular internal geometric form, are called **amorphous** solids. ("Amorphous" means without shape or form.) There are three crystalline solids—salt, quartz, and gypsum.

A **liquid** has the characteristic of having its particles move freely while still retaining a definite volume. The particles in a liquid are still held together by strong attractive forces, but are not held in a rigid form as with solids. The mobility of the particles gives a liquid its fluidity and causes it to take the shape of the container in which it is stored. If a glass of water is poured onto a flat surface, the water will flow and spread over the surface, demonstrating the fluidity of its liquid state.

A **gas** has the characteristic of having no fixed shape, with its particles moving independently of each other. The particles in the gaseous state have gained enough energy to overcome the attractive forces holding them together as liquids or solids. A gas presses continuously and in all directions upon the walls of the vessel in which it is contained. Because of this quality, a gas completely fills the vessel. The particles of a gas are relatively far apart, compared to those of solids and liquids, and occupy only a very small volume of the space in which the gas is confined. A gas may be compressed into a very small volume and may also be expanded practically indefinitely. Liquids cannot be compressed to any great extent, and solids can be compressed even less.

When a bottle of ammonia solution is opened in one corner of the laboratory, one can soon smell its familiar odor in all parts of the room. The ammonia gas escaping from the solution proves that gaseous particles (1) move freely and rapidly, (2) expand considerably, and (3) completely fill the area into which they are released.

Although matter is discontinuous, attractive forces exist that hold particles together and give to matter its appearance of continuity. These attractive forces are strongest in solids, giving them rigidity; they are weaker in liquids, but still strong enough to hold them in a definite volume; and they are so weak in gases that their particles are practically independent of each other.

SUBSTANCES AND MIXTURES

The term "matter" refers to the total concept of material things. There are thousands of distinct and different kinds of matter. Upon closely examining different samples of matter, we can observe them to be either homogeneous or heterogeneous. The term "homogeneous" is used in many different ways. If we have a group of students, all of whom are men, we may say that this group is homogeneous, since they are all of the same gender. In contrast, a class consisting of both men and women is said to be a heterogeneous, or mixed, group. Matter is either homogeneous or heterogeneous. Material that has identical properties throughout is **homogeneous.** Material consisting of two or more phases is **heterogeneous.** A system of ice and water is heterogeneous, containing both solid and liquid phases, although the water itself is uniform in composition and is homogeneous.

A **substance** is a particular kind of matter that is homogeneous and has a definite, fixed composition. Substances, sometimes known as pure substances, occur in two forms: elements and compounds. Several examples of elements and compounds are copper, gold, oxygen, salt, sugar, and water. Elements and compounds are discussed in more detail in Chapter 4.

Matter that contains two or more substances mixed together is known as a **mixture.** Mixtures are variable in composition and may be either homogeneous or heterogeneous. When sugar is dissolved in water, a sugar solution is formed. All parts of this solution are sweet and contain both substances, sugar and water, uniformly mixed. Solutions are homogeneous mixtures. Air is a homogeneous mixture (solution) of several gases. If we examine ordinary concrete, granite, iron ore, and other naturally occurring mineral deposits, we observe them to be heterogeneous

mixtures of several different substances. Of course, it is very easy to prepare a heterogeneou
mixture just by physically mixing two or more substances, such as sugar and salt.

How do we recognize substances? Each substance has a set of **properties** that are charac
teristic of the substance and give it a unique identity. Properties are the personality traits c
substances, and are classified as either physical or chemical. **Physical properties** are th
inherent characteristics of a substance which may be determined without altering the com
position of that substance; they are associated with its physical existence. Common physica
properties are color, taste, odor, state of matter (whether solid, liquid, or gas), densit
melting point, and boiling point. **Chemical properties** are those characteristics associate
with the changes in composition of a substance. Chemical properties describe the behavior c
a substance when it reacts or combines with other substances, as in a chemical reaction.

We can select a few of the physical and chemical properties of chlorine as an exampl
Chlorine is a yellowish-green gas with a disagreeable odor. It will not burn, but will suppo
the combustion of certain other substances. Chlorine is used as a bleaching agent, as
disinfectant for water, and in many chlorinated substances such as refrigerants and insect
cides. When chlorine combines with the metal sodium, it forms a salt, sodium chlorid
These properties, among others, help to characterize and identify chlorine. Substances, the
are recognized and differentiated by their properties.

PHYSICAL CHANGES

Matter can undergo two types of changes, physical and chemical. A substance may chang
its appearance without undergoing a change in composition: **Physical** changes are main
changes in size, shape, or state of matter without an accompanying change in compositio
The changing of ice into water and water into steam are physical changes from one state c
matter into another. No new substances are formed in these physical changes.

If we heat a platinum wire in a burner flame, the wire will become red hot. It returns to i
original silvery, metallic form after cooling. The platinum undergoes a physical change
appearance while in the flame, but its composition remains the same under both condition

CHEMICAL CHANGES

If a clean copper wire is heated in a burner flame, a change in the appearance of the wire
readily noted after it cools. The copper no longer has its characteristic color, but now appea
black. The black material is copper oxide, a new substance formed when copper is combine
chemically with oxygen in the air during the heating process. The starting material wa
essentially 100 percent copper, whereas the black copper oxide produced contains only 79
percent copper, the rest being oxygen. When both platinum and copper are heated und
identical conditions, platinum changes only physically, but copper changes chemically a
well as physically. In a **chemical change,** substances are formed that are entirely differen
having different properties and composition from the original material. The new substance
need not in any way resemble the starting material before the change took place.

Mercuric oxide is an orange-red powder which, when subjected to high temperature, decomposes into a colorless gas (oxygen) and a silvery, liquid metal (mercury). The composition of both of these products, as well as their physical appearances, is noticeably different from that of the starting compound. From these observations, we can conclude that a chemical change has taken place.

Chemists have devised *chemical equations* as shorthand methods of expressing chemical changes. These equations may take several forms. The two examples of chemical changes presented above may be represented by the following word equations:

> Copper plus Oxygen plus heat produces Cupric oxide
> Mercuric oxide plus heat produces Mercury plus Oxygen

These equations may also be written as

> Copper + Oxygen $\xrightarrow{\Delta}$ Cupric oxide
>
> Mercuric oxide $\xrightarrow{\Delta}$ Mercury + Oxygen

The arrow means "produces"; it points to the products. The delta sign (Δ) is used to represent heat. The starting substances are called the *reactants*; and the substances produced are called the *products*. In later chapters, equations will be presented in a still more abbreviated form, with symbols used for each substance.

In an overwhelming majority of cases, a physical change will accompany a chemical change. The student should realize that, where a chemical change occurs, a physical change occurs also. Where a physical change is listed, we mean that only a physical change occurs.

From the discovery that fire could be used to warm shelters and cook food, to the conquering of the atom, which may soon light our cities, man's progress has been directed by his ability to harness, produce, and utilize energy.

Energy is the capacity of matter to do work. In this respect, matter can have both potential and kinetic energy. **Potential energy** is the energy an object possesses due to its relative position. For example, a ball located 20 feet above the ground has more potential energy than another ball located 10 feet above the ground, and will bounce higher when allowed to fall. Water backed up behind a dam represents potential energy that can be converted into useful work in the form of electrical energy. Gasoline represents a source of chemical potential energy that can be released during combustion.

Kinetic energy is the energy matter possesses due to its motion. When the water behind the dam is released, its potential energy is changed into kinetic energy, which may be used to drive generators and produce electricity.

ENERGY IN CHEMICAL CHANGES

Common forms of energy are mechanical, chemical, electrical, heat, and radiant or light energy. In all chemical changes, matter either absorbs or releases energy.

Chemical changes produce different forms of energy. Electrical energy to start automobiles is produced by chemical changes in the lead storage battery. Light energy for photographic purposes occurs as a flash during the chemical change in the magnesium flashbulb. Heat and light energies are released from the combustion of fuels.

Conversely, energy is used to cause chemical changes. For example, a chemical change occurs in the electroplating of metals when electrical energy is passed through a salt solution in which the metal is submerged. A chemical change also occurs when radiant energy from the sun is utilized by plants in the process of photosynthesis. And, as we saw, a chemical change occurs when heat causes mercuric oxide to decompose. Chemical changes are often used primarily to produce energy rather than new substances. The heat or thrust generated during the combustion of fuels is more important than the new substances formed.

QUESTIONS

Study and understand the terms introduced in this chapter.

1. Matter	*10.* Physical properties
2. Solid	*11.* Chemical properties
3. Amorphous	*12.* Physical change
4. Liquid	*13.* Chemical change
5. Homogeneous	*14.* Conservation of mass
6. Heterogeneous	*15.* Energy
7. Substance	*16.* Potential energy
8. Mixture	*17.* Kinetic energy
9. Properties	*18.* Conservation of energy

REVIEW QUESTIONS

1. Give three examples of matter in each of the physical states.
2. Discuss the relationship of the particles of matter to each other as they occur in the solid, liquid, and gaseous states.
3. Distinguish between physical and chemical changes.
4. Classify the following as physical or chemical changes.
   a. Digesting food.
   b. Evaporating gasoline.
   c. Stretching rubber.
   d. Generating steam in a boiler.
   e. Winding a clock.
   f. Tarnishing of silver.
   g. Souring of milk.
5. Distinguish between potential and kinetic energy.
6. Is chemical energy potential or kinetic?
7. What are properties of substances?
8. Why are ice, water, and steam (water vapor) not classified as three different substances?
9. Why are gases highly compressible?

PREPARE Questions

1. What are the three physical states of matter?

_____

_____

_____

2. What are two characteristics of a gas?

_____

_____

3. What is the purpose of a chemical equation?

_____

4. What are the two types of changes that matter can undergo?

_____

_____

5. Define *energy*.

_____

_____

6. What is kinetic energy?

_____

_____

7. Name three forms of energy.

_____

_____

_____

8. What does the arrow mean in a chemical equation?

_____

9. What is the relationship between chemical changes and energy?

_____

_____

10. What is a mixture?

_____

_____

Comprehension-Skill Questions

1. What is an amorphous solid? How is it different from a crystalline material?

_____

_____

2. What is meant by the physical property of a substance? Give two examples of physical properties.

_____

_____

_____

3. How are the chemical properties of a substance different from its physical properties?

_____

_____

4. In a chemical equation, what do the following mean?

Reactant _____

Product _____

A delta (Δ) sign _____

5. What is the difference between potential energy and kinetic energy?

_____

_____

6. What is the difference between the physical changes and the chemical changes of substances? Give an example of each kind of change.

_____

_____

_____

7. What is homogeneous matter? Give an example.

_____

_____

8. What is heterogeneous matter? Give an example.

_____

_____

9. How would you define *matter*?

_____

_____

10. When a bottle of ammonia solution is opened in one corner of a room, one can soon smell its odor in all parts of the room. What three characteristics of ammonia does this fact demonstrate?

   a. _____

   b. _____

   c. _____

Reading Rate

IMPROVING READING RATE

What is reading? Before we can begin to consider how to read faster, we must understand just what reading really is. Read the following sentence.

> Sam drove his sweetheart to the dance in his new automobile.

Now read this.

> Sam drock pid girl at home septurk chesim.

Now try this.

M + 5 ⊔ ⊓ Ξ ‖ = ⊓ ⊓ ∕ =

In how many of these three situations were you *reading*? Most people would agree that in the third instance *no reading* was done. How about the second group? No reading was done there, either. Only in the first instance was reading really done. Why is this so? It is because reading is a thinking process and involves making sense of (interpreting) symbols. It is a meeting of the author's mind with the reader's mind. The reader must examine the printed symbols on the page and come up with the same IDEAS that the author had when he or she set those symbols down. Only to the extent that the reader can do this is he or she a successful reader.

Reading is an active process and requires concentration. Have you ever had the following experience? You prepare to read a textbook (or perhaps a novel). You make yourself comfortable and begin to glance at the reading material. You go through one page, two, three, four, five pages. Suddenly you look up and say, "My Gosh! What have I read?" You don't know. You've done an eye exercise. Although your eyes faithfully followed every word on these pages, your mind was elsewhere. You were thinking about what you planned to wear to the dance Saturday night or what time class would be over tomorrow or even that it was warm or cool or noisy outside. Reading is an active thinking process. When you read—really read—your whole mind is on the task at hand.

Can you read a foreign language just because you can verbalize or sound out the letters? No. Reading is thinking. Therefore, a reader has to understand the author's *thoughts*, not merely the words. The words are an intermediary step, just as the score is in music. An author expresses thoughts in meaningful groups of words (meaningful phrases). The word *the* by itself means nothing. *Boy* by itself means little. *Run* by itself means little. Put the three words together, and you have a thought. Now it has meaning. You see the sentence "The boy runs" and think the IDEA "The boy runs." We even have an expression that points this up. The expression "I read you" means "I understand you." Reading is understanding, making sense of symbols.

How does this definition of reading relate to so-called speed reading? If reading is really understanding, then speed reading is really speed understanding. When we increase reading rate, we increase the rate at which we understand materials. The title of this section is "Improving Reading Rate." No mention is made of comprehension because the title *means* improving rate of *understanding*. To read fast, you must think fast. You must concentrate. In order to drive at 60 miles an hour, you must be in high gear. Reading words and not ideas is like racing the car in neutral. You go nowhere fast.

How Fast Should You Read?   Asking "How fast should I read?" is like asking "How fast should I drive?" Before you can answer, you must have some information. Over what kind of road will you be driving? What is the weather like? Is there an emergency or are you simply out to admire the scenery? Actually, the answer to the question "How fast should you drive?" is "It depends." It depends on the difficulty of the driving conditions and on why you are driving.

Just as it is with the auto, so it is with reading. How fast does a good reader read? The answer: "It depends." It depends on three things: (1) the difficulty of the material, (2) the reader's purpose in reading, and (3) the condition of the reader. Good readers don't read a chemistry textbook, for example, at the same rate of speed that they would read a magazine article about the private life of a celebrity. Chemistry is a more difficult subject and so it takes more careful reading. Similarly, good readers will read an article on income tax law at one speed if they are simply passing time in a doctor's office and at another speed if they are preparing a tax return. The material is the same, but the purpose is different. Finally, as in everything we do, our condition affects our performance. If we were awake most of the night, if we have a cold, if we are taking certain medications, if we've had some tragedy in our lives, if we're worried about an upcoming test—a multitude of physical and emotional influences will, and should, cause us to change our reading rate.

Good readers are flexible readers. They read at different rates depending on their purpose, their condition, and the type of material they're reading. Without realizing it, they will read at one rate for detailed, factual reading; at another rate when their purpose is to get the "gist" of an article; and at still another rate for scanning. Good readers find themselves reading at different rates from article to article, from section to section, from page to page, from paragraph to paragraph, even from phrase to phrase. They read more slowly and methodically when they are studying factual material (refer to PQ3R). When their purpose is to discover main ideas, they read faster than when they are reading the same material for minor details. Sometimes their purpose is to scan material. Good readers do this fastest of all.

What Is Scanning?   Have you ever looked for somebody's telephone number in a telephone book? Have you ever had to find specific information in an encyclopedia or look up a word in a dictionary? Have you ever searched a chapter in a textbook to find a particular date or name? If you did a good job in these tasks, you SCANNED for this information.

Scanning is a narrowing-down process. Let's assume you're looking in a history textbook to find out what kind of schooling Benjamin Franklin had. What would you do?

1. Locate the general area that would contain the information. (In this case, you might find a chapter on Franklin or some likely pages by looking in the book's index.)
2. Glance over the area looking for key words. (Try to find an appropriate heading, such as "Franklin's Early Years" or "Education.")
3. Read the section that contains the key word.
4. Decide which words give the needed information.

What are some of the things you should *avoid* if you are to read faster?

Some Don'ts

DON'T LIP READ.   Many people form the words silently with their lips as they read. Some people whisper the words quietly. Why is this a bad habit? When you move your lips to pronounce words, you are forcing yourself to pay attention to *words*, not thoughts. You also limit your reading speed to the fastest speed at which you can talk. It is most certainly possible to read much faster than that.

DON'T POINT.   Many people are afraid of losing their place or, for some reason, feel more secure when they can point at the material as they read it. Once again, this practice forces attention to *words* rather than thoughts.

DON'T LOOK BACK.   Looking back can take two forms: rereading and regressing. Rereading is looking back to check on what you just finished reading. Sometimes you need to be sure of a name or a number, so you reread. Sometimes the passage doesn't make sense, so you reread and find, for example, that you skipped the word *not* or looked at *every* and thought it was *very*. Rereading, because it remedies these problems, is sometimes necessary and good, but if overdone it wastes time and causes a lack of concentration. When you habitually reread, you don't force yourself to "get it" the first time; when you don't reread, you concentrate during the first reading.

Regressing, the other form of looking back, is an *unconscious* act. The reader's eyes automatically flick back over the preceding material, not for better understanding but strictly out of habit. The reader isn't even aware of doing it. Regressing has two unfortunate results—it slows down reading rate and it interferes with good understanding. Many regressions cause the reader to lose the chain of thought. In studying regressive eye movements of poor readers, researchers have found that many people read a sentence in the following way.

> John scheduled scheduled an appointment scheduled an appointment with his counselor his counselor with his counselor so that he that he so that he could arrange his program program of courses program of courses for the coming semester coming semester for the coming semester.

Is it any wonder that people who read in this fashion are confused when they get to the end of the sentence—and even more so when they go through whole paragraphs and even chapters in the same way?

DON'T MOVE YOUR HEAD.   Take in as large a meaningful thought unit as possible. Then go to the next one. The fewer times your eye has to stop to take in thoughts, the faster you will read.

Although we should be aware of the factors that *interfere* with good reading, it is even more important to be aware of *positive* factors that will help increase speed.

What Should I Do?

BE AWARE OF YOUR PURPOSE.   When you are aware of what you are looking for, you are able to sift information and pay most attention to that which is most important at the moment.

CONCENTRATE.   After determining your purpose for reading, concentrate on reading for that purpose. Force concentration by looking away and telling yourself what you have read about. Don't look back when you do this. Try to visualize the *ideas* as you read.

THINK AS YOU READ.   Relate the ideas to what you already know. Increased rate comes about only as your comprehension skills increase.

PRACTICE.   Compete with yourself. Time yourself reading a specific number of pages of the same type of material each day. (A section in the same novel would be excellent.) Read the material as fast as you can. Then try to beat your own score the next day. Try to read the same amount of material in *less* time.

HAVE A POSITIVE ATTITUDE.   When you have confidence in your own ability to increase rate through better comprehension, you will work at it more effectively. As you become more sensitive to and proficient at the skills discussed in this book, you will be able to use these skills to increase reading rate.

In Brief

Reading is a thinking process—getting ideas from print. Speeding up reading means speeding up the idea-gathering process. Without the ideas (comprehension), speed is meaningless.

The successful reader

—gets the same ideas that the writer had
—is flexible, changing rate according to
    1. purpose
    2. physical or emotional condition
    3. difficulty of the material

Rates for reading:

Slowest: reading for details
Medium: reading for main ideas
Fastest: scanning

SCANNING: partial reading to locate a particular bit of information
Steps in scanning:

    1. Locate the general area that may contain the information.
    2. Glance over the area, looking for key words.
    3. Read the section that contains the key word.
    4. Decide which words give the needed information.

Don't do the following (because rate suffers; because understanding suffers):

Don't lip read.
Don't point.
Don't regress.
Don't move your head.

Do the following: (because rate improves; because understanding improves)

Be aware of your purpose.
Concentrate.
Think.
Practice.
Have a positive attitude.

How to Use
This Section

This section of the book is composed of ten short reading selections, each followed by two sets of questions: (1) a set of ten short-answer comprehension questions, to be used only if the selection is read as a rapid-reading exercise; and (2) a set of ten skill-development questions, designed to test ability in ten skills discussed in this book. The arrangement of each set of skill-development questions approximately parallels the sequence of the chapters: Question 1 always measures vocabulary; question 2—main idea; 3—details; 4—relationships; 5—more relationships; 6—organization; 7—locating information; 8—following directions; 9—figurative language; 10—purpose and tone.

After reading two or three of these selections and answering the skill-development questions, you may notice that you missed several questions of the same number. If this happens, it could mean you need additional practice in the skill those questions measure. Check the part of the selection that the question covers to see *why* the right answer is correct. Perhaps you need to review the appropriate chapter and redo some of the exercises.

If these readings are used as rapid reading selections in class, follow your instructor's directions.

If you are working independently, you can use the following procedure:

1. Make certain you know the meaning of the words in the vocabulary review.
2. Preview the comprehension questions carefully. They will help you to set your purpose in rapid reading.
3. Jot down the time that you begin to read.
4. Keep your purpose for reading in mind and read as rapidly as you can to understand the concepts presented.
5. Jot down the time that you finish reading.
6. Answer the comprehension questions.
7. Determine the number of minutes and seconds it took to read the selection, then check your rate by referring to the table on pages 434–436.
8. Enter your scores on the rapid-reading progress chart on page 437.

Becoming a Successful Student

VOCABULARY REVIEW

- *mitigating* circumstances
- *self-discipline* is needed
- to become *harried* and *stressed*
- ask *relevant* questions

A BALANCED PEP SCHEDULE

1   So you've finally made it to college. You've been accepted, and you have
2 received registration materials, and you've been assigned a time to sign up for
3 your classes. Now, how do you decide which courses you should take? Oh,
4 you know the courses you need or want to take during your first year or two.
5 But how should you schedule your courses?

6   If you have read the chapters preceding this one, you know about the
7 importance of balance and skill in order to be a successful student. If you
8 spend almost all your time working on school assignments you really will not
9 feel successful, because you need some time for a social life, for recreation,
10 and possibly for a job. Only if your college life is well balanced can you really
11 enjoy it and feel a sense of accomplishment and self-worth. What do you need
12 to know in order to plan your course schedule each semester?

13   First, as a successful student you should try to balance your course load
14 with other facets of your life. Unfortunately, too many students feel that there
15 is a rule that insists that unless you take 15 course hours per semester you are
16 an inadequate student. Nonsense! You should proceed at a rate which meets
17 your needs and which balances your life. The key word is *balance*. If you need
18 or desire to work 20 or more hours per week, you are probably doing an
19 injustice to yourself if you take a full load. If your subjects include one or
20 more laboratory courses, you will probably want to balance them with other
21 courses that are not as demanding. If you have a family and have personal
22 and social obligations, a full load is just too much. Better to do well with fewer
23 courses, and feel good about yourself and your academic accomplishments,

24 rather than to feel frustrated and possibly withdraw from a class or two.
25 Incidentally, you have no right to expect your instructor to lower his or her
26 standards because you have mitigating circumstances. It is your responsibil-
27 ity to adjust your selection of classes to your unique situation.

28   Even when you can take a full load, there are some things to consider in
29 order to maintain balance. There are three general classifications of courses,
30 called PEP. You can balance your course load if you take a mixture of PEP
31 each semester. What is PEP and what should you know about it?

32   The first P stands for PLUG AWAY courses. These are courses that require
33 continuous day-by-day study and preparation for class and laboratory work.
34 These courses usually involve lots of practice and many tests. Any of the
35 laboratory science courses, such as chemistry or biology, come under this
36 grouping. Skills courses, such as mathematics, English, or reading, also ap-
37 pear here, as do courses such as foreign languages or accounting. They are
38 demanding and require that you do the following if you are to be successful.

39   **1.** Try not to miss any classes for any reason. These classes are usually
40   taught in sequence, so you can't understand the second lesson if you
41   didn't understand the first lesson, and you can't understand the third
42   lesson if you didn't understand the second, and so on.
43   **2.** Because of the above situation, it is important that you keep up with
44   each lesson. You can't let yourself fall behind. This, of course, means
45   that daily study and review are absolutely necessary. In other courses
46   you sometimes have more time to prepare lessons, but not in PLUG
47   AWAY courses.
48   **3.** If you don't understand a point made in your classes or in your read-
49   ing, see your instructor immediately. If you wait, you will fall behind. If
50   too much time elapses, you will fall hopelessly behind and may have to
51   withdraw from the class—an unnecessary and costly step.

52   E stands for ENJOYMENT. Take a fun-type course which you know you
53 will enjoy, or perhaps a course which will help you relax. This category
54 includes courses in art appreciation, drawing, ceramics, music appreciation,
55 speech, or physical education, perhaps golfing, swimming, volleyball, or
56 modern dance. These courses normally have few exams, although they may
57 have long-range goals such as the creation of a ceramic object or drawing or
58 the development of a physical skill. Don't take these courses too lightly,
59 however. There are some dangers that you need to watch out for.

60   **1.** Self-discipline is needed. In these courses you are often left on your
61   own with a long-range project. Sometimes you need to practice to
62   develop a skill. Although the particular scheduling of time is left up to

63 you, you must be sure to schedule that time on a regular basis. You
64 should not allow it to wait until the end of the semester, or you will
65 become harried and stressed and all of the fun will be gone. You must
66 discipline yourself (no one will be looking over your shoulder to scold
67 you if you don't) and set up a regular schedule in order to succeed.
68 2. Don't look upon this course as a "snap" or as something unimportant.
69 To do so puts you into the position of taking it for granted, which is a
70 position that can lead to failure.

71 The third type of course (the second P) is the POWER course. These
72 courses do not usually require a lot of daily work, but they do require a lot of
73 outside reading which, more often than not, can be done on a weekly basis.
74 Also, there are often long-range projects to be done. Although there are fewer
75 tests, this very fact means that these tests take on added importance, because
76 you have fewer opportunities to show what you know. A poor grade in one of
77 these tests is difficult to overcome. English literature, history, sociology, psy-
78 chology, and anthropology are examples of POWER courses. In order to be
79 successful in this type of course, you should note the following suggestions.

80 1. Once again, you must have self-discipline. You should not leave the
81 weekly reading until the night before it is required. Plan your work for
82 the semester in relatively equal, but manageable steps.
83 2. It is important that you take good notes and that you study them
84 regularly so that you don't fall behind. Because there are so few tests
85 (usually no more than two or three plus the final exam), they will cover
86 work done over a long period of time. Only by taking and then keeping
87 up with your notes can you study effectively for these tests.

88 You should try to balance your course load each semester by taking one or
89 two courses from each of these categories. An ideal situation is to take one, or
90 two at the most, PLUG AWAY courses in one semester. If you need to take
91 more than two, you might want to consider taking a smaller course load that
92 semester so that you can do justice to these courses.
93 There are two other items that you should consider. If this is your first
94 semester at a particular school, you should take a limited load, perhaps no
95 more than ten credits. This will give you time to become adjusted to a new
96 situation without having to spend the time and energy involved in carrying a
97 full load. A second and very important point—take "preparatory" courses
98 first. If you know that you need help in mathematics or in reading, or perhaps
99 even in typing, be sure to sign up for these courses during your first semester,
100 if possible. Get these hang-ups out of the way once and for all so that you can
101 zero in on the course work in full possession of the skills needed for success.

CHARACTERISTICS FOR SUCCESS

102   What are some other characteristics of successful students? As a successful
103   student, you should:

104   **1.** *Think positively.* You need to have a good self-image so you can turn
105   what seems like defeat into a positive learning situation. If you expect
106   that you can do better, and you try to do better, then overall you will do
107   better. Babe Ruth was known as the home-run king. He was also the
108   strike-out king. However, if he thought of himself as the strike-out
109   king, it could have defeated him and he would not have been the
110   home-run king. You might want to read a book that discusses the
111   importance of thinking positively. Read *Positive Plus: the Practical Plan*
112   *for Liking Yourself Better* by Dr. Joyce Brothers (G. P. Putnam's Sons,
113   1994).

114   **2.** *Be interested in your courses.* Even if you think a course is the most
115   boring one in the world, force yourself to be interested. Take a minor
116   point and read as much as possible about it in order to become an
117   expert in just that little bit of information. Talk about it, live and breathe
118   that minor point for a few days. That kind of interest can beget interest
119   in the entire course.

120   **3.** *Seek help when you need it, before it's too late.* If you have special problems,
121   don't be afraid to seek help. See your teacher, your counselor, your
122   advisor, anyone that you think may be able to help you. It is important
123   that you be aware of where you can go for help. As a student, find out
124   what kind of help is available, and where, before you need it. Some
125   schools have special courses in reading and mathematics and other
126   basic skills. Some have tutoring centers where you can get help in
127   understanding the material for a particular course. Special counselors
128   are usually available to help you with personal problems. Most cam-
129   puses can help with money—student loans, scholarships, special stu-
130   dent aid funds, or work-study programs. Some campuses will help you
131   find housing. Find out what is available at your school, and be pre-
132   pared to use it when you need it.

133   **4.** *Attend classes and be active in class.* Attending class and arriving on time
134   are subtle points that indicate that you are serious about your commit-
135   ment to learning. Take part in classroom discussions and hand in as-
136   signments on time. Speaking up in class forces you to think about the
137   points being made and keeps you interested in what is being discussed.
138   However, ask relevant questions, such as for further explanations of
139   points that you need to have clarified or for a definition of an item
140   not fully understood. Ask questions about the implications of the

141 information learned. This will help you to understand and absorb in-
142 formation more fully.

143 **5.** *Have a good attitude about college life.* Know your strong points and your
144 weaknesses, understand your goals and work toward them, and most
145 important, understand what a college can and cannot do for you. Take
146 responsibility for your own education. You should realize that attend-
147 ing college offers you the raw material for success and education—
148 libraries, teachers, textbooks. However, only you can educate yourself.
149 Take advantage of what is around you and use it to your best advan-
150 tage according to your own needs.

151 **6.** *Have the "know-how" to be successful.* Make sure that you know how to
152 study, take notes, take tests, use time wisely. Be sure you can use
153 reference sources such as the library. Develop memory skills. Try to get
154 along with your teachers and your fellow students. You should be at
155 ease in expressing yourself and in understanding words. Learn from
156 experience. Always look for ways to do things better. Notice that this
157 book covers most of these needs—take advantage of it.

158 **7.** *Know the rules and be familiar with the various college calendars.* You should
159 know about various social, cultural, and sports events. You should
160 know deadlines for withdrawal from classes without penalty, and
161 deadlines for making up incomplete grades. Be aware of prerequisites
162 and other requirements for the program you are enrolled in. Know
163 which student government activities are available and how they can
164 help you.

Skill-Development Questions

1. What does the word *demanding* mean as it is used on lines 37–38?

2. What is the main idea of the paragraph on lines 13–27?

3. Name three characteristics of plug-away courses.

4. How does the sentence on line 49 relate to the sentence before it?

5. How does the sentence on lines 44–45 relate to the sentence before it?

6. In the PEP part of this article, assume that one of the major divisions is called *Plug-Away Courses.* What should you call its subdivision, the one that would include math and English?

7. Which words in the paragraph on lines 93–101 tell you why you should take a limited load during your first semester?

8. List the seven characteristics for success in alphabetical order. Then, next to each one, describe that characteristic in eight words or less.

   a.

   b.

   c.

   d.

e. _____

f. _____

g. _____

9. What is meant by the word *snap* as it is used on line 68?

_____

10. Which words best describe the tone of this selection?
    a. demanding and serious
    b. discouraging and negative
    c. lighthearted and fun
    d. hopeful and upbeat

Improve Your Memory

By Irwin L. Joffe

VOCABULARY REVIEW

- your senses are *psychologically conditioned*
- *mnemonic* techniques

1   How is your memory? When you are introduced to a woman at a social
2 gathering, do you remember her name or do you almost immediately forget it
3 and then spend several minutes trying to find some sneaky way to get her to
4 repeat it? If you do the food shopping for your family, do you always refer to
5 a shopping list (which you sometimes forget to take with you)? At school, is it
6 a problem to remember the ten causes or the eight qualities or the nine
7 characteristics or perhaps basic formulas or statistical information? Well, if so,
8 it's time for a change. You can improve your memory fantastically if you want
9 to. You can learn to remember anything you want to remember for as long as
10 you want to remember it. Business executives can learn to remember names
11 and faces and important appointments and critical statistical information.
12 Waitresses can learn to remember orders without having to write them down.
13 Postal workers can learn to remember street names and numbers. Inventory
14 clerks can remember numbers relating to stocked parts. You can learn to
15 remember your Social Security number, your license plate number, important
16 telephone numbers, and at least a three-year calendar without looking it up.
17   All over the country memory experts are conducting seminars and work-
18 shops to help people improve their memory. The author of this book, Profes-
19 sor Irwin L. Joffe, conducts a memory workshop for groups of business
20 people, or students, or the general public and has helped many hundreds of
21 people to improve their memories fantastically and to feel just great about it.
22 It does take work and practice, but it can be done and it is well worth it.
23 Whether fortunately or unfortunately, more than 75 percent of the material
24 covered in college classes is a memory task rather than concept development,
25 and students with good memory skills can get good grades with less effort.
26   How can you do all of this? Memory is composed of three factors—input,
27 storage, and retrieval. Input is achieved through the senses. Information

335

28 enters your physiological system through one or more of the sense organs—
29 you hear or see or smell or touch or taste something. This sense impression is
30 translated into impulses that travel via your nervous system to the brain
31 where, under normal conditions, it is stored. One problem here is that if your
32 senses perceive information incorrectly because they are damaged or under
33 the influence of alcohol or other drugs or otherwise psychologically condi-
34 tioned, that incorrect information will be translated and carried to the brain
35 that way, and it will be stored that way. Your brain is now holding that
36 information, whether correctly or incorrectly perceived, and it holds it there
37 for future retrieval.

38   How many times have you tried to remember something and you know
39 it's there (on the "tip of the tongue") but you just can't seem to remember it?
40 You need a retrieval system, which is what memory workshops are all about.
41 A mnemonic device is a retrieval technique. The word *mnemonic*, which
42 comes from Mnemosyne, the Greek goddess of memory, refers to a technique
43 for remembering. Memory workshops emphasize these techniques, such as
44 pegging, linking, and strategies of progressive elaboration. These techniques
45 refer to ways of associating items. Let us say that two items on your shopping
46 list are eggs and milk. One way to remember these is to link them so that they
47 are locked together. If you think of one of them, the other will automatically
48 come to mind. You do this by using as much of ASOE as you can. ASOE
49 stands for action, substitution, out of proportion, and exaggeration. You also
50 need to develop as lively and as strong an imagination as possible. The wilder
51 your imagination, the better.

52   To return to eggs and milk—how can you link them in as imaginative a way
53 as possible? You might want to imagine a chicken laying small milk cartons; or
54 you might see yourself opening a milk carton to pour a glass of milk, but eggs
55 come out instead of milk. You might open an egg carton and see a dozen milk
56 cartons smiling at you, or you might see yourself cracking eggs open and milk
57 comes out, or you might be milking a cow but eggs fall into the pail. The
58 important thing is don't just see a carton of milk standing next to a carton of
59 eggs. This probably will not help you to remember them because it is too weak a
60 link. It doesn't have enough ASOE. Also, it is important to imagine the two
61 items rather than to intellectualize them. You must see them in your mind's eye,
62 not just think about them. Then you will lock them together.

63   Everything you remember is remembered by association (of which linking
64 is only one technique). What is the second line of our national anthem? Think
65 about it before reading on. Didn't you have to say the first line ("Oh, say can
66 you see") before you could remember the second line ("By the dawn's early
67 light")? You really don't remember the second line. You only remember the
68 first line, which reminds you of the second line, which reminds you of the
69 third line and so on.

70   The linking technique is one of the least sophisticated mnemonic systems
71 and yet it is amazingly effective. Return to the shopping list. Suppose that in
72 addition to eggs and milk you plan to purchase the following six items: peas,
73 apples, hot dogs, cigarettes, cake, and strawberries. You have already imag-
74 ined an egg carton that you open and find a dozen little milk cartons smiling
75 and waving at you. (The smiling and waving strengthens the link because of
76 the action component of ASOE.) Pick up one of the milk cartons and open it.
77 Now pour. Peas tumble into the glass. Look at the peas in your mind. They
78 are filling up the glass and overflowing onto the table where they run and
79 jump. Now look at one of the peas. It is very proud and is swelling up and
80 getting bigger and bigger and bigger and look—it has become an apple. Do
81 you see that green, smiling apple? Pick it up and squeeze it hard. As you
82 squeeze, hot dogs emerge from the apple. See the hot dogs clearly in your
83 mind. Forget the apple temporarily. See the hot dogs jumping into a cigarette
84 package and the package sealing up. You now see a pack of cigarettes (any
85 brand you desire, but do see a particular brand). Forget the hot dogs tempo-
86 rarily. See the cigarettes. The package is opening and the cigarettes are climb-
87 ing out, one at a time, and placing themselves on top of a cake as if they were
88 candles. Do you see those cigarettes on the cake? Now look at the cake. Forget
89 the cigarettes temporarily. Just see the cake. It is a strawberry shortcake and
90 the strawberries are very deep red and stand out vividly against the white
91 cream.

92   Now stop for a moment. Go back to the first picture that you saw in your
93 mind. Can you recall the egg carton and the dozen little milk cartons in it? Now
94 think only of the milk cartons. What do you see? The peas are pouring out. Look
95 at the peas, or at least look at one of them. Can you recall it puffing up and
96 becoming an apple? Now look at the apple. Does it help remind you of the hot
97 dog? Look at the hot dogs. What are they doing? (Becoming cigarettes?) Look at
98 the cigarettes. Are they on the (birthday) cake? See the cake. What kind of cake
99 do you see? Don't the strawberries look delicious? Now try to recite the eight
100 items of your shopping list from memory. Can you remember them? (Eggs,
101 milk, peas, apples, hot dogs, cigarettes, cake, and strawberries.)

102   Two important points should be made here. First, the illustration just given
103 is a modified form of linking sometimes known as progressive elaboration,
104 where the items are linked into a kind of story. This isn't always possible or
105 even desirable. However, just pure linking would be equally effective. You
106 might have seen the milk in the egg carton, then the milk carton pouring peas,
107 then perhaps peas being picked off of an apple tree, then an apple on a stick
108 except that the stick is a hot dog, then the hot dog being smoked by someone,
109 and finally strawberries rising from the lit end of a cigarette instead of smoke.
110 A second important point is that the research has shown that it is the things
111 that *you* make up and imagine that are most effective. The above ways of

112 linking the eight items are the author's suggestions and they may work, but
113 the most effective strategy is for *you* to make up your own links.

114   What should you do if you forget one or two items on a list? Strengthen
115 these with more ASOE; especially give them more action.

116   There are other even more effective techniques that are used to remember
117 lists of items or to remember names and faces and numbers or formulas.
118 Mnemonic techniques really work effectively and can allow students, busi-
119 ness executives, and other people to remember more things in less time, thus
120 taking a lot of hassle out of school and/or the job. It can help you to improve
121 grades or advance on the job or even be a winning card player. Some people
122 feel that using mnemonic techniques is not a good thing to do because it
123 makes the mind lazy or because a person becomes too dependent upon it.
124 That is not so. If you need to remember certain information several times over
125 a period of time, you will find that you will soon remember the information
126 and forget the mnemonic device that you used to arrive at it. This author
127 remembers certain telephone numbers that are needed once or twice a month
128 that were originally learned through a mnemonic device (a phonetic peg).
129 However, the peg is no longer remembered. It is like using a crutch to help
130 you walk when you need it, but when your foot no longer needs the crutch,
131 you throw it away.

132   You *can* learn to improve your memory. It can make your life easier and
133 even happier. Wouldn't it be foolish not to give it a try?

Comprehension Questions

Decide whether each of the following statements is true or false according to the selection. Then mark T or F in the appropriate place.

1. _____ Using mnemonic techniques makes the mind lazy.

2. _____ Information enters your physiological system through the sense organs.

3. _____ In order to develop a good memory, you need to develop a good imagination, and you must lie a lot.

4. _____ School work is about 25 percent memory and 75 percent concept development.

5. _____ Linking is a type of association.

Choose the correct answer for each of the following and circle the letter preceding it.

6. The reason just seeing a carton of milk standing next to a carton of eggs is not a good link is:
   a. It has too much ASOE.
   b. It is too ridiculous.
   c. It doesn't have enough action.
   d. It might make you hungry, which is distracting.

7. Which of the following items was *not* on the shopping list?
   a. peas
   b. whipped cream
   c. hot dogs
   d. cigarettes

8. Mnemonic systems are really systems for achieving
   a. psychological conditioning
   b. development of the sense organs
   c. imagination
   d. retrieval

9. Which of the following is a correct statement according to the selection?
   a. Using alcohol or other drugs sharpens your mind and helps you to develop a good memory.
   b. Memory workshops are only 75 percent effective.

      c. People become too dependent upon memory techniques.

      d. You can learn to remember anything you want to.

10. Which two items are needed for a good memory?

      a. imagination and association

      b. a lazy mind and imagination

      c. ASOE and good intelligence

      d. the ability to understand concepts and the ability to exaggerate

Skill-Development Questions

1. What are the meanings of the following words as they are used on the lines indicated?

   a. Conducting (line 17) _____

   b. Translated (line 30) _____

2. Circle the letter before the sentence that best expresses the main idea of the selection.
   a. Using mnemonic techniques makes the mind lazy and should only be used in emergency circumstances.
   b. You can learn to improve your memory fantastically, and it can make your life easier and happier.
   c. Linking is a mnemonic device that will help develop a fantastic memory.
   d. Memory workshops are given around the country.

3. What is the difference between linking and progressive elaboration?

   _____

   _____

4. Which relationship is shown by lines 55–60?

   _____

5. Which of the following sentences represents a cause-effect relationship?
   a. lines 27–29
   b. lines 59–60
   c. lines 31–35

6. The paragraph in lines 27–37 introduces a major idea, input, which would become a heading in an outline. This heading can be divided into two parts (called details in an outline). The first detail could be expressed as "method" or "process." How should you express the second detail?

   _____

7. Which words tell why you should make up your own links?

   _____

8. Arrange the items on the shopping list in alphabetical order. Then, to the left of the list, number them according to the order in which they are linked in the article. To the right of the list, number them according to the order in which you might purchase them in a store.

_____

_____

_____

_____

_____

_____

_____

_____

9. What is meant by the words *in your mind's eye* on line 61?

_____

10. The major purpose of this article is to
   a. share an experience
   b. inform
   c. prove a theory
   d. promote a controversial point of view

Clearing a New Path to the Top

By Tommye Jo Daves of

Levi Strauss

VOCABULARY REVIEW

- the program has been *replicated*
- one *maxim* that has guided me
- I was *pegged* as supervisor material

1 Tommye Jo Daves only wanted to earn enough money to buy a washing
2 machine when she began working at Levi Strauss & Co. 33 years ago. But
3 today, as head of Levi's Murphy, N.C., plant, she is one of the few female
4 plant managers in her company and her industry. Daves convincingly dem-
5 onstrated her management skills to her supervisors in an unorthodox way: by
6 setting up a successful employee-training and adult-education program at
7 Levi's Blue Ridge, Ga., plant—a program that has been replicated at all 31
8 Levi Strauss plants in the United States. In designing the extensive evening
9 curriculum, meant to help blue-collar workers like herself get the training and
10 education they need to become eligible—or better equipped—for promotions,
11 Daves blazed her own fast track to the top. And even though actions are
12 supposed to speak louder than words, speaking up was also crucial to her
13 success. Here's how she did it.

14 'They say your talents are only good if you give them away. And if there's
15 one maxim that has guided me throughout my career, that's it. I started as a
16 sewing-machine operator at Levi's Blue Ridge factory, a pilot plant housed in
17 an old gymnasium. My husband and I were a struggling young couple with a
18 small daughter. I hadn't planned to work outside the home, but I thought that
19 if I could just get a washing machine, my life would be much easier. So I
20 became one of the first 30 people on the plant's payroll; the starting pay was
21 80 cents an hour.

22 My first job was sewing jeans pockets. After about three months, I was
23 selected to become a supervisor trainee. As a trainee, I had to learn the whole
24 business—every job. I had long since saved up enough money for the wash-
25 ing machine, but I was enjoying my newfound career. I have no earthly idea

343

26 why I was pegged as supervisor material, except that I always tried to main-
27 tain a positive attitude and was very quality-conscious. Within 2 years I was
28 promoted from supervisor to training instructor, and over the next 12 years I
29 worked my way up the ranks to line manager in charge of several hundred
30 people, where I stayed for 13 years.

31 **Realizing Your Ambitions.** On the surface, I was happy as a lark. But
32 in the back of my mind, I was thinking about the plant manager's job. Of
33 course, I didn't want to ask for it, because that wasn't the sort of thing women
34 did. And when they did ask, they were usually told they'd have to be willing
35 to relocate. Funny thing, though—I noticed that the same standard didn't
36 apply to the men. Time after time I'd help train them, and then they'd be
37 promoted to positions above me.
38 I didn't know how resentful this made me until the company held a meet-
39 ing in November 1986 to discuss equal-opportunity issues. Management
40 stood up and said, "Of course, there are equal opportunities for men and
41 women within the company." Suddenly, my blood began to boil. I stood up,
42 and the words started to pour out of my mouth. "That isn't exactly the way it
43 is," I said. "Women are not happy. I'm letting you know right now that I'd like
44 to be the assistant plant manager. It's overdue. And it's time for some changes
45 in my life."
46 The reaction was dead silence. My first thought was "Oh my God, what
47 have I done now!" It was really emotional for me to admit to myself that I had
48 this anger inside, that I felt I had been overlooked. But afterward my immedi-
49 ate supervisor came up to me and we talked. He had repeatedly suggested
50 that I be made assistant plant manager, and he told me he was planning to
51 recommend me again.

52 **Finding Opportunities.** I was determined to change the company
53 practice of telling people they weren't qualified for a promotion without
54 telling them why. I had gotten where I was without a college education, and I
55 knew firsthand that if people were motivated, they could learn what they
56 needed to know on the job. As a line manager, I decided to establish a
57 procedure whereby we asked employees what their goals were—and when
58 we told a person they weren't ready for a promotion, I felt it was only fair to
59 tell them how to become qualified.
60 But I didn't want to leave it at that. I wanted to make sure people were able
61 to get the proper training. That's when I got the idea to hold night classes.
62 Some of our older women wanted to be plant mechanics. The problem was
63 that many of them didn't have the math skills or any experience in reading
64 construction specifications. So I asked the vocational high school director if I
65 could get a math teacher to come to our plant two nights a week for two

66 hours. We were able to get funding from the state to pay the teacher, and the
67 employees bought their own books. Since there wasn't a budget for anything
68 like this at the time, we told the plant management that all they had to do was
69 make the cafeteria available and provide soft drinks and cookies. We soon
70 had four women who passed the mechanic's test with flying colors.

71   That first course was so successful that we decided to offer one that would
72 allow employees to earn their high school equivalency diplomas. Those who
73 had not graduated from the 12th grade had always been unlikely choices for
74 supervisory positions. But after the GED class, 22 workers became strong
75 candidates to move up in the ranks.

76   We began to offer typing, communications, reading, electronics, and ad-
77 vanced electronics classes. The demand eventually became so great that we
78 had to move from the cafeteria to the high school building next door. Since we
79 had funding from the state, it cost the company next to nothing. I attended
80 nearly every session, just to make sure the quality remained high and to show
81 I was committed. My relationship with my staff was strengthened because
82 they were seeing me in a more informal setting. We never guaranteed that if
83 you took a class, you'd get a promotion, but we let people know we'd give
84 them the best shot. At the same time, setting up this program was a chance to
85 showcase my leadership skills. While I don't think my volunteer work was
86 the sole reason for my ultimately becoming plant manager, it sure didn't do
87 me any harm.

88   In October 1987, I was promoted to assistant plant manager. And early last
89 year, I got the news that I was being named the Murphy plant manager—I
90 would be responsible for 385 employees. As plant manager, I create a road
91 map to make sure that all the work gets done. Since some of the best ideas
92 come from employees on the floor, I try to get out into the plant as much as I
93 can every week and talk about whatever ideas and concerns people might
94 have. Much of the rest of my time is spent meeting with department manag-
95 ers to make sure everything is running smoothly.

96   Being a volunteer lets you put yourself in the workers' shoes. These proj-
97 ects have made me aware of how important it is for a boss to communicate
98 and provide clear instructions. You realize that lots of times when things go
99 wrong in an operation, it's because the workers didn't get the full picture.

100   Today, Levi Strauss has company-funded adult-education programs at all
101 of its U.S. plants. I've also long been an active member of Levi's community-
102 involvement teams, which encourage volunteer activities of all sorts. It's not
103 unusual for employees to strike out on their own to address community
104 needs. After Hurricane Andrew hit Florida, for example, one of our employ-
105 ees went there with a load of supplies donated by a local church group. We
106 decided to pay her salary while she was gone and call it a business trip—
107 that's the least a company can do, I think.

108   I've learned a lot since the day I stood up at the equal-opportunity meeting.
109 I've tried to use my experience to make things better for women in the
110 company. Today, the top five managers who report to me are all women.
111 When I started out 33 years ago, I had no idea I'd have the opportunity to lead
112 an all-woman management team. I've worn out four washing machines since
113 I got here. And I plan to wear out a few more before I'm through.'

Comprehension Questions

Decide whether each of the following statements is true or false according to the selection. Then mark T or F in the space provided.

1. _____ At first, the classes were held in the high school cafeteria.

2. _____ Ms. Daves became plant manager as a direct result of her volunteer work in setting up the classes.

3. _____ Today, Levi Strauss pays for the classes at all of its U.S. plants.

4. _____ The first class was set up so that employees could earn their high school equivalency diplomas.

5. _____ Ms. Daves started at Levi Strauss as a sewing machine operator.

Choose the correct answer for each of the following questions and circle the letter that precedes it.

6. Ms. Daves was selected to become a supervisor after being with the company
   a. six months
   b. three months
   c. two years
   d. one year

7. Why did Ms. Daves take the job in the first place?
   a. She wanted to become a supervisor.
   b. She wanted a career outside the home.
   c. She wanted a washing machine.
   d. She needed a sewing machine.

8. What is one reason Ms. Daves didn't want to be plant manager?
   a. She felt that she would have to relocate.
   b. She felt she would be embarrassed.
   c. She felt that she wasn't qualified.
   d. She loved what she was doing—she didn't want to change jobs.

9. Who paid the teacher for the first class?
   a. the state
   b. the employees who took the class
   c. the company
   d. the teacher taught the class as a volunteer

10. What percent of Levi plants have employee classes?
   a. 10%
   b. 25%
   c. 50%
   d. 100%

Skill-Development Questions

1. What is meant by the word *standard* as it is used on line 35? Decide its meaning from the context.

   standard _____

2. Circle the letter before the sentence that best expresses the main idea of the paragraph on lines 31–37.
   a. On the surface she was happy as a lark.
   b. She really wanted to be plant manager.
   c. The standards that applied to women did not apply to men.
   d. She was angry because men that she trained were promoted to positions above her.

3. What is significant about the top five managers who report to Ms. Daves?

   _____

4. How does the second part of the sentence on lines 79–81 relate to the first part of the sentence?

   _____

   _____

5. How does the sentence on lines 64–66 relate to the sentence before it?

   _____

   _____

6. The paragraph on lines 76–87 states that the classes had some results. One was that the workers got a better shot at promotion. What were the two results for the author?

   _____

7. There are six events that are mentioned as happening at a specific time. Assuming that Ms. Daves started work in 1960, find the time of each of the six events and tell what each one was.

   _____

   _____

   _____

_____

_____

_____

8. Following is a list of some of the events that occurred during the thirty-three years that Ms. Daves worked for Levi Strauss. Number these events in the order in which they occurred.

_____ She became a training supervisor.

_____ She set up advanced electronics courses.

_____ The company held a meeting to discuss equal opportunity issues.

_____ A GED class was offered.

_____ She became plant manager.

9. What is meant by the words "Suddenly, my blood began to boil" as it is used on line 41?

_____

10. Which words best express the tone on lines 31–37?
   a. sarcasm and bitterness
   b. resentful but hopeful
   c. frustration and anger
   d. frustration and sarcasm

The Interview

VOCABULARY REVIEW

- one important *caveat*
- a *keystone* of any effective interview
- *attune* yourself to the interviewer
- make very *astute* judgments
- he wants to *regale* you with stories
- you can *segue* into questioning him

1 More often than not, it is the small things that occur in an interview that
2 spell the difference between getting an offer and being rejected. As you will
3 learn as you read on, the basic objective of a candidate in an interview is to
4 spark a positive feeling in the interviewer. It's a purely subjective feeling, so
5 your close attention to the little things is essential.

THE BASICS

6 **Be certain of the time and place of the interview and the name of**
7 **the interviewer.** Sometimes candidates are so excited to get an interview
8 that they neglect to ask for this essential information. Write it down and keep
9 it with you until after the interview. If no one tells you your interviewer's
10 name, ask. Sometimes the situation precludes finding out, but you're ahead of
11 the game if you know it going in.

12 **Arrive early for the interview.** If you plan on arriving at least fifteen
13 minutes before the appointed time, you will have a cushion against any
14 unforeseen delays, such as a traffic tie-up or an elevator breakdown or an
15 inability to find the right building or office, any of which could cause you to
16 be late if you depended on split-second timing. Being early can also give the
17 interviewer a good initial impression of your reliability and interest.

18   **Bring a pen and notebook with you.**   The notebook should fit in a
19 pocket or purse so that you don't walk into the interview room with it in
20 hand. Its purpose is twofold. First, the interviewer may give some informa-
21 tion for you to write down. If you're prepared with your own writing mate-
22 rial, it will save him or her from trying to find something for you during the
23 interview.
24   Second, immediately after the interview you should write down what
25 occurred: what you said, what the interviewer said, and what your reactions
26 were. This information can be very important in future interviews so that you
27 can be sure that what you tell the interviewer is consistent.

28   **Remember the interviewer's name.**   There is possibly no sweeter
29 sound to the human ear than the sound of one's own name. If you don't know
30 the interviewer's name prior to meeting him, concentrate on it when he
31 introduces himself and remember it. For some people this is very difficult.
32 They are concentrating on themselves so much and thinking about how ner-
33 vous they are that they completely forget the name or don't pay close atten-
34 tion when they hear it for the first time.
35   When he introduces himself, repeat his name immediately by saying some-
36 thing on the order of, "How do you do, Mr. Smith." Then repeat the name a
37 couple of times during the first part of the interview. This repetition will help
38 you to remember the name. It will also have a pleasing effect on the inter-
39 viewer, who undoubtedly likes to hear the sound of his name.
40   One caveat: do not call the interviewer by his or her first name unless
41 invited to do so (something that is very unlikely). Calling people by their first
42 name without being asked is a familiarity that offends many people.

43   **Don't offer to shake hands unless the interviewer offers a hand
44 first.**   All interviewers are different. Some will not offer to shake hands. A
45 male interviewee should not offer to shake hands if his interviewer does not
46 first offer. For a woman, this is not so crucial. You may find a chivalrous
47 interviewer who believes it is offensive for a man to offer his hand to a
48 woman but would not be offended for a female interviewee to offer her hand
49 to him. The safe rule, in any event, is not to offer your hand unless the
50 interviewer makes the first move.
51   If you do shake hands, make it a firm grip. A weak handshake can be a real
52 turnoff. But don't go overboard and show your Charles Atlas grip. If you
53 break a few bones in his hand or bring him to his knees by your hearty
54 handshake, he won't remember you with good feelings.

55   **Don't smoke unless invited.**   Many people are allergic to cigarette
56 smoke. Further, the interviewer may have to occupy the room for the entire

57 day, and he doesn't want it filled up with smoke. Smoking has generally
58 become so controversial that you shouldn't take the chance on offending him
59 by lighting up without being invited. No matter how addicted you are to
60 tobacco, you should be able to survive a few minutes without your dose.
61 Many nonsmokers have an almost religious antagonism to smoking. Why risk
62 offending?

63 **Don't chew gum.**   Gum chewing can communicate a distinctly negative
64 impression. It may not offend some interviewers, but it is still better not to
65 take the risk of doing something that may rub him the wrong way.

66 **Wait for your interviewer to sit down or offer you a chair before**
67 **seating yourself.**   Most of these suggestions are items of common cour-
68 tesy, but they are often overlooked, particularly in the context of the interview
69 when you are nervous and thinking about yourself.
70   It is a keystone of any effective interview for you to come across as an
71 honest person. "Here I am with all my warts" is the impression that is best to
72 leave. You don't want to expound on your warts, but you want to leave the
73 impression that you accept yourself for what you are and that you want the
74 interviewer to know you as the person you are.
75   But that's just the *impression* you want to leave. You must attune yourself to
76 the interviewer early, and this requires strict attention to him and his reactions
77 to you.
78   You will have to make some very astute judgments in the early moments of
79 the interview about the interviewer. In order for you to conduct an effective
80 interview, you must concern yourself with the interviewer's problems, preju-
81 dices, desires, and feelings. Is he dynamic, a take-charge guy who wants to
82 regale you with stories? Let him. Is he somewhat shy and insecure in his
83 position? Help him out. Does he exhibit any prejudices that you are able to
84 perceive? Don't run afoul of them.
85   You must exercise the perception to categorize him early and then the
86 discretion to guide the interview along the lines that help him arrive at the
87 conclusion you wish.
88   Being interviewed and being interviewed well are two entirely different
89 matters.

YOU MUST SELL YOURSELF

90   As an interviewee you are primarily a salesman. The product you are
91 selling is yourself, and the assets of the product consist of your experience,
92 skills, and personality. You communicate your experience and skills in your
93 résumé. Your personality comes across in the interview.

94 You should be outwardly oriented. You should think about the interviewer
95 and gear the interview toward his concerns. If you talk intelligently about
96 something in which he is concerned, he will be more interested in the areas of
97 your concern. Interviewers are like everyone else: they are selfish, and their
98 own concerns are paramount in their minds. If you show a genuine interest in
99 them and can discuss them intelligently, the interest in you will be sparked. If,
100 on the other hand, you are unable to communicate your interest with sincer-
101 ity, the likely consequence will be a loss of confidence in you, and you'll be
102 worse off than when you started.

KEEP THE INTERVIEWER'S ATTENTION

103 Pay strict attention to how you are being received by the interviewer. If you
104 determine that his interest is lagging, there are a few tricks you can use to
105 bring him back around.

106 **You can vary the tone of your voice (for example, by lowering it or**
107 **making it louder).** Television advertisers often do this by making their
108 commercials louder than the show they sponsor. Theoretically this change in
109 tone beckons and makes the viewer more attentive to something he may have
110 little desire to hear.

111 **You can vary the tempo at which you speak (by speeding it up or**
112 **slowing it down).** Essentially any change that you make from the manner
113 in which you have been behaving will act as a lure to bring the interviewer's
114 attention back from its wandering. You must capture and retain the inter-
115 viewer's interest, or the remainder of the interview will be a mere formality
116 and probably result in rejection.
117 What you do with that attention once you capture it will determine
118 whether your interview is going to be successful. If, for example, you con-
119 vince the interviewer that you don't have the experience for the job or the
120 skills required or that your personality is abrasive or bland, you're no better
121 off than you were before you walked in the door.
122 Once you have captured his attention, you must continue your salesman-
123 ship and create the desire in the interviewer to have you as an employee.

FACT FINDING

124 If you can get the interviewer to talk about himself or reveal something
125 personal in an early part of the interview, you can reinforce or verify some of
126 your assumptions before you act on them. The first part of the interview can

127 be a jousting period while you feel him out and vice versa. What you must
128 realize is that he has probably assumed that you are the typical interviewee
129 who will meekly sit and wait for him to conduct the interview. Therefore, he
130 will not be prepared for subtle probes.

131   You must take your key from him. If he starts boldly by asking questions
132 and gives you no signal that he will entertain personal queries, you have to
133 wait until the time is propitious.

134   If you are unable to penetrate his shield, you can still work on some
135 existing beliefs you may safely assume that he has from interpreting his
136 actions. For example, if you have submitted your résumé in advance and then
137 been called in for an interview, you may safely assume that the interviewer
138 has made a preliminary determination that you are qualified for the position
139 based upon the data you provided. You may then proceed to work upon this
140 belief by verifying and amplifying the facts on your résumé and by detailing
141 specific experience and skills.

142   You can also assume that the interviewer knows what he wants out of the
143 position, and you may query him on how he views the position and the tasks
144 he wants accomplished. After he has discussed this, you can tailor your
145 experience and skills to the desires he has revealed.

146   Some interviewers will tell you something about the job before they start
147 questioning you, but most won't. Most interviewers are inwardly oriented,
148 just as are most interviewees, and they may not really focus on the inter-
149 viewee. They may be thinking instead about asking the right questions in the
150 interview.

151   Therefore if you can easily segue into questioning him about the position
152 early on, he may give you some valuable keys that you can use to guide the
153 rest of the interview and create in him the realization that you are the right
154 person to fill the position.

CONTROL

155   **An interviewer can be expected to control the flow of the**
156 **interview.**   Some interviewers may begin by asking general questions to
157 ease your nervousness and will then move on to more specific questions
158 about areas in which they are interested that are not covered on your résumé.

159   But although the interviewer controls the flow of the interview, the inter-
160 viewee controls the content. After all, an interview generally consists of an
161 interviewer's asking questions and the interviewee's answering them. What
162 the interviewee does with the questions is up to him or her. Thus you should
163 go into the interview knowing the points that you want to cover, for example,
164 your achievements.

THINK ABOUT THE INTERVIEWER

165   Don't think about yourself so much. Most interviewees think about them-
166 selves to the exclusion of everyone else. When you walk into a room, you may
167 be worrying about how you look, whether your palms are sweaty, whether
168 your voice will crack.

169   But we all think about ourselves. The interviewer is thinking about him-
170 self. Maybe he doesn't have the same insecurities attacking him, but he's
171 thinking about himself all the same. He may be worried about his job or
172 making the plane that night. He may have a million things on his mind other
173 than this interviewee sitting in front of him.

174   So there you are worrying about yourself and your sweaty palms and there
175 he is thinking about something else. In fact the interviewer may have the
176 same insecurities. He may not have conducted many interviews and be wor-
177 ried that he's going to make a fool of himself. He may even be worried that
178 his palms are sweaty or that he won't ask the right questions. Or, worse, if he
179 is really inexperienced, he may feel that he won't be able to think of anything
180 to say and there will be gaps of silence.

181   Whatever his thoughts, there's a good possibility that he's not thinking
182 what you think he's thinking. He's not taking you apart piece by piece in his
183 mind, coolly evaluating your every movement.

184   It's your responsibility to think about him.

185   If you determine that he is insecure and unsure of himself, try to make the
186 interview go as smoothly as possible for him. If you do and you control the
187 interview to the extent that there are no gaps and you say what you want to
188 say, probably you will have conducted a very good interview.

189   If you go into the interview thinking about the interviewer, you will relieve
190 yourself of the tremendous tension that most interviewees feel about an inter-
191 view. You will feel that you have some control of the situation and a plan of
192 attack.

Comprehension Questions

Decide whether each of the following statements is true or false according to the selection. Then mark T *or* F *in the appropriate place.*

1. _____ Never arrive early for an interview because it shows that you are too anxious.

2. _____ Offer to shake hands with the interviewer as soon as you meet in order to make a positive impression.

3. _____ Smoking while being interviewed is a good idea because it helps you relax.

4. _____ Most interviewers will tell you about the job before they start to question you.

5. _____ Although the interviewer controls the flow of the interview, the interviewee controls its content.

Choose the correct answer for each of the following questions and circle the letter preceding it.

6. Why should you bring a pen and notebook with you to the interview?
   a. It impresses the interviewer because it shows interest in what is said during the interview.
   b. The interviewer may want to check to see that your handwriting is neat and legible.
   c. If you write down, immediately after the interview, what occurred during the interview, you can be consistent in what you say in future interviews.
   d. If you have many different interviews, your notes of each one will help you remember what was said and it will aid in making a job choice.

7. Which is *not* mentioned as a way to keep the interviewer's attention?
   a. Make eye contact.
   b. Speak at a faster tempo.
   c. Lower your voice.
   d. Speak more slowly.

8. Why should you think about the interviewer during the interview?
   a. If you can make the interview go as smoothly as possible for the interviewer, you will relieve yourself of tension and have better control of the situation.
   b. If you find a weakness in the interviewer, you can embarrass him or her into offering you the job.

c. It will show the interviewer that you are a sensitive and caring person who deserves the job.

d. You may be an interviewer some day, and thinking about and watching this one gives you valuable insights.

9. Which of the following suggestions for having a good interviewer is mentioned in the selection?

a. If you look at the interviewer when you talk, you show confidence in yourself.

b. Sweaty palms always leave a negative impression.

c. It helps create a positive impression if you call the interviewer by his or her first name.

d. It is important to come across as an honest person.

10. Which of the following suggestions for having a good interview is *not* mentioned in the selection?

a. Try to remember the interviewer's name.

b. Learn as much as you can about the company before coming to the interview.

c. Wait for the interviewer to sit down or offer you a chair before you sit down.

d. Remember that you must sell yourself.

Skill-Development Questions

1. What is the meaning of the word *initial* as it is used on line 17?

   _____

2. Write the main idea of the paragraph on lines 169–173.

   _____

   _____

3. What are two reasons given by the author for arriving early for the interview?

   _____

   _____

4. *a.* How does the sentence on lines 26–27 relate to the one before it?

   _____

   b. How does the sentence on lines 99–102 relate to the one before it?

   _____

5. *a.* How does the sentence on lines 128–129 relate to the one before it?

   _____

   b. What relationship is shown in the sentence on lines 49–50?

   _____

6. How many major divisions does this article have? _____

   Write the third major division. _____

7. Which words tell why you should go into the interview knowing the points that you want to cover?

   _____

   _____

8. What are three things to do to help you remember the interviewer's name?

   _____

   _____

   _____

9. Explain in your own words the meaning of the expression "Here I am with all my warts" as used on line 71.

_____

_____

10. How does the author want you to feel after reading this selection?
    a. confident and upbeat
    b. cautious and worried
    c. nervous but optimistic
    d. knowledgeable but fearful

The Garbage Man

VOCABULARY REVIEW

- what *contemporary* society buys
- a one-man garbage *guru*
- *queasy* stomachs
- early morning *forays*
- a seeming *anomaly*
- an *esoteric* subject

1 Outfitted in surgical gown, face mask, and rubber gloves, the doctor looks
2 ready to perform delicate surgery. However, he and his students head not for
3 the operating room but instead for the Tucson city dump.
4 The garbagemobile picks them up at 2:00 P.M. promptly six days a week,
5 and as the old blue limousine bearing the official emblem, "Le Projet du
6 Garbage" glides toward its destination, Dr. William Rathje earnestly explains
7 the significance of his garbage. Though some might think this University of
8 Arizona professor is kidding, he is perfectly serious in proclaiming, "I love
9 my trash! When you look at a bag of garbage, you see only moldy orange
10 peels, half-eaten TV dinners, and spoiled scraps of steak, but I carefully sort
11 through the bags, and the items show me evidence of what contemporary
12 society buys and how it lives. It seems perfectly logical to me that if archaeol-
13 ogists could use garbage from the past to reconstruct what was going on in
14 ancient societies, we can use today's garbage to see what's going on in our
15 own society."
16 Rathje has been a one-man garbage guru for the last 10 years, and through
17 a course called "Independent Study in Archaeology," he has allowed hun-
18 dreds of students the opportunity of getting college credit for following him
19 into a truly stinking job. "We lose about one in 20 whose queasy stomachs just
20 can't be calmed in the name of science," says Rathje, "but they're more than
21 made up for by students who repeat the course because of the exciting infor-
22 mation gained from ripping through the trash." Still, it would be only honest
23 to say that even the most stalwart garbage sorter's blood runs cold when he
24 whiffs rancid chicken.

25   Students undergo two weeks of intensive training to become part of the
26   garbage guerrillas. They have to learn how to tell a peach pit from an apricot
27   pit and to know whether deodorant falls into the classification of personal
28   sanitation or cosmetics. In all, there are over 200 categories to memorize and
29   students are tested to make certain they know, for example, that found
30   saltpork fat is classified differently from encountered meat trimmings.
31   It takes a team of two dedicated students about 45 minutes to sort through
32   a bag of garbage. One calls out the items giving identifying number, type,
33   weight or volume, cost, composition of container and brand name of each
34   thing. The other student records this information on a form for transfer to
35   computer tape.
36   Of course the program didn't achieve such sophisticated status overnight.
37   In fact, in the earliest stages, it involved Rathje and eight students choosing
38   three census tracts representing low, middle, and upper income households,
39   and then "garbage-napping" the contents of the refuse cans before the city
40   sanitation trucks arrived for them. The results of these early morning forays
41   confirmed the group's suspicions that population groups say one thing about
42   their behavior and do another. Excited by all the possibilities, the group
43   decided to expand, and get their trash legally. Rathje checked and found out
44   that once trash is set on the curb it belongs to the city, so he went to the Tucson
45   Sanitation Division and asked if his students could borrow some garbage.
46   At first, the Sanitation Department was a little skeptical, but after Rathje
47   persuaded them of his serious intent, and enthusiastically spoke of all the
48   important things garbage could show, the department not only gave ap-
49   proval, but offered to have workers pick up the refuse for the scholars to
50   study. Tom Price, then Tucson's chief of operations, jokingly commented that
51   policemen and firemen had gotten their day of glory on television, and it was
52   high time the sanitation men got some.
53   That settled, Rathje and Wilson Harris, one of the first student volunteers,
54   spent almost two years setting up the methodology for sampling garbage.
55   Their sampling unit includes 19 of the city's 67 census tracts. The tracts were
56   selected in clusters to get the full range of ethnic and socioeconomic charac-
57   teristics of the total population. Two bags of garbage are randomly chosen
58   from each designated census tract and are picked up by foremen from the city
59   sanitation department on regular collection days. The bags are marked only
60   with the number of the census tract and the date. They are then deposited in a
61   special part of the city's maintenance yard for inspection.
62   Harris is now in charge of all field operations and he tells students that any
63   letters or other forms of identification found while sorting should immedi-
64   ately be discarded to keep the garbage anonymous. Harris also extracts a
65   pledge from all student workers—they may not eat, drink, or smoke anything
66   they find.

67   Although Rathje, a Harvard Ph.D., initially had trouble convincing anyone
68 that "Le Projet du Garbage" wasn't just a bunch of rubbish, it now seems that
69 the United States government as well as corporations such as Chevron, General
70 Mills, and Alcoa accept the value of garbage research enough to finance it.

71   "Garbage cans don't lie," says Rathje solemnly. "You are what you throw
72 away." In other words, garbage tends to give a much more accurate picture of
73 market research than the traditional interview process. Rathje points out a
74 study on beer drinking that was done by having interviewers go door to door
75 asking about the amount of household beer consumption within a single
76 week. The results showed that 75 percent of the families drank no beer within
77 a week's time, 25 percent drank 1–7 containers, and none drank more than 7
78 containers. But back door research "said it all," when it revealed just how
79 many people actually had "gone for the gusto." Fifty percent of the house-
80 holds surveyed in interviews had more than seven containers of beer in the
81 garbage and some of the households had more than an empty case of beer
82 bottles in the trash.

83   "It's not really that people mean to lie," surmises Rathje, "it's just that they
84 want to impress the interviewer." Rathje also found that it is the blue-collar
85 households who drink the "best" imported beers. The upper crust settles for
86 domestic, cheaper brands.

87   That isn't the only seeming anomaly in Rathje's findings. When the 1973
88 meat shortage hit and prices went sky high, the expected assumption was that
89 people would waste less meat. Instead, the amount of trashed meat rose
90 significantly. In fact, in a time when everyone was complaining that he
91 couldn't afford beef, Rathje, extending his figures nationwide, estimated that
92 more than $500,000 worth of meat was thrown away. However when prices
93 went down, so did the amount of waste.

94   Although Rathje usually leaves the interpretation of such facts to others, he
95 says that in this case, he feels that during the shortage people bought cheaper
96 cuts of meat which they didn't know how to fix and ended up throwing out,
97 or they bought whole sides of beef to save money, and then, lacking proper
98 storage, let the meat spoil.

99   The packaging industry has used Rathje's data to study the amount of solid
100 waste it creates and to determine whether its packaging is sturdy enough and
101 the right size. The EPA has used "Le Projet du Garbage" to test the effective-
102 ness of different types of advertising in encouraging recycling. The results:
103 The type of ads didn't matter much. When the prices for the recycling items
104 rose, so did the number of items recycled.

105   "Garbage," claims Rathje, "may contain the last real evidence of the Amer-
106 ican dream." For, surprisingly enough, garbage cans in rich and poor neigh-
107 borhoods share many more similarities than differences. For example,
108 stereotypes were shattered when, in one study, it was found that poor

109 Mexican-American families bought as much milk, took more vitamins, and
110 bought more educational toys for their children than middle-class Anglos.
111 Still, Rathje admits that there are some indicators of upper-class garbage
112 including such items as squeezed oranges and diet soft drink cans. "In fact,"
113 he says, "one law of trash is that as you go down the socioeconomic ladder,
114 you eat farther up the asparagus stalk."

115   Lacking either the time or the knowledge to use leftovers, it is the middle
116 class that is the most wasteful when it comes to edible food. "Maybe," says
117 Rathje, "it's because both husband and wife work and are too busy, or maybe,
118 it's because they now feel that the new house is too expensive to afford so
119 they get their status by buying expensive convenience foods and tossing out
120 the leftovers."

121   Leaving statistics behind, Rathje claims that every bag of garbage tells its
122 own story. He leaves to the listeners' imaginations the circumstances behind
123 the contents of a garbage bag which contained several empty disposable
124 diaper cartons, one worn baby bootie, and a package of birth control pills
125 missing only one pill.

126   Rathje also likes the bag within the garbage bag which contained every-
127 thing for a fine picnic lunch. Nothing had been touched. "Someone probably
128 threw out the picnic and took a sack of garbage by mistake. Can't you just
129 imagine the way they felt upon traveling to the perfect spot and opening their
130 great lunch to find a bag of garbage? Of course," add Rathje wryly, "if it's
131 anything like the average bag of garbage there was probably more than
132 enough edible food to feed them."

133   For in a single year, Tucson residents waste some 15 percent by weight of
134 all the edible food they buy. Their current food waste in a single week could
135 provide enough meat, poultry, and fish for 4,000 people. In the space of a year,
136 Tucson residents throw away more than $500,000 worth of beef, $1 million of
137 vegetables, and about $75,000 worth of pastries.

138   In the average household 500 whole glass bottles are tossed out each year, as
139 are 1,800 plastic items (both wraps and containers), 850 steel cans, 500 recyclable
140 all-aluminum cans, and more than 13,000 items of paper and cardboard.

141   "There are worldwide similarities in urban garbage. I predict that the
142 whole concept of garbology will grow, and in 10 to 20 years, you'll see
143 garbage being studied in every major city of this country. Would I ever love to
144 be at the helm of those studies.

145   "We're beginning to treat garbage with a lot more respect. As the throw-
146 away era of cheap energy and unlimited mineral by-products comes to an
147 end, we realize that garbage is more than an unsightly nuisance that can be
148 gotten rid of," concludes Rathje.

149   Rathje takes a professional view of his garbology. He scorns any compari-
150 son to what he calls Peeping Tom Garbologists a la *National Enquirer* who, for

151 example, stole Henry Kissinger's garbage and used it for a gossipy story. By
152 contrast, he proudly states, "Our garbage analysis has been used by the
153 Federal Government's General Accounting Office to report food waste and by
154 the U.S. Senate's Select Committee on Nutrition and Human Needs."

155   When told he is often considered the Carl Sagan of garbage and asked to
156 explain the comparison, Rathje says, "Sagan took the rather esoteric subject of
157 astronomy and made it applicable and interesting to the general public. I took
158 the subject of garbage which was considered gross and of no use and showed
159 the public how their buying and wasting habits affect the quality of life.
160 Besides," he added, " both Sagan and I love our topics of study."

161   Rathje smiles. "We've modeled our official emblem after the ceiling of the
162 Sistine Chapel. There the hand of man is reaching for life from the hand of
163 God. Here the gloved hand of man is reaching for knowledge from the can of
164 garbage."

Comprehension Questions

Decide whether each of the following statements is true or false according to the selection. Then mark T or F in the appropriate place.

1. _____ Dr. Rathje looks through garbage in order to find gossipy information about people.

2. _____ At first Dr. Rathje and his students acted illegally in order to get the garbage.

3. _____ Sorting through garbage is an important form of market research.

4. _____ Advertising campaigns help to encourage people to recycle items.

5. _____ Dr. Rathje's study proves that people waste less when prices go up.

Choose the correct answer for each of the following questions and circle the letter before it.

6. How long does it take to record the information from a bag of garbage? How many people does it take?
   a. three people, 30 minutes
   b. one person, 45 minutes
   c. four people, 30 minutes
   d. two people, 45 minutes

7. Who collects the garbage for Dr. Rathje?
   a. students
   b. a sanitation department foreman
   c. Wilson Harris, student volunteer
   d. local corporations

8. Dr. Rathje is
   a. a historian
   b. a sociologist
   c. a psychologist
   d. an archaeologist
   e. a chemist

9. Which two items are part of the official emblem?
   a. the gloved hand of a man and a can of garbage
   b. the hand of man and the hand of God

c. the hand of man and the Sistine Chapel

d. the hand of God and the Sistine Chapel

10. Who is the most wasteful when it comes to edible food?

a. the lower class

b. the middle class

c. the wealthy

d. the large family

Skill-Development Questions

1. What does the word *gross* mean as it is used on line 158? Circle the letter before the correct answer.
   - *a.* unrefined, in bad taste
   - *b.* easily seen
   - *c.* bulky or fat
   - *d.* immediately noticeable

2. Circle the letter that best expresses the main idea of the paragraph on lines 25–30.
   - *a.* Students need to memorize over 200 categories in order to be a garbage researcher.
   - *b.* Some students flunk and don't make the garbage-research team.
   - *c.* Students undergo intensive training to be a garbage researcher.
   - *d.* Students have to pass an aptitude test in order to be a garbage researcher.

3. How has Dr. Rathje's project helped industry?

   _____

   _____

   _____

4. Which relationship is shown on lines 101–104?

   _____

5. Which relationship is shown by the sentence on lines 94–98?

6. Lines 83–86 state that lower-income families drink expensive beer and upper-income families drink cheap beer. Lines 87–93 state that people wasted more meat when meat prices were high than when they were low. Write a heading appropriate for these two points.

   _____

   _____

7. Which words give an example of a "Peeping Tom Garbologist"?

   _____

   _____

8. How have each of the following been related to garbage research? List this information in the order in which it appears in the selection: the EPA, the Chevron Corporation, the General Accounting Office, Alcoa, the packaging industry, a U.S. Senate committee, the Tucson Sanitation Department, General Mills.

_____

_____

_____

_____

_____

_____

_____

_____

9. What does the term *back door research* refer to as it is used on line 78?

_____

_____

10. Which of the following best describes the purpose of this selection?
   a. to make you more conscious of what you throw out
   b. to show the value of garbology
   c. to interest you in taking Dr. Rathje's course
   d. to show a way in which students can earn college credit

I Have a Dream

by Martin Luther King Jr.

- five *score* years ago
- *languished* in the corners of American society
- neither rest nor *tranquility*
- their freedom is *inextricably* bound to ours
- *wallow* in the valley of despair
- *prodigious* hilltops of New Hampshire

1   Five score years ago, a great American, in whose symbolic shadow we
2 stand today, signed the Emancipation Proclamation. This momentous decree
3 came as a great beacon of light and hope to millions of Negro slaves who had
4 been seared in the flames of withering injustice. It came as a joyous daybreak
5 to end the long night of their captivity.
6   But one hundred years later, the Negro is still not free. One hundred years
7 later, the life of the Negro is still sadly crippled by the manacles of segregation
8 and the chains of discrimination.
9   One hundred years later, the Negro lives on a lonely island of poverty in
10 the midst of a vast ocean of material prosperity. One hundred years later, the
11 Negro is still languished in the corners of American society and finds himself
12 an exile in his own land. So we have come here today to dramatize a shameful
13 condition.
14   In a sense we have come to our nation's capital to cash a check. When the
15 architects of our republic wrote the magnificent words of the Constitution
16 and the Declaration of Independence, they were signing a promissory note to
17 which every American was to fall heir. This note was a promise that all men,
18 yes, black men as well as white men, would be guaranteed the unalienable
19 rights of life, liberty, and the pursuit of happiness.
20   It is obvious today that America has defaulted on this promissory note
21 insofar as her citizens of color are concerned. Instead of honoring this sacred

22 obligation. America has given the Negro people a bad check, which has come
23 back marked "insufficient funds."

24 But we refuse to believe that the bank of justice is bankrupt. We refuse to
25 believe that there are insufficient funds in the great vaults of opportunity of
26 this nation. So we have come to cash this check—a check that will give us
27 upon demand the riches of freedom and the security of justice.

28 We have also come to this hallowed spot to remind America of the fierce
29 urgency of now. This is no time to engage in the luxury of cooling off or to
30 take the tranquilizing drug of gradualism. Now is the time to make real the
31 promises of democracy. Now is the time to rise from the dark and desolate
32 valley of segregation to the sunlit path of racial justice. Now is the time to lift
33 our nation from the quicksands of racial injustice to the solid rock of brother-
34 hood. Now is the time to make justice a reality for all of God's children.

35 It would be fatal for the nation to overlook the urgency of the movement
36 and to underestimate the determination of the Negro. This sweltering sum-
37 mer of the Negro's legitimate discontent will not pass until there is an invig-
38 orating autumn of freedom and equality. 1963 is not an end but a beginning.
39 Those who hope that the Negro needed to blow off steam and will now be
40 content will have a rude awakening if the nation returns to business as usual.

41 There will be neither rest nor tranquility in America until the Negro is
42 granted his citizenship rights. The whirlwinds of revolt will continue to shake
43 the foundations of our nation until the bright day of justice emerges.

44 But there is something that I must say to my people who stand on the
45 warm threshold which leads into the palace of justice. In the process of
46 gaining our rightful place we must not be guilty of wrongful deeds.

47 Let us not seek to satisfy our thirst for freedom by drinking from the cup of
48 bitterness and hatred. We must forever conduct our struggle on the high
49 plane of dignity and discipline. We must not allow our creative protest to
50 degenerate into physical violence. Again and again we must rise to the majes-
51 tic heights of meeting physical force with soul force.

52 The marvelous new militancy which has engulfed the Negro community
53 must not lead us to a distrust of all white people, for many of our white
54 brothers, as evidenced by their presence here today, have come to realize that
55 their destiny is tied up with our destiny and they have come to realize that
56 their freedom is inextricably bound to our freedom. This offense we share
57 mounted to storm the battlements of injustice must be carried forth by a
58 biracial army. We cannot walk alone.

59 And as we walk, we must make the pledge that we shall always march
60 ahead. We cannot turn back. There are those who are asking the devotees of
61 civil rights, "When will you be satisfied?" We can never be satisfied as long as
62 the Negro is the victim of the unspeakable horrors of police brutality.

63   We can never be satisfied as long as our bodies, heavy with fatigue of
64 travel, cannot gain lodging in the motels of the highways and the hotels of the
65 cities. We cannot be satisfied as long as the Negro's basic mobility is from a
66 smaller ghetto to a larger one.

67   We can never be satisfied as long as our children are stripped of their
68 selfhood and robbed of their dignity by signs stating "for whites only." We
69 cannot be satisfied as long as a Negro in Mississippi cannot vote and a Negro
70 in New York believes he has nothing for which to vote. No, we are not
71 satisfied, and we will not be satisfied until justice rolls down like waters and
72 righteousness like a mighty stream.

73   I am not unmindful that some of you have come here out of excessive trials
74 and tribulation. Some of you have come fresh from narrow jail cells. Some of
75 you have come from areas where your quest for freedom left you battered by
76 the storms of persecution and staggered by the winds of police brutality. You
77 have been the veterans of creative suffering. Continue to work with the faith
78 that unearned suffering is redemptive.

79   Go back to Mississippi; go back to Alabama; go back to South Carolina; go
80 back to Georgia; go back to Louisiana; go back to the slums and ghettos of the
81 Northern cities, knowing that somehow this situation can, and will be
82 changed. Let us not wallow in the valley of despair.

83   So I say to you, my friends, that even though we must face the difficulties
84 of today and tomorrow, I still have a dream. It is a dream deeply rooted in the
85 American dream that one day this nation will rise up and live out the true
86 meaning of its creed—we hold these truths to be self-evident, that all men are
87 created equal.

88   I have a dream that one day on the red hills of Georgia, sons of former
89 slaves and sons of former slave-owners will be able to sit together at the table
90 of brotherhood.

91   I have a dream that one day, even the state of Mississippi, a state sweltering
92 with the heat of injustice, will be transformed into an oasis of freedom and justice.

93   I have a dream that my four little children will one day live in a nation
94 where they will not be judged by the color of their skin but by the content of
95 their character. I have a dream today!

96   I have a dream that one day, down in Alabama, with its vicious racists,
97 with its governor having his lips dripping with the words of interposition and
98 nullification, that one day, right there in Alabama, little black boys and black
99 girls will be able to join hands with little white boys and white girls as sisters
100 and brothers. I have a dream today!

101   I have a dream that one day every valley shall be exalted, every hill and
102 mountain shall be made low, the rough places shall be made plain, and the
103 crooked places shall be made straight and the glory of the Lord will be
104 revealed and all flesh shall see it together.

105   This is our hope. This is the faith that I go back to the South with.

106   With this faith we will be able to hew out of the mountain of despair a
107 stone of hope. With this faith we will be able to transform the jangling dis-
108 cords of our nation into a beautiful symphony of brotherhood.

109   With this faith we will be able to work together, to pray together, to strug-
110 gle together, to go to jail together, to stand up for freedom together, knowing
111 that we will be free one day. This will be the day when all of God's children
112 will be able to sing with new meaning—"my country 'tis of thee, sweet land
113 of liberty, of thee I sing; land where my fathers died, land of the pilgrim's
114 pride, from every mountainside, let freedom ring"—and if America is to be a
115 great nation, this must become true.

116   And so let freedom ring from the prodigious hilltops of New Hampshire.

117   Let freedom ring from the mighty mountains of New York.

118   Let freedom ring from the heightening Alleghenies of Pennsylvania.

119   Let freedom ring from the snow-capped Rockies of Colorado.

120   Let freedom ring from the curvaceous slopes of California.

121   But not only that.

122   Let freedom ring from Stone Mountain of Georgia.

123   Let freedom ring from Lookout Mountain of Tennessee.

124   Let freedom ring from every hill and molehill of Mississippi, from every
125 mountainside, let freedom ring.

126   And when this happens, and when we allow freedom to ring, when we let
127 it ring from every village and hamlet, from every state and city, we will be
128 able to speed up that day when all of God's children—black men and white
129 men, Jews and Gentiles, Catholics and Protestants—will be able to join hands
130 and to sing in the words of the old Negro spiritual, "Free at last, free at last;
131 thank God Almighty, we are free at last."

Comprehension Questions

Decide whether each of the following statements is true or false according to the selection. Then mark T or F in the appropriate place.

1. _____ The dream of the author is that all people in this country will be treated equally and fairly.

2. _____ The speaker was talking to an assembled crowd of both blacks and whites.

3. _____ Dr. King warns his people not to trust white people and not to work with them.

4. _____ Dr. King was in no way critical of Northern cities.

5. _____ Dr. King was also critical of countries other than the United States.

Choose the correct answer for each of the following and circle the letter preceding it.

6. When does Dr. King say there will be an end to unrest in America?
   a. When African Americans are granted their citizenship rights and justice is done.
   b. Never. There will always be unrest.
   c. When African Americans have a chance to blow off steam.
   d. When job and housing discrimination stops.

7. Which type of discrimination or injustice is *not* mentioned in this selection?
   a. police brutality
   b. "for whites only" signs
   c. job discrimination
   d. discrimination in lodging

8. Which type of discrimination or injustice is mentioned in this selection?
   a. unequal education
   b. discrimination in medical care
   c. voting discrimination
   d. help for the elderly

9. Which of the following is *not* part of Dr. King's dream?
   a. Sons of former slaves and sons of former slave-owners will be able to sit down together as brothers.

b. Black boys and black girls will be able to join hands with white boys and white girls.

c. Dr. King's children will not be judged by the color of their skin but by the content of their character.

d. African Americans everywhere will unite and help each other in developing their own businesses and in getting each other jobs.

10. Which of the following statements is true according to the selection?

a. In his speech Dr. King feels that faith in his dream will give African Americans everywhere the strength to make the dream a reality.

b. Dr. King feels that African Americans should run for political office in order to achieve needed gains.

c. African Americans should develop their own businesses and patronize them exclusively.

d. African Americans should seek to educate themselves to the fullest extent possible.

Skill-Development Questions

1. What is the meaning of the word *heavy* as it is used on line 63?

_____

2. Circle the letter before the sentence that best expresses the main idea of the first two paragraphs, lines 1–8.
   a. The Emancipation Proclamation was a beacon of light that blacks all over the country should look for hope.
   b. The African American today is poor in a land of prosperity.
   c. In spite of the freedom granted by the Emancipation Proclamation, the African American in the United States is still crippled by segregation and discrimination.
   d. The Emancipation Proclamation was unjust and ignored by most people.

3. In what year was this speech made?

_____

4. How does the sentence on lines 6–8 relate to the one before it?

_____

_____

5. How does the sentence that begins on line 26 relate to the one before it?

_____

_____

6. The paragraph on lines 83–87 presents the unifying thought (heading) for the next four paragraphs. What is that unifying thought (heading)?

_____

_____

7. What proof does Dr. King offer that many white people realize that their freedom is bound to the freedom of black people?

_____

8. List in alphabetical order the various states that Dr. King asks that freedom ring from. Then number them in the order in which they appear in the speech. Next to each state write the geographical description indicated about that state.

_____

_____

_____

_____

_____

_____

_____

9. For the figurative expression "a lonely island of poverty in the midst of a vast ocean of material prosperity" tell:
   a. What things are being compared

   _____

   _____

   b. What qualities are characteristic of the figurative language

   _____

   _____

   c. What qualities are appropriate to this context

   _____

   _____

   d. What this figurative language means in the context in which it is used

   _____

   _____

10. Which of the following words best describes this speech?
    a. threatening
    b. pleading
    c. joyous
    d. inspirational

Driving Force

VOCABULARY REVIEW

- a *U-turn* in attitude
- an object of *derision*
- the *contrite suitor*
- women are a *driving force*

1　The attractive blonde in the tailored suit steps adroitly from a big red
2　sedan, drops the keys into the palm of a waiting car-wash attendant and turns
3　to the camera: "To all of you attracted to Buick's growing reputation for
4　quality but . . . who think a new Buick is beyond your means, may I make the
5　following suggestion? Go and see the new Buick Skylark Custom."

6　With her confident manner and soft-sell pitch, this woman is contemporary
7　and appealing. Like Candace Bergen's, her approach works for both female
8　viewers, who relate to her casual charm, and male viewers, who are supposed
9　to be drawn in by her legs and low voice. The dual attraction is intentional. In
10　an attempt to reach both men and women, Buick has the ad, called "the
11　Ellen," playing all over the airwaves, from so-called women's shows to Mon-
12　day Night Football. Unlike the traditional heroes of car ads, this savvy driver
13　is not only female, she's unaccompanied by husband, kids, or boyfriend. Ford
14　dealers have taken the same tack with Susan Lucci and Lindsay Wagner,
15　using female spokespeople who appeal to both sexes. It's a way of covering
16　their bets: Don't alienate the guys by peddling a "woman's car," and try not
17　to aggravate female buyers by selling sex.

18　In other ads, women pitch exclusively to women. Whether it's the Mercury
19　Tracer's "Girl, You Got to Look Good" spot, a Saturn commercial showing a
20　sweet-faced schoolteacher eagerly awaiting her new car, or Geo's "Getting to
21　Know You" campaign, women are popping up all over. Nissan's current
22　Maxima spot features a female narrative that begins, "I want a choice:
23　whether I pick up my kids, my clients or just pick up and go." Infiniti was one
24　of the first to show young women enjoying a midpriced sedan; two female
25　accountants in a G20 (priced at over $19,000) gleefully toss the car phone over
26　their shoulders and into the back seat.

27   Call it a U-turn in attitude. Once, a woman driver was an object of derision.
28 Now she is the prize. To observe the auto industry in America today is to
29 witness a romance of epic proportions. Playing the part of the contrite suitor
30 is Detroit, trying to win back the female car buyer. She, meanwhile, has been
31 having a foreign affair, spending her money and her time with Japanese and
32 European models. Who can blame her? For decades the Big Three—Ford,
33 GM, and Chrysler—turned their backs on women. When she *was* part of the
34 picture, it was usually as the girlfriend, cooing over her guy's new wheels, as
35 the suburban station-wagon mom, or as a talking hood ornament. As late as
36 1980, Ford felt the need to advise its dealers that "the same dainty little hand
37 that pushes the shopping cart has a viselike grip on the economic pulse of the
38 nation," urging salesmen to "talk to women as you would to any young-
39 thinking, intelligent people."

40   Now, at last, women are talking back, and their say in the automotive
41 market extends to the way cars are designed, priced, and sold. U.S.
42 automakers are now meeting demands for safety features like air bags, anti-
43 lock brakes, automatic door locks. and built-in child seats. Even dealerships,
44 one of the last macho bastions, are starting to turn more female-friendly, with
45 single-price "no-dicker stickers" and better arrangements for leasing and
46 maintaining a car.

47   In the process, Detroit has discovered that men like these innovations,
48 too—and that's helping fuel a sales recovery. Irma Elder, the owner of two
49 Troy Ford dealerships outside Detroit (and one of a handful of women deal-
50 ers), says, "I've seen huge progress in the last four or five years. It's just like
51 everything else. It's taken them a long time to understand that we're here to
52 stay."

53   How did women finally get into the driver's seat? It wasn't the sight of
54 Thelma and Louise in their '66 T-bird (although the popularity of a female
55 road movie wasn't lost on Detroit's image makers). It was the numbers. In
56 1992, women bought 50 percent of all new cars sold in the U.S.—a $67 billion
57 share. By the year 2000, that figure is expected to hit 60 percent. Women
58 already influence between 80 and 85 percent of all new-car purchases, accord-
59 ing to industry estimates, meaning they have substantial input in discussions
60 of what to buy. They are the primary drivers of roughly half the cars on the
61 road, and 90 percent of all minivans. Women were major players in some of
62 Detroit's few success stories of recent years: the surprising takeoffs of the
63 Ford Explorer and the Jeep Cherokee, as well as other sport/utility vehicles.
64 And they account for a growing part of the luxury market. Women buy nearly
65 50 percent of all Infiniti J30s, a luxury car with a $34,000 price tag, says Debbie
66 Thayer, Infiniti's creative/media manager.

67   Still, the most vital statistic in recent times may be the fact that women buy
68 the majority of less expensive cars, those priced at less than $20,000. Such

69 sales have become crucial during the recession; from 1986 to 1991, domestic
70 sales plunged from 11.5 million cars to 8.1 million (domestic exports dipped
71 from 648,000 to 542,000 during that period). "It all comes back to economics.
72 The recession is what made these companies market to women," says Betsy
73 Folks of the Office for the Study of Automotive Transportation, who tracks the
74 role of women in the auto industry. "Before 1987, they just didn't bother. Now
75 they need every dime they can lay their hands on."

76   The women's market didn't arise overnight, of course, The number of
77 female buyers doubled from 1972 to 1992, as women surged into the work-
78 place; by 1980, they were already buying nearly 40 percent of new cars. But
79 Detroit persisted in treating this huge consumer cohort just as it always had—
80 as a specialty market. After all, this was the industry that, in 1956, brought
81 forth the Dodge La Femme, a pink convertible with rose tapestry upholstery
82 that came with matching rain bonnet, lipstick, purse, and compact. (Surprise:
83 Women hated it.)

84   "Thinking of women as a single niche or market segment instead of the
85 mainstream is incredibly stupid," says Laurel Cutler, formerly a vice presi-
86 dent of Chrysler and now vice chair of Foote, Cone & Belding/Leber Katz
87 Partners. Tom Healey, director of media and advertising for the leading re-
88 search firm of J.D. Power & Associates, agrees. "It's a classic mistake. If you
89 position a car as a woman's car, that's more of a turnoff for a woman than
90 anything—and it's going to lose you the guys."

THE JAPANESE INVASION

91   Marketing has been only one part of the equation. The other important
92 factor has been the changing nature of the industry. In the late '70s, the top-
93 selling car in America was the full-size Chevy, with sales of about a million
94 cars a year. By the time the Accord inherited the title, in 1989, it needed only
95 about 400,000 buyers to be the nation's best-seller. Today there are 50 brands
96 and 600 nameplates selling in America; up through 1991, the largest piece of
97 the pie any car had taken in recent years went to the Accord, with 4 percent.
98 The niche trend hurt American automakers more than foreign importers, who
99 had higher technology and could produce several models in one plant and
100 update models faster.

101   While Detroit fiddled during the early '80s, the Japanese burned rubber.
102 Honda, the number-three automaker in Japan, introduced a line of compacts
103 with more standard equipment and dependability and better quality at lower
104 prices than anything Americans had to offer. "They studied the American
105 market with a humility not known in Detroit or even in Tokyo at that time,"
106 says Cutler. "They gained an understanding of the consumer." That included
107 consumers of both sexes, who were treated seriously in informational ads that

108 stressed the car, not the person who should drive it. The unisex strategy paid
109 off. It's no accident that in 1989 in the U.S., more than half of all Honda
110 Accords were bought by women.

111   One Japanese company that has paid increasing attention to the needs of
112 women drivers is Mazda. Much of the credit goes to Jan Thompson, Mazda's
113 U.S. marketing vice president and the nation's highest-ranking woman in
114 auto sales. "Women have been buying by default, so if you show them any
115 interest, they really respond," says Thompson, 43, who urged Mazda to spon-
116 sor top women's tournaments in golf and tennis, host golf clinics for female
117 executives, and raise money for breast-cancer research.

118   One of the reasons Mazda has been able to reach this market so well,
119 Thompson says, is that half of its top 14 U.S. marketing managers are women.
120 "The most important thing we've done is to mirror our target audience," says
121 Thompson. "The same type of people who are buying our cars are selling our
122 cars." Indeed, Thompson has been known to insist that more women be
123 assigned to Mazda's advertising account. "You have to have some of your
124 target buyers inside the business," she says. "It comes across in the way you
125 advertise and the media you select."

126   After witnessing several of these foreign success stories, American
127 automakers finally caught on. "The wake-up call was the numbers, the defec-
128 tion to the imports," says John Damoose, vice president of marketing at
129 Chrysler. "One of the cautions we learned is that many of the things women
130 want today are the same things men want: They want a reliable car, they want
131 value, they want not to have to come back in for service to begin with, and
132 they want to be handled professionally."

133   Each of Detroit's Big Three now has a women's advisory committee to
134 review ads and suggest design changes. They have also added more women
135 designers and engineers. The automakers have found some differences in the
136 importance female consumers attach to certain features; by and large, women
137 are more concerned with getting a good price than men are, and are more
138 eager for safety refinements, like remote-control locks with "panic buttons"
139 that cause the lights to flash and the horn to sound to repel carjackers and
140 other assailants. As with air bags, however, the adjustments benefit everyone.
141 If, for example, control buttons are enlarged to make them easier for women
142 with long fingernails to use, they'll also be better for men with large hands.
143 The same is true of adjustable-height seat belts, which make buckling up
144 easier for both sexes. "We used a lot of women's input in the design develop-
145 ment of the Explorer," says Bruce Gordon, a marketing manager at Ford. "We
146 put in features we knew would appeal to women, like the touch drive that
147 puts it into four-wheel, and touch windows and locks." The attentiveness
148 has paid off: Women buy 32 percent of all Explorers, and Ford hopes to push
149 that percentage higher with new luxury models. In general, the sport/utility

150 vehicles have been a huge hit with women, who enjoy the luxuries of a car
151 packaged in the ruggedness of a truck. Women buy 34 percent of Jeep Chero-
152 kee base models and almost 50 percent of the $29,341 Grand Waggoneer. At
153 Ford, one out of four small trucks is sold to a woman, up from one in 10 a
154 decade ago.

155   All this would seem to indicate that women are satisfied and that the
156 necessary changes have been implemented, but Detroit still has a lot of catch-
157 ing up to do. GM, Ford, and Chrysler lag miles behind Mazda, for example,
158 when it comes to making women a driving force within the company. Accord-
159 ing to a new transportation study by the University of Michigan and the
160 *Detroit Free Press*, women held 12 percent of GM's management positions in
161 1991, up 1.2 percentage points from 1987; the comparable numbers were 6.6
162 percent at Ford (versus 5 percent in '87) and 6.8 percent at Chrysler (the 1987
163 level was 3.5 percent). Some numbers have actually worsened: In 1989, there
164 were five female vice presidents among the Big Three; now there are two—
165 one at Ford and one at GM.

CAVEAT VENDOR

166   The biggest gender gap, however, is in the showroom. Women often feel
167 unfairly treated by salesmen, and a 1990 study by Northwestern University
168 Law School showed their concern is justified: White males consistently paid
169 less for cars than white females or blacks.

170   "When a woman enters a dealership—that's where the problems lie," says
171 Zvia Herrmann, marketing director of *Car and Driver* and *Road & Track* maga-
172 zines. "She's done her homework, asks logical questions and isn't treated
173 with respect." Herrmann thinks part of the problem now is salesmen's igno-
174 rance: "A woman will ask about limited-slip differential, and the dealer is
175 intimidated because *he* doesn't know the answer."

176   When Judi Hamilton, 51, a legal secretary in Minneapolis, wanted to trade
177 in her minivan late last year, she and her daughter first test-drove a Toyota
178 Camry. No go. "I liked the way it drove, but the price was high and they
179 didn't want to negotiate." Buick lost her business because "the salesman
180 asked if I could bring in my husband. I don't have a husband," says Hamil-
181 ton, who is divorced. "I looked at him and said, 'If I had a husband, I
182 wouldn't ask his opinion.'"

183   Finally, she went to Pontiac. There she found a salesman "who acted like I
184 might know what I was doing," she recalls. "I had a list of criteria: I wanted
185 antilock brakes, automatic locks, cruise-control, an air bag, front-wheel drive.
186 And I wanted specific things done to the car, like undercoating. Everything
187 was no problem," she says. "Within two hours, I bought a Grand Am."

188   More radical changes at the dealership level will have to come about if
189 American car companies are to continue on the road to recovery. "Like any
190 huge industry, it takes forever for the culture to change," concludes Betsy
191 Folks. "The attitudes are so entrenched. But as soon as they start getting
192 scared and getting their pink slips—how appropriate, pink—that's when
193 things start to change."

Comprehension Questions

Decide whether each of the following statements is true or false according to the selection. Then mark T or F in the appropriate place.

1. _____ In 1992, half of all new car buyers in the U.S. were women.

2. _____ Women loved the Dodge La Femme, a pink convertible with rose upholstery.

3. _____ Ford is the only company of the big three that has a women's advisory committee.

4. _____ Women are the primary drivers of most minivans.

5. _____ After years of neglect, American automakers are now trying to capture the women's market.

Choose the correct answer for each of the following questions and circle the letter preceding it.

6. The company with the largest percentage of women marketing managers is
   a. Ford
   b. Mazda
   c. Chrysler
   d. General Motors

7. A major factor in the surge of women car buyers is
   a. Women wanted to feel independent.
   b. More women had jobs.
   c. Housewives needed cars to transport their children to different activities.
   d. Women had more control of family finances.

8. One problem in many showrooms is that
   a. Most women who buy cars can't afford them.
   b. Women can't make a decision as to interior colors and design features.
   c. Women won't deal with male salespeople—they want to buy from a female salesperson.
   d. Women are not treated with respect.

9. When buying a car, women are more concerned with
   a. safety features
   b. color
   c. comfort
   d. a good radio

10. In 1989, the car women bought more than any other in the U.S. was the
   a. Mazda
   b. Honda Accord
   c. Ford Taurus
   d. Toyota Camry

Skill-Development Questions

1. Which of the following dictionary definitions of the word *fuel* reflect its meaning as it is used on line 48?

    _____ *a.* material used to produce heat or power by burning

    _____ *b.* to support or stimulate

    _____ *c.* to dispense fuel

    _____ *d.* nutritive material

2. Write the main idea of the paragraph on lines 118–125 in the space provided.

    _____

    _____

3. Why did so many women buy Honda Accords in 1989?

    _____

    _____

4. How does the sentence on lines 143–144 relate to the sentence on line 140?

    _____

    _____

5. How does the last part of the sentence on lines 88–90 relate to the first part?

    _____

    _____

6. The paragraph on lines 111–117 lists several ways that Mazda showed interest in women. This information can be organized under four headings or in three headings with subpoints under one of the headings. Write the information as three headings with appropriate subheadings.

    _____

    _____

    _____

    _____

    _____

7. What does Buick call the ad that is described in the first paragraph of this selection?

_____

8. In Part B, list the ways in which Honda appealed to women car buyers. Then, in Part A, list the ways Mazda appealed to women car buyers.

A. _____

B. _____

9. What is meant by a "romance of epic proportions," as stated on line 29?

_____

10. Decide whether each of the following statements is fact or opinion, according to the selection. Write *F* or *O* in the space provided to indicate your answer.

_____ *a.* Women have caused changes to be made in the way automobiles are made and marketed.

_____ *b.* Women will probably be the major buyers of automobiles in the future.

_____ *c.* The surge in women car buyers is the direct result of the increase in women-owned auto dealerships.

Tracer of Missing Heirs

By Phyllis Zauner

VOCABULARY REVIEW

- an unknown *bequest*
- the man was *penurious*
- a *contingency contract*
- a *propensity* for *innovative* thinking

1   Some days William Linhart finds work to be just sheer pleasure.

2   Like the day he knocked on a stranger's door down in Las Vegas. The man
3   on the other side of that door was down on his luck—behind in his rent, with
4   one solitary silver dollar to his name. But the moment he opened that door,
5   his luck was due for a change. A tall, graying man greeted him with some
6   good news. "If your name is Williams, you've just inherited $6,000."

7   Bill Linhart is a tracer of missing heirs, one of perhaps a dozen such sleuths
8   in the country who find missing heirs for a price—from 30 to 50 percent of the
9   inheritance.

10   Linhart has spent weeks searching for this man named Williams, flying
11   from one end of California to the other, checking old phone books, talking to
12   telephone operators, inspecting county records, scanning voter lists. He got
13   his first break when he discovered a few scribbled numbers in a phone book
14   that had been left behind by Mrs. Williams in an apartment she had once
15   occupied. With that and a few phone calls, he was hot on the trail of giving
16   away money.

17   In this case, Linhart recognized the tight squeeze Williams was in and said,
18   "Look, this is going to take six weeks. Can I advance you $100?"

19   Six weeks later, Williams told him, "You don't know what that hundred
20   bucks meant to me. I paid half of it on the rent. I went down to the Goodwill
21   and bought a new suit and some shoes, got a haircut and went out and got a
22   job in the electronics industry."

23   On days like that, Linhart knows he's in the right business.

24   He used to be a private eye, chasing deadbeats, tailing fathers who were
25   behind in their child-support payments, working on divorce cases. But he

26 says he feels much better about his job now. "It's much nicer work: now I'm
27 the bearer of good tidings."

28   He drifted into freelancing as a missing heirs sleuth almost by accident. An
29 attorney he was working with on a divorce case said, "Bill, I've got a probate
30 case here I'd like to settle; one of the heirs can't be found. Do you suppose you
31 could locate this woman for me? An aunt has left her $35,000."

32   Linhart found her, all right. It took a while, but it was the most satisfying
33 work he had done in twenty-six years as a private detective. "When this
34 woman was sixteen," he says, "her mother had shamed her and had her
35 sterilized because of an illegitimate child. After that the daughter became a
36 prostitute and a family disgrace. But when I found her, she was living happily
37 with a rich husband. She didn't need the money, but I was able to reunite her
38 with the son she had borne twenty years before, and that made her happier
39 than all the money I could have given her. It turned out her son was in debt,
40 so she used the inheritance to help him."

41   After that experience, Linhart gave up playing Sam Spade and took on the
42 role of Robin Hood.

43   Perhaps one person out of fifteen may be up for some sort of unknown
44 bequest, according to Linhart. He estimates that there's more than $25 billion
45 in unclaimed assets, scattered from coast to coast, tied up in abandoned
46 stocks, insurance proceeds, forgotten safe deposit boxes. Lost money is com-
47 monplace. Some people keep hidden bank accounts, set aside for a rainy day
48 because of a husband who drinks or a wife who gambles. Or maybe a hus-
49 band takes a flier on a stock that goes sour; later the firm recovers, the stock
50 rises, but it's never listed in his will. And money orders are frequently stashed
51 away and forgotten.

52   A bank in Grass Valley, California, lists a cashier's check for $33,000 bought
53 in 1962 that's never been cashed. And there's a bond that was purchased in
54 1885 for $75 now worth $2 million to somebody—if Linhart could only find
55 the unknowingly lucky person entitled to it.

56   "Many of these unclaimed estates come from people who were, in their life-
57 times, highly secretive about their wealth," says Linhart. "Right now I'm looking
58 for the son and daughter of a former San Francisco school janitor. The man was
59 penurious. He never ate lunch. Everyone thought he was living in poverty. What
60 he was really doing with his lunch hour was calling his stockbroker."

61   Unless the missing heirs are found for these unclaimed estates before the
62 statute of limitations runs its course, the state simply takes the money. Under
63 California law, if you're a named heir and the money goes to the state, Linhart
64 says, you have eleven years to claim it. If a relative dies *without* a will, the
65 next-of-kin has five years to make a claim. Laws of other states are much the
66 same, although there may be a slight variation in the number of years allowed
67 in which to stake your claim.

68 The state controller publishes a list each year of unclaimed money, but
69 beyond that the government has neither the time nor the inclination to search
70 out its rightful owners. Last year Linhart's home state, California, collected
71 $9 million in such funds. "There's $25 million right now, here in the West, that
72 I could recover if I could only find the people," Linhart says with a sigh.

73 When Linhart does find those heirs—and sometimes it takes years—he
74 immediately gets their signature on a contingency contract legally binding
75 them to pay him a percentage, usually about 30 percent, sometimes up to 50
76 percent of the inheritance, depending on the work involved. (The state of
77 Washington puts a ceiling of 5 percent on such an agreement.) He gets the
78 contract signed *before* he tells where the money is or who left it. He works
79 strictly on speculation, paying his own expenses. He finds maybe 15 percent
80 of the people he's looking for; the other 85 percent frustrate him. "You wind
81 up with a bunch of cases that are only half done. The only ones that pay off
82 are the ones you solve."

83 Some come easy. One missing heir was reported to be in Oakland, though
84 no address was known. Linhart checked the birth and death records and
85 found that the man had died in 1949, but the widow was listed on the death
86 certificate. Within twenty-four hours Linhart had located her, got his contract
87 signed and collected $2,400 for himself.

88 Other cases may never be solved, though he has worked long and hard on
89 them. He'd like to find Robert Leopold Forster and his sister (once a San
90 Francisco schoolteacher) who are entitled to $360,000 from the estate of their
91 father, a former Los Angeles businessman whose wife died in an accident
92 right after his death.

93 Some of the people he finds don't want the money. One woman refused an
94 inheritance because she always hated the uncle who left her the money. One
95 oldster turned down a $5,600 bequest because she was happy on her Social
96 Security income and "would rather not be bothered." Some won't step for-
97 ward because they're in trouble with the law and would rather not surface.

98 On the other hand, he uncovers some unsuspecting heirs, in desperate
99 financial straits, for whom the money is a lifesaver.

100 When he found one missing heir in Phoenix, she was living with her
101 husband and a new baby and another couple in a one-room apartment. "I was
102 washing diapers when I heard about it," she said. "We had been trying to
103 stretch one order of liver and onions for four days." The woman had once
104 served a term in a California prison for forgery and had changed her name
105 when she got out. California authorities were reluctant to release information,
106 and Linhart spent a year trying to find her. He finally traced her through a
107 Drug Abuse Control group. Total amount of the inheritance, from a great
108 aunt, was $4,300. The day after she got the money, she and her husband
109 moved into a rented house.

110   Linhart meets all kinds in his business. One of his favorite cases was
111 tracking down a San Francisco topless-bottomless dancer. She was entitled to
112 $6,000 from the estate of a distant relative back in her home state of Virginia.
113 Linhart had scouted for weeks, trying to find her under her real name, Diane
114 Beaver.

115   Not everyone wants to sign a contract to pay Linhart for all his work,
116 even on the threshold of a windfall. They figure if *he* found *them*, they ought
117 to be able to find out who left the money and thus circumvent the fee.
118 "Usually after spending a lot of money on fruitless phone calls, they call me
119 and tell me I'm a phony. I tell them if they sign the agreement I'll produce
120 the money."

121   The success of a "probate investigator" depends on having a network of
122 contacts, plenty of experience in locating and reading public records, a
123 dogged determination and—the vital ingredient—a propensity for innova-
124 tive thinking. "The formula for finding people is 90 percent drudgery and
125 10 percent inspiration," the ex-detective explains. He's a positive thinker.
126 Deep down inside he believes he can accomplish the unlikely and some-
127 times even the impossible.

128   Many of the heirs Linhart finds are skeptical. He found one of them, a
129 former Ziegfeld Follies girls, in a skid row hotel. "The first thing she said to
130 me was, 'How much do you want?' She was already giving $10 to some guy
131 who claimed he could prove she was a real Swedish princess. When I gave
132 her the inheritance check she went right down to the local saloon and ordered
133 'drinks for the house.' Within a month she had gone through everything she
134 got and called me up to ask if I could find some more for her."

135   But Linhart believes a certain amount of skepticism is healthy. There are
136 crooks in the business, too. "If anyone offers to find inherited money for you
137 but demands up-front money, beware." An honest man, he says, gets paid
138 when he gets the money for you. Until then he works purely on speculation.

139   Linhart makes it a practice to find the cash, then the inheritor. He finds out
140 about uncollected funds through court records, which are open to the public.
141 Attorneys sometimes ask him for help. And he has friends and contacts in
142 banks and insurance companies.

143   Occasionally someone will call and say they know where there's an un-
144 claimed estate, asking for a cut. He's agreeable to that, too. "If you know of an
145 estate with no heirs, tell me about it. If I find the heirs, I'll pay a finder's fee."

146   The past nine years have been satisfying times for Linhart. He's made a lot
147 of people happy.

148   To a lady in San Bernardino who was on welfare, he handed $8,000. To a
149 family in Los Angeles with five children, a jobless father and a broken-down
150 car, he handed $7,000. He has passed out hundreds of dollars to people who
151 never expected it.

152   In the process, he's made a few bucks for himself. He says a probate
153 investigator, pressing hard and with a touch of good luck, could make from
154 $10,000 to $25,000 working four months out of the year.

155   But for Bill Linhart, the important thing is that at the age of sixty-three, he's
156 able to say he's working at something he enjoys.

157   Now, if he could just find the Kasper brothers whose uncle left them
158 $10,038. Or a lady whose maiden name is Azarov and who may have married
159 a Chicago doctor and has $47,000 coming. Or Edmund Johann Shiffer who
160 has $22,000 coming. Or Denise Michaelle Quinn . . . or Delia Riordan . . . or
161 Edwin S. LaPierre. . . .

162   Or, who knows? Maybe one of these days William Linhart will come look-
163 ing for *you*!

164   But be prepared, He'll want a little for his trouble.

Comprehension Questions

Decide whether each of the following statements is true or false according to the selection. Then mark T or F in the appropriate place.

1. _____ If missing heirs can't be found, the money eventually goes to the state.

2. _____ Linhart manages to find most of the people that he looks for.

3. _____ Linhart gets paid a standard 30 percent of the inheritance.

4. _____ Linhart's home state is New York.

5. _____ Some people Linhart finds don't want the money.

Choose the correct answer for each of the following and circle the letter preceding it.

6. Which of the following is *not* one of the people Linhart has found?
   a. a former Ziegfeld Follies girl
   b. a famous Hollywood movie star
   c. a San Francisco topless-bottomless dancer
   d. a former prostitute

7. Which of the following is a person Linhart has found?
   a. the children of a stingy former school janitor
   b. the children of a man whose wife died in an accident right after his death
   c. a girl who was really a Swedish princess
   d. a woman who hated the uncle who left her the money

8. Which of the following statements is true, according to the selection?
   a. Each state tries to find the rightful heirs of unclaimed money.
   b. Linhart sometimes takes years to find an heir.
   c. If an heir is very poor, Linhart doesn't take any money from him.
   d. Under California law, if a person dies without a will, the next of kin must file a claim within three months or the state gets the money.

9. How many partners does Linhart have?
   a. None. He works by himself.
   b. one
   c. two
   d. three

10. What did Linhart do before he became a tracer of missing heirs?

 a. He was a private detective.

 b. He was a psychologist.

 c. He was a banker.

 d. He was a lawyer.

Skill-Development Questions

1. Circle the letter before the answer that best expresses the meaning of the word *positive*, as it is used on line 126.
   a. confident
   b. arrogant
   c. not subject to argument
   d. always certain

2. Circle the letter before the statement that best expresses the main idea of the selection.
   a. William Linhart finds missing heirs who have mixed feelings about their inheritance.
   b. William Linhart is a successful tracer of missing heirs who thoroughly enjoys his work.
   c. Tracing missing heirs is a profitable business in which very few people are involved.
   d. People who inherit money have all kinds of problems.

3. What eventually happens to the money if an heir isn't found?

   _____

4. How does the sentence on lines 89–92 relate to the sentence before it?

   _____

5. Which relationship is shown by the sentence on lines 122–125?

   _____

6. Line 47 introduces reasons for hidden bank accounts. List those reasons.

   _____

   _____

7. What precautions does Linhart suggest that you take if someone offers to find an inheritance for you?

   _____

8. Make two lists. (1) List the names of the people Linhart found and the amount of the inheritance. (2) List the names of people Linhart would like to find and how much they would inherit. Give the description of the person if the name is not given. Do not list it if the amount of money is not given. If a name is not given, put the information at the end of the list.

_____

_____

_____

_____

_____

_____

_____

9. Explain the meaning of the sentence on lines 41–42.

_____

_____

10. Which of the following words best describes Linhart?
    a. proud and demanding
    b. happy and helpful
    c. arrogant and stingy
    d. continuously frustrated

Car Theft: Growth Industry

VOCABULARY REVIEW

- an insurance *scam*
- the stolen car was *laundered*
- operators are becoming more *sophisticated*
- the *interminable* mountain of *paperwork*

1   It was a warm summer night when a Colorado teenager named Tom bor-
2 rowed his big brother's 1976 Corvette and went for a ride in the countryside
3 north of Denver. On a two-lane stretch of the roadway, Tom tried to pass
4 another car at high speed and lost control.

5   The Corvette flew off the road and bounced down the side of a steep
6 canyon, over great boulders, into the streambed below.

7   Tom's life ended at that moment—1:30 A.M., Friday the 13th—but the
8 crushed yellow Corvette would be born again. The names that follow have
9 been changed, but the story is true. Not only true, but typical. The insurance
10 scam happens repeatedly and is one of the ways thieves regularly rip off
11 America's auto insurance companies—and therefore their policyholders—to
12 the tune of more than $4 billion a year.

13   Tom's brother was promptly paid the full value of the $7,400 car by his
14 insurance company, which sold the wreck at a salvage auction. The parts
15 dealer who bought it was secure in his $900 investment. He knew the
16 twisted wreckage contained a small metal plate—the Vehicle Identification
17 Number (VIN) —worth a lot of money. All he needed to do was wait a few
18 months, until Peter T., a young man he hadn't met yet, got in a bind for
19 cash.

20   Peter, the owner of the yellow 1976 Corvette, was late with his car pay-
21 ments. "I'm about to lose my car to the repo man," he told a buddy.

22   "No problem," said the friend. "Just leave it at the shopping center where I
23 can steal it, and report the theft to the sheriff. The car won't be found, I can
24 promise you. Then your insurance company will have to pay you full value."

25 And that's the way it happened: Peter's fancy car disappeared, and his
26 insurance company paid him and his mortgage-holder $8,000 for the loss.

27 Peter's friend drove the hot car directly to a shop operated by Felix M. and
28 collected $1,500 for an hour's work. In the world of auto thieves, Felix's place
29 was known as a "chop shop."

30 Felix knew Peter's car was coming. The day before he'd paid a parts dealer
31 $1,350 for a totally wrecked yellow Corvette. Felix could afford the price
32 because the wreck held the magic number needed to make the stolen Corvette
33 salable. It was the VIN from the car that had carried Tom to his death six
34 months earlier.

35 Felix removed the VIN plate from the stolen Corvette. He knew the plate
36 would betray him if it were checked on the state's computer. Then he
37 replaced it with the VIN plate from Tom's wreck, secured a Utah title for the
38 reborn Corvette, duly used it to reregister in Colorado, and the stolen car
39 was laundered.

40 Things moved smoothly. Felix sold the Corvette for $6,000—more than
41 twice his investment—to a used-car dealer, who resold it to a franchised
42 Chevrolet dealer. Every time the doctored car changed hands—on what's
43 known as Auto Row—someone made money. The Chevy dealer found a
44 private buyer who paid $9,800.

45 The proud new owner—we'll call him William N.—enjoyed the flashy car
46 and kept making his $300 monthly payments for more than a year. Then
47 William's world collapsed. A stranger appeared displaying a badge that iden-
48 tified him as a Denver detective, and took the yellow Corvette away.

49 Felix's chop shop had been under investigation, and the trail finally had
50 led to William. His title to the car was invalid. The law says a thief cannot pass
51 a valid title, even to a good-faith purchaser. The car really belonged to the
52 insurance company that had paid Peter for his loss.

53 A grand jury indicted Peter, his good buddy, Felix, and several others
54 2$^1/_2$ years after Tom went for a drive in his brother's car.

55 Peter's yellow Corvette was a high-theft model, according to the National
56 Highway Traffic Safety Administration (NHTSA), the kind of car in demand
57 by auto-theft rings because of high resale values and, therefore, high profit
58 margins. The penalty for stealing and altering a high-price Corvette, after all,
59 is no greater than for stealing a humble Subaru or Ford Escort. Other cars
60 high on chop-shop wish lists include the Pontiac Firebird, the Chevrolet
61 Camaro, the Oldsmobile Toronado, and the Oldsmobile Cutlass Supreme.
62 Foreign cars such as BMW, Mercedes-Benz, and Toyota's Celica Supra are on
63 the high-theft list, too. Even Volkswagen's Rabbit Convertible stands a high
64 risk of being stolen.

65 Professional thieves are not the only hazards; owners of inexpensive cars
66 are likely to be ripped off by joyriding teenagers, by illegal immigrants

67 searching for a quick way home across the border, or drug users who can
68 resell parts, such as tires or stereos, for quick cash.

69   The NHTSA is keeping track of high-risk cars to learn which ones should
70 have their parts serialized under a new law that will begin with 1987 models.
71 The law also prohibits tampering with serial numbers or counterfeiting titles.

72   But while it is designed to frustrate the chop shops, the new law could
73 have unwelcome side effects. Sgt. Jimmy Jones of the Denver Police Depart-
74 ment auto-theft squad, for instance, predicts that pre-1987 cars will get more
75 attention from thieves because of the new law. And he says more stolen cars
76 will vanish across the border into Mexico and other foreign markets.

77   Mexico has no central registry for serial numbers; already an estimated
78 20,000 hot cars cross our southern border every year. About half come back.
79 Mexico agreed in 1982 to report serial numbers of suspicious cars found there,
80 and 10,000 are located every year. The remaining 10,000 disappear without a
81 trace. Some four-wheel-drive models go on to Central America. Colorado
82 State Trooper Gordon Smith thinks they may be used in guerrilla warfare.

83   If your car is taken by a juvenile joyrider, you have about a 50-50 chance of
84 getting it back soon, according to the National Automobile Theft Bureau
85 (NATB)—but chances are the valuable contents will be missing.

86   The NATB is a private organization funded by 600 insurance companies. It
87 has been chasing car thieves since 1912, and has become so expert that police
88 agencies frequently tap NATB computers for leads. The chase, however, is
89 getting harder.

90   For every 100 cars reported stolen, only 15 suspects are arrested—about
91 half the arrest rate of 30 years ago. The NATB concludes that the chop-shop
92 operators are becoming more sophisticated, and therefore harder to nab. The
93 Chicago Crime Commission tagged two ranking members of that city's crime
94 syndicate as principals in a 26-member auto theft ring broken up last year.
95 The commission says a car thief can earn up to $100,000 a year stealing autos.

96   The temptation to steal cars reaches into respectable ranks, too. A recent
97 Ohio insurance fraud involved the dean of a dental school, an attorney, and
98 seven other Cleveland residents. A roundup of participants in an Illinois
99 auto-theft scheme bagged the owners of a restaurant, a construction company,
100 and, yes, an insurance agency.

101   Although it is the insurance industry that pays directly, auto theft is not a
102 victimless crime. The real victims are the policyholders whose premiums go
103 up to cover the illegal losses. Auto theft costs insurers $4 billion a year. No
104 one knows the exact number of false auto-theft claims, but industry estimates
105 range from 10 to 15 percent of the total. That would put the annual loss from
106 phony claims somewhere between $400 million and $600 million.

107   Long experience with fraud has helped the NATB draw a profile of poten-
108 tial crooks. There are 23 key indicators that cause an adjuster to look extra

109 carefully at a claim; when three or four of these suspicious factors come
110 together on one claim, they warrant further investigation.
111   If you're the owner of a stolen car, you are a victim, too. Even though most
112 insurance settlements are immediate after an auto is stolen, there is the hassle
113 factor. You must deal endlessly with the police, especially if your car was used
114 in the commission of a crime or in a hit-run accident. You have to shop again
115 for personal valuables that were in the car—if they are replaceable at all. And
116 there is the disruption in work and in your family routine, and the intermina-
117 ble mountain of paperwork that breeds resentment.
118   Even so, auto theft clearly is a growth industry, increasing each year by
119 more than 3 percent. And one day, you may be the victim. If that happens,
120 you can do only one thing: Right away, call the police. Then call your insurer.

Comprehension Questions

Decide whether each of the following statements is true or false according to the selection. Then mark T *or* F *in the appropriate place.*

1. _____ Auto theft is a victimless crime.

2. _____ The NATB is a police agency that has been exceptionally successful in catching car thieves.

3. _____ Peter and Tom both owned yellow 1976 Corvettes.

4. _____ William did not know that the yellow 1976 Corvette he bought from a Chevrolet dealer was stolen.

5. _____ Felix owned a "chop shop."

Choose the correct answer for each of the following questions and circle the letter that precedes it.

6. Which one of the following people was an honest recipient of money for a yellow Corvette?
   a. Peter's friend
   b. William
   c. Tom's brother
   d. Peter

7. Which one of the following people was not involved in auto theft?
   a. William N.
   b. the dean of a dental school
   c. a restaurant owner
   d. an attorney

8. Different kinds of people and reasons for stealing cars are listed below. Which choice is mentioned in the article?
   a. drug users who want to resell parts for cash
   b. Chevrolet dealers who want to replace their inventory of cars
   c. individuals who want a flashy car
   d. insurance people to make up for their payoff of claims

9. Why might someone overpay for a wrecked car?
   a. to sell it back to the insurance company for a big profit
   b. to sell the parts in Mexico for a big profit

c. to fix it up in his spare time and joyride it

d. to get the VIN plate

10. Which of the following statements is true according to the selection?

    a. Most of the cars that go to Mexico are recovered.

    b. Even the owner of a car that has been stolen is a victim.

    c. If you buy a car in good faith from a legitimate dealer, it's yours even if it eventually turns out to be stolen.

    d. All types of cars are equally in demand by auto theft rings.

Skill-Development Questions

1. Following are four dictionary definitions of the word *flew*. Circle the letter before the choice that gives the meaning as it is used on line 5.
   a. to float in the air
   b. to rise in the air with wings
   c. to escape
   d. to move rapidly

2. Circle the letter before the sentence that best expresses the main idea of the paragraph on lines 72–76.
   a. The new law is designed to frustrate the chop shops.
   b. The new law could have unwelcome side effects.
   c. More stolen cars will vanish across the border.
   d. More pre-1987 cars will be stolen when the new law goes into effect.

3. Why did the parts dealer think the wrecked yellow Corvette was worth as much as $900?

   _____

4. How does the sentence on lines 96–98 relate to the sentence before it?

   _____

5. How does the sentence on lines 5–6 relate to the sentence before it?

   _____

6. Lines 111–117 discuss the "hassle factor." List five possible headings (no sub-headings) under the hassle factor.

   _____

   _____

   _____

7. Which lines tell how Peter's stolen car was laundered?

   _____

CHAPTER 4

A. 1. E, E, E, O   3. E, E, O, O   5. E, E, O, E
B. 1. XP, O, XP, XP   3. XP, XP, O, XP   5. XP, XP, XP, O
C. 1. E, XP, E, XP   3. E, XP, E, XP   5. XP, XP, XP, E
D. 1. CC, CC, CC, CC   3. CC, CC, O, CC   5. CC, O, O, CC
E. 1. CC, E, E, O   3. E, CC, E, E   5. XP, E, CC, E

CHAPTER 5

A. 1. D, O, D, O   3. D, O, O, O   5. O, O, D, D
B. 1. O, R, O, R   3. O, O, R, O   5. R, O, O, R
C. 1. D, D, O, R   3. O, O, R, D   5. R, O, D, O
D. 1. CE, CE, CE, O   3. CE, CE, CE, O   5. CE, O, CE, CE
E. 1. R, D, CE, CE   3. CE, D, R, CE   5. CE, R, O, O
F. 1. CN, O, CN, O   3. CN, O, CN, CN   5. O, CN, CN, O
G. 1. D, D, R, CN   3. CE, CN, D, CN   5. CE, D, CN, O

CHAPTER 6

Practice Exercise A

1. countries
3. baked goods
5. domesticated animals
7. parts of speech
9. rooms in a house
11. metals, or minerals
13. heads of government
15. types of money
17. occupations
19. senses

Practice Exercise B

1. women's clothing
3. carpenter's tools
5. U.S. presidents
7. animals
9. measurements

Gently Does It: Walk Your Way to Health

VOCABULARY REVIEW

- she *advocates* walking
- walking can be *recuperative*
- various *sedentary* groups
- a *sustained* pace
- the *rigor* of brisk walking

1 Say good-bye to runner's knees and jogging's stress fractures, shin splints,
2 and bad backs. Instead, enjoy what is fast becoming the exercise of choice:
3 walking. It's fun, easy, and inexpensive, and it's surprisingly good for you.
4 "Walking is the most underrated exercise in the world," says Dr. Christine L.
5 Wells, an Arizona State University professor in the Department of Health and
6 Physical Education and author of the book *Women, Sport and Performance*. "Also,
7 it's very worthwhile for weight loss and its health benefits are significant."
8 Wells advocates walking for a number of reasons. It is invigorating, yet
9 nowhere near as exhausting as jogging or running. And walkers are less likely
10 to get injured than joggers.
11 Almost anyone can take up walking, including people with low-back-
12 pain complaints. As an exercise, walking can even be recuperative. What's
13 more, walking allows you to go at your own pace, while getting you out in
14 the fresh air.
15 Walking is of benefit because it's an aerobic exercise, like running, swim-
16 ming, cross-country skiing, and the currently popular aerobic dancing. By
17 increasing the supply of oxygen to the muscles and skin, aerobic exercises
18 help build the body's capacity for expending energy and physical endurance.
19 In addition, because it strengthens the heart and lungs, aerobic exercise is
20 believed to be an important factor in preventing heart disease.
21 And the results from walking can be impressive. Test studies of various
22 sedentary groups have shown that walking can improve significantly cardio-
23 vascular functioning and general body tone and conditioning. Moreover, the
24 benefits of walking compare favorably with those obtained from bicycling
25 and jogging.

CHAPTER 4

A. 1. E, E, E, O   3. E, E, O, O   5. E, E, O, E
B. 1. XP, O, XP, XP   3. XP, XP, O, XP   5. XP, XP, XP, O
C. 1. E, XP, E, XP   3. E, XP, E, XP   5. XP, XP, XP, E
D. 1. CC, CC, CC, CC   3. CC, CC, O, CC   5. CC, O, O, CC
E. 1. CC, E, E, O   3. E, CC, E, E   5. XP, E, CC, E

CHAPTER 5

A. 1. D, O, D, O   3. D, O, O, O   5. O, O, D, D
B. 1. O, R, O, R   3. O, O, R, O   5. R, O, O, R
C. 1. D, D, O, R   3. O, O, R, D   5. R, O, D, O
D. 1. CE, CE, CE, O   3. CE, CE, CE, O   5. CE, O, CE, CE
E. 1. R, D, CE, CE   3. CE, D, R, CE   5. CE, R, O, O
F. 1. CN, O, CN, O   3. CN, O, CN, CN   5. O, CN, CN, O
G. 1. D, D, R, CN   3. CE, CN, D, CN   5. CE, D, CN, O

CHAPTER 6

Practice Exercise A

1. countries
3. baked goods
5. domesticated animals
7. parts of speech
9. rooms in a house
11. metals, or minerals
13. heads of government
15. types of money
17. occupations
19. senses

Practice Exercise B

1. women's clothing
3. carpenter's tools
5. U.S. presidents
7. animals
9. measurements

110 backpack, which allows additional weight to be supported by the body. The
111 idea, of course, is that the heavier you are, the more energy you typically
112 expend.

113   Posture in walking is also important. As you walk, keep your shoulders
114 back, pelvis forward, abdomen flat and head erect. Point your toes straight
115 ahead in the direction of your walk and step forward so that your heel
116 touches the ground first. Then roll forward to the ball of your foot to drive off
117 the next step. Striders recommend that you slightly tilt your foot to the
118 outside edge of your shoe. This allows the outside shoe edges to act as
119 "rockers" to give you a smooth heel-to-toe motion. As you rock, lock your
120 ankle to keep it from dropping toward the inside, thus preventing any knee
121 strain.

122   Try for a rhythmic stride. Arms should swing loosely and freely at your
123 sides. As you walk, breathe deeply from the diaphragm.

124   A large part of walking's universal appeal is its low-key enjoyment. There
125 is no need to compete with others or to strain for distance or speed. Called the
126 "world's greatest exercise," walking is a gentle activity that can convince
127 even the most lethargic among us to begin a fitness regime. All exercise
128 should be this easy.

Comprehension Questions

Decide whether each of the following statements is true or false according to the selection. Then mark T or F in the appropriate place.

1. _____ Breathe deeply as you walk.

2. _____ Walking can result in severe back problems.

3. _____ Walking is becoming the exercise of choice.

4. _____ When you walk, wear shorts and a light top so that you don't perspire.

5. _____ The faster you walk, the more calories you burn.

Choose the correct answer for each of the following questions and circle the letter that precedes it.

6. Which of the following will burn as many calories as forty minutes of walking?
   a. twenty-five minutes of jogging
   b. thirty minutes of swimming
   c. twenty minutes of bicycling
   d. twenty minutes of dancing

7. Which of the following is mentioned as a nonphysical benefit of walking?
   a. It saves gasoline.
   b. It is a way to "let off steam."
   c. It builds up a hearty appetite.
   d. It can be a sociable activity.

8. Which of the following is not mentioned as a benefit of walking?
   a. It gets you outdoors.
   b. It's an inexpensive exercise.
   c. It's an aerobic exercise.
   d. It's competitive.

9. Physicians recommend that, for best benefit, you should walk how many days per week?
   a. two
   b. three
   c. four
   d. five

10. Which of the following can running be compared to?
    a. cross-country skiing
    b. sailing
    c. weight lifting
    d. acrobatics

Skill-Development Questions

1. What is the meaning of the word *pall* on line 69 as it is used in this selection? Do not look the word up; try to guess its meaning from the context.

   Pall _____

2. Write the main idea of the paragraph on lines 91–95 in the space provided. ‑

   _____

   _____

3. More than ten advantages of walking are given in this selection. Name five of them.

   _____

   _____

   _____

   _____

   _____

4. How does the sentence on lines 9–10 relate to the sentence before it?

   _____

5. How do lines 33–36 relate to line 32?

   _____

6. Lines 1–73 list results of walking like *increases endurance, prevents heart disease,* and *increases muscle tone.* These could be presented as details under the subheading "Physical." Line 74 starts a list that could appear under another subheading. Name that subheading. _____

   These two subheadings in turn could appear under a more comprehensive heading. Name that heading.

   _____

   _____

7. Which words on lines 96–101 tell why you should wear sunscreen and a wide-brimmed hat?

   _____

8. Check to see what limits your heart rate must meet by calculating the "target range" as suggested on lines 61–67. Write your answer on the line below.

_____

9. "An apple a day keeps the doctor away" might be a figurative way to express the author's message (walking can keep your healthy). If the figurative expression is used in this way, (a) what two things are being compared, and (b) what quality of the figurative item being compared is appropriate to this context?

   a. _____
   b. _____

10. Which word best describes the author's feeling about walking? Circle the letter before your choice.
    a. tiresome
    b. soothing
    c. enthusiasm
    d. boring

Appendix

The suggested answers provided here are for the odd-numbered practice exercises and the skill-development questions that follow the reading selections. You can find other answers to exercises in the separate Instructor's Manual. It should be emphasized that all the answers are *suggested* only. They are not meant to be exclusive or final. Although they do represent the best judgment of the author, other possible answers should be accepted if, in the judgment of the instructor, they are adequately supported by the student.

Answers to Practice Exercises

CHAPTER 1

Practice Exercise A

1. *semihectennial:* fiftieth
   fidgamy: faithful marriage
3. *multimort:* many deaths
   beneviv: good life
   retroceed: go back
5. *gloop:* classroom
   runding: studying
   sootuk: communication
7. *chronotender:* time stretcher
9. *gruck:* seek, or desire
   blim: school

Practice Exercise B

1. *b*   3. *a*   5. *d*   7. *a*   9. *c*   11. *b*   13. *b*   15. *d*

Practice Exercise C

1. *taxonomy:* classification
3. *vicariously:* second hand, indirectly
5. *inundated:* flooded
7. *innocuous:* harmless
9. *corpora allata:* tiny pair of glands behind the brain
11. *origin:* upper end
    insertion: lower end

13. *carnivorous:* meat eater
    herbivorous: plant eater
15. *antipathy:* dislike
    dolorous: sad
17. *novice:* beginner
    fecund: fertile
19. *adamant:* stubborn, firm

Practice Exercise D

1. *b*   3. *d*   5. *a*   7. *b*   9. *b, d*

Practice Exercise E

1. salt	wages
3. to arms	warning
5. Latin *Aprillis*	fourth Gregorian month
7. Babel (?)	talk foolishly
9. room	friend
11. out + center	deviating from the norm
13. capture	long, pointed tooth
15. single	member of a religious brotherhood
17. seasickness	stomach disturbance
19. wanderer	nonluminous celestial body

CHAPTER 2

Practice Exercise A

1. *a*   3. *b*   5. *d*   7. *d*

Practice Exercise B

1. *d*   3. *c*   5. *c*   7. *a*

Practice Exercise C

1. *b*   3. *a*   5. *d*   7. *a*   9. *c*   11. *a*   13. *d*   15. *a*
17. There are variations in the social behavior of the great apes.
19. In Australian tribes great respect and status are given to older people.
21. Sometimes the actual words of conversation contradict other forms of communication.
23. The American family today is smaller than it used to be in several ways.
25. The voyage across the Atlantic was very unpleasant.
27. Teachers and students behave in predictable ways.

29. In his youth, Newton showed no promise.
31. *a.* Transportation workers have certain traits in common.
    b. Transportation workers have certain traits in common.
    c. Transportation workers must be conscientious and pay close attention to detail.
    d. Transportation workers should be able to work under pressure.
    e. Transportation workers should have easygoing personalities.
    f. Some transportation workers need to work as part of a team.
    g. Some transportation workers need to work independently.
    h. Transportation workers need to have good health and physical stamina.

CHAPTER 3

1. Answered in text.
3. *a.* to make up deficiencies in their high school preparation
   b. because they are working part-time and attending school part-time
5. Keeps track of positions available
   arranges interviews with company representatives
   publishes bulletins giving job information
   maintains files on student applications
7. Ordain and establish the U.S. Constitution
9. *a.* stun prey for leisurely consumption
   b. detect the presence of others
11. Allows leisure time for arts and crafts
13. *a.* lies at center of Africa-Eurasian land mass
    b. faces toward Americas
    c. ideal climate
    d. excellent harbors
    e. navigable rivers
15. *d*   17. *c*   19. *a*   21. *c*
23. *a.* served as convention recorder
    b. participated vigorously in debates
25. *a.* Production might be discontinued while costs remain high.
       Employees might lose some income.
    b. Money in excessive inventory will be tied up.
       Excessive inventory may be misplaced or stolen.
       Excessive inventory may become spoiled or obsolete.
       Excessive inventory must be insured.
    c. The source may go out of business.
       Employees at the source may strike.
       Production facilities at the source may break down.
       Natural disasters may interrupt delivery.

CHAPTER 4

A.	1. E, E, E, O	3. E, E, O, O	5. E, E, O, E
B.	1. XP, O, XP, XP	3. XP, XP, O, XP	5. XP, XP, XP, O
C.	1. E, XP, E, XP	3. E, XP, E, XP	5. XP, XP, XP, E
D.	1. CC, CC, CC, CC	3. CC, CC, O, CC	5. CC, O, O, CC
E.	1. CC, E, E, O	3. E, CC, E, E	5. XP, E, CC, E

CHAPTER 5

A.	1. D, O, D, O	3. D, O, O, O	5. O, O, D, D
B.	1. O, R, O, R	3. O, O, R, O	5. R, O, O, R
C.	1. D, D, O, R	3. O, O, R, D	5. R, O, D, O
D.	1. CE, CE, CE, O	3. CE, CE, CE, O	5. CE, O, CE, CE
E.	1. R, D, CE, CE	3. CE, D, R, CE	5. CE, R, O, O
F.	1. CN, O, CN, O	3. CN, O, CN, CN	5. O, CN, CN, O
G.	1. D, D, R, CN	3. CE, CN, D, CN	5. CE, D, CN, O

CHAPTER 6

Practice Exercise A

1. countries
3. baked goods
5. domesticated animals
7. parts of speech
9. rooms in a house
11. metals, or minerals
13. heads of government
15. types of money
17. occupations
19. senses

Practice Exercise B

1. women's clothing
3. carpenter's tools
5. U.S. presidents
7. animals
9. measurements

Practice Exercise C

1. Refer to text.
3. Christmas
    Giving gifts
    Sending cards
  Easter
    Sending cards
    Attending church
    Displaying clothes
      New hats
      New dresses
      New accessories

Figure A.1

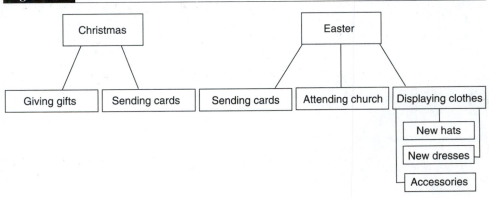

5. How to study
  Survey the chapter
    Read titles
    Read illustrations
      Pictures
      Maps
      Charts and graphs
    Turn titles into questions
    Read subsections
    Recite from memory
    Review
  How to take tests
  How to take notes
    From lectures
    In textbooks

Figure A.2

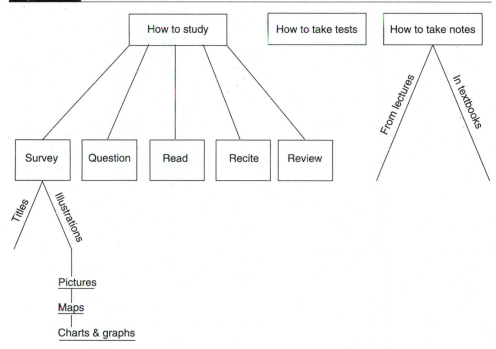

Practice Exercise D

   1. Refer to text.

   3. I. Vision

         A. Structure of the eye

            1. Lens

            2. Retina

            3. Optic nerve

         B. Eye conditions

            1. Cataract

            2. Glaucoma

     II. Hearing

         A. Structure of the ear

            1. Outer ear

            2. Inner ear

         B. Ear diseases

Figure A.3

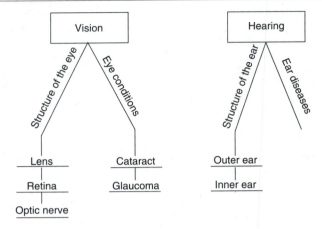

Practice Exercise E

1. Refer to text.
3. I. Avoid tension
        A. Take practice swings
        B. Blot out spectators from mind
        C. Hit ball as if practice shot
      II. Take the offensive
     III. Allow for mistakes
        A. When slicing
        B. When pulling pitch shots
      IV. Don't gamble
       V. Concentrate

Figure A.4

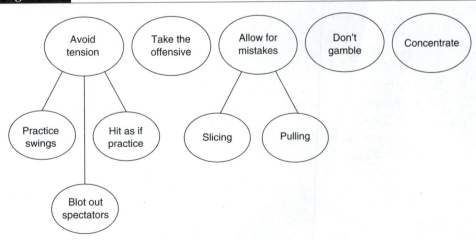

F. Materials Used in Making Self Bows
   I. Wood
      A. Yew
      B. Osage orange
      C. Lemonwood
      D. Hickory
   II. Other materials
      A. Fiberglass
      B. Steel
      C. Aluminum

Figure A.5

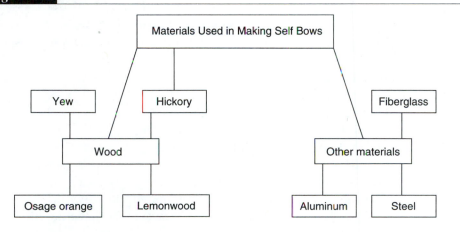

CHAPTER 7

Practice Exercise A

1. a. Changes in the economy
   b. Changes in consumer behavior
   c. Changes in the population

Practice Exercise B

1. a. Life insurance
   b. Property insurance
   c. Auto insurance
   d. Liability insurance
3. Straight life insurance requires payments for the insured person's entire life, but limited payment life insurance has payments that end after a specified time.

Practice Exercise C

1. *b* (no)
3. The temperature required

Practice Exercise D

1. Revolution in science
3. Revolution in commerce or trade

CHAPTER 8

1. I, G, A, F, H, E, B, C, D
3. Use moderate temperature and short cooking time.
5. There would be fewer doctors, nurses, and hospitals available to care for them. Fallout could prevent doctors and nurses from reaching injured or sick persons.
7. They are not as good.
9. To find your own identity.
11. The average person does not do it well.
13. To seize privateers.
15. Its activity is destroyed at high temperatures.
17. It was . . . the ship they had been sent to find.
19. *a.* (1) High cost is the great disadvantage.
   (2) Television commercials have a very limited life.
   (3) Commercials are wasted on many viewers who have no interest in the product.
   b. The hours between 6:00 and 10:00 A.M. and between 3:00 and 6:00 P.M.
   c. Time between placement of ad and its publication.
   d. The largest number of people have their TVs turned on.

CHAPTER 9

1. *a.* Flex knees slightly.
   b. Perform a preliminary waggle.
   c. Place feet apart with weight pulled toward inside of ankles, slightly forward on balls of feet.
3. *a.* 2
   b. 1
   c. Number 1 involves a strong feeling about the statement, but in 4 you may not have a strong feeling about the answer.
5. *a.* Select a topic (do a preliminary survey).
   Research the topic completely.

Develop an outline.
Write the first draft.
Reread it after a day or two.
(Write revisions if necessary.)
Write the final version.

b. A preliminary survey.

c. Any four of the following: first, before, then, now, the next step.

7. 45123

9. 11342

11. 52341 or 51342

13. 42131

15. 32142

17. 21312

19. 13245

CHAPTER 10

1. Refer to text.

3. *c, b*

5. *a, a*

7. *d, a*

9. *b, a*

11. Refer to text.

13. *a.* her money and medicine

    b. Medicine cures illness.

    c. Her money rejuvenated (saved) the business.

15. *a.* his life and an open book

    b. Information is easily seen in an open book.

    c. Nothing in his life was hidden.

17. *a.* a grade for a course and an iceberg

    b. Only a small part of an iceberg is apparent.

    c. The course grade is only a small part of the value of the course.

19. *a.* Harry and putty

    b. Putty is easily shaped.

    c. Mary controlled Harry.

21. Life is compared to the open sea, on which the individual is adrift on a raft. The pounding of the sea is compared to the troubles of life. The calm sea is likened to life's pleasant times. Sea salt and pressures refer to the erosive pressures of living. One can never be sure how the sea (life) will deal with one; it may keep on supporting one, or it may suddenly deprive one of everything one has.

CHAPTER 11

1. Figure 11.4

1. to show how and when various land areas came into the Union
2. 1898
3. Louisiana Purchase
4. Alaska, Gadsden Purchase, Louisiana Purchase

2. Figure 11.6

1. two
2. Accounting and chemistry
3. sixteen
4. Yes, earlier and later hours can be adjusted.

5. Figure 11.8

1. Say, "May I speak to Pat?"
2. Say, "Thank you," put the receiver down, groan, think.
3. (1) Say, "I didn't recognize your voice." (2) Start talking to Pat.
4. (1) If you get a busy signal (2) If you may not talk to Pat

7. Figure 11.10

1. 543 words per minute
2. 4:50 minutes
3. selection 3
4. 4:00 minutes

9. Figure 11.12

1. It will operate.
2. *N*, or Neutral
3. reverse

CHAPTER 12

Practice Exercise A

1. O	6. O	11. O	16. O
2. O	7. O	12. F	17. F
3. F	8. O	13. O	18. O
4. O	9. O	14. F	19. O
5. O	10. F	15. F	20. O

Practice Exercise B

    1. Refer to text.

    3. *b*

    5. *c*

    7. *c*

    9. *a*

  11. *c*

  13. *d*

  15. to provide the student with directions for preparing the paper

  17. *c*

  19. to explain why the book is organized as it is

Answers to Quizzes

Answers to the Quizzes are in the Instructor's Manual.
PQ3R PRACTICE SELECTION

PQ3R Practice Selection

PREPARE QUESTIONS

1. solid, liquid, gas
3. a short method of expressing chemical changes
5. Energy is the capacity of matter to do work.
7. (any three) mechanical, electrical, chemical, heat, radiant or light
9. Chemical changes either use or produce energy.

COMPREHENSION-SKILL QUESTIONS

1. Amorphous solids have no internal geometric form. Crystalline solids have a geometric form.
3. Chemical properties describe behavior of a substance when it reacts or combines with other substances.
5. Potential energy is energy due to position, while kinetic energy is energy due to motion.
7. Homogeneous matter has identical properties throughout. Example: water.
9. Matter has mass and occupies space.

Answers to Comprehension Questions

Selection Number

	1	2	3	4	5	6	7	8	9	10
1	F	F	F	F	F	T	T	T	F	T
2	T	T	F	F	T	T	F	F	F	F
3	T	F	T	F	T	F	F	F	F	T
4	T	F	F	F	F	F	T	F	T	F
5	F	T	T	T	F	F	T	T	T	T
6	c	c	b	c	d	a	b	b	c	b
7	a	b	c	a	b	c	b	d	a	d
8	c	d	a	a	d	c	d	b	a	d
9	d	d	a	d	a	d	a	a	d	b
10	a	a	d	b	b	a	b	a	b	a

Answers to Skill-Development Questions

Selection 1

1. requiring lots of careful work
2. You should try to balance your course load with other aspects of your life.
3. require daily study, lots of practice, many tests
4. explanation
5. cause-effect
6. skills courses
7. This will give you time to become adjusted to a new situation . . .
8. Teacher judgment on the following:
    a. Think positively.
    b. Be interested in your courses.
    c. Seek help, if needed, before it's too late.
    d. Attend classes and be active in classes.
    e. Have a good attitude toward college life.
    f. Have the skills needed for success.
    g. Know the college rules.
    h. Know the college calendar.
9. easy
10. d

Selection 2

1. a. teaching
   b. changed
2. b

3. In linking, two things are associated together independent of any other. In progressive elaboration, all items are linked together in a story.
4. example
5. *c*
6. problems
7. "most effective strategy"
8. 4   apples   *
     7   cake   *
     6   cigarettes   *
     1   eggs   *
     5   hot dogs   *
     2   milk   *
     3   peas   *
     8   strawberries *

   * Right-hand numbers are teacher judgment. However, items in the same department of the store (e.g., apples, peas, strawberries) should be together.
9. in your imagination
10. *b*

Selection 3

1. basis, or criterion
2. *b*
3. All of them are women.
4. explanation
5. cause-effect
6. *a.* The relationship with her staff was strengthened.
   b. It showed her leadership qualities. (It helped get her the job.)
7. three months later—supervisor trainee
   two years later—training instructor
   twelve years later—line manager
8. 1-5-3-4-2
9. "Suddenly I became angry."
10. *d*

Selection 4

1. first
2. The interviewer is thinking about herself.
3. Provides a cushion against unforeseen delays
   Gives the interviewer a good first impression of reliability and interest
4. *a.* explanation
   b. comparison-contrast

5. *a.* cause-effect
   b. conclusion
6. *a.* six
   b. keep the interviewer's attention
7. "What the interviewee does with the question is up to him."
8. Concentrate on it when he introduces himself.
   Repeat her name when she introduces herself.
   Repeat the name a couple of times during the first part of the interview.
9. I have faults, problems, and concerns like anybody else, but I'm being honest about it and I accept myself as I am.
10. *a*

Selection 5

1. *a*
2. *c*
3. teacher judgment
4. example
5. conclusion
6. seeming anomalies
7. "stole Henry Kissinger's garbage and used it for a gossipy story."
8.

Tucson Sanitation Department	provided garbage
Chevron	financed research
General Mills	financed research
Alcoa	financed research
packaging industry	studied waste it created; studied package strength and size
EPA	tested effectiveness of ads for recycling
General Accounting Office	reported on food waste
U.S. Senate committee	(not stated)

9. what was found in the garbage
10. *b*

Selection 6

1. tired
2. *c*
3. 1963
4. example
5. cause-effect
6. the dream that one day this nation will live the creed that all men are created equal
7. Line 56: "as evidenced by their presence here today"

8. (5) California—curvaceous slopes
   (4) Colorado—snow-capped Rockies
   (6) Georgia—Stone Mountain
   (8) Mississippi—every hill and molehill, every mountainside
   (1) New Hampshire—prodigious hilltops
   (2) New York—mighty mountains
   (3) Pennsylvania—heightening Alleghenies
   (7) Tennessee—Lookout Mountain
9. *a.* an isolated island and a vast ocean
   b. An island is land that is small and isolated, surrounded by water.
      An ocean is a large body of salt water; it surrounds an island.
   c. the small size of the island and its isolation
   d. Negro communities are small isolated areas of poverty, surrounded by
      white prosperity.
10. *d*

Selection 7

1. *b*
2. (The first sentence of the paragraph tells the main idea.)
3. Women were treated seriously in informational ads that stressed the car,
   not the driver.
4. example
5. conclusion
6. (Mazda showed interest in women by)
   > sponsoring women's sports tournaments
   >> golf
   >> tennis
   > hosting golf clinics for female executives
   > raising money for breast cancer research
7. "The Ellen"
8. *a.* Sponsored women's golf and tennis tournaments, hosted women's golf
   clinics, raised money for breast cancer research, increased the number of
   women managers.
   b. Made compact cars with more dependability, with more standard equipment, and with better quality at lower prices. Treated both sexes seriously in their ads.
9. teacher judgment
10. *a.* F
    b. O
    c. O

Selection 8

1. *a*
2. *b*
3. It goes to the state.
4. example
5. conclusion
6. hidden from a husband who drinks or a wife who gambles
7. Don't give any money in advance.
8. (1) Williams—$6,000; Diane Beaver—$6,000; former prostitute—$35,000; Oakland widow—$2,400; woman on Social Security—$5,600; Phoenix woman—$4,300; San Bernadino woman—$8,000; Los Angeles woman—$7,000.

   (2) Robert Forester and sister—$360,000; Kasper brothers—$10,038; Azarov—$47,000; Edmund Shiffer—$22,000
9. Sam Spade was a fictional private detective who was an expert at solving crimes. Robin Hood was a folklore hero who robbed the rich to give money to the poor.
10. *b*

Selection 9

1. *d*
2. *b*
3. He used the VIN plate, which was worth a lot of money.
4. example
5. cause-effect
6. dealing with the police
   shopping for personal belongings that were stolen
   disruption in work
   disruption in family routine
   paperwork
7. Lines 35–39
8. Felix—chop-shop owner
   Peter—couldn't make car payments
   Tom—died in a car crash
   William—bought a stolen car in good faith
9. teacher judgment
10. *b*

Selection 10

1. loses attractiveness, has short lasting appeal
2. You should have proper shoes for walking.
3. (any five of the following)
    promotes weight loss, burns calories
    leads to fewer injuries
    aids in recuperation
    helps build physical endurance
    improves cardiovascular functioning
    reduces blood pressure
    provides an activity with long-lasting appeal
    soothes and relaxes
    helps in clear thinking
    provides a sociable activity
    provides an affordable activity
4. explanation
5. cause-effect
6. psychological
    benefits of walking
7. because of concern about skin cancer
8. teacher judgment
9. (a) an apple and walking
    (b) It's healthful
10. c

Reading-Rate
Table and Progress
Chart

If your reading time was between 1 and 15 minutes, your rate in words per minute (WPM) can be read directly from the table. If your reading time was less than 1 minute or more than 15 minutes, you may calculate your rate directly by using the formula

$$\frac{\text{number of words}}{\text{number of seconds}} \times 60$$

Time (min. + sec.)	Selection Number									
	1	2	3	4	5	6	7	8	9	10
1:00	1970	1738	1448	2310	1945	1645	2419	2095	1527	1495
1:15	1576	1390	1158	1848	1555	1316	1936	1676	1222	1196
1:30	1313	1159	965	1540	1296	1096	1613	1397	1018	997
1:40	1182	1043	869	1386	1167	987	1451	1257	916	897
1:50	1075	948	790	1260	1061	898	1319	1143	833	816
2:00	985	869	724	1155	972	823	1209	1047	764	748
2:10	909	802	668	1066	897	759	1116	967	705	690
2:20	844	745	621	990	833	705	1037	898	654	641
2:30	788	695	579	924	778	658	968	838	611	598
2:40	739	652	543	866	729	617	907	785	573	561
2:50	695	613	510	815	686	583	854	739	539	528
3:00	657	579	483	770	648	548	806	698	509	498
3:10	622	549	457	730	614	521	764	662	482	472
3:20	591	521	434	693	583	494	728	628	458	449
3:30	563	497	414	660	557	472	691	598	436	427
3:40	537	474	395	630	530	449	660	571	417	408

3:50	514	453	378	603	507	430	631	546	398	390
4:00	493	434	362	578	486	411	605	524	382	374
4:10	473	417	348	554	466	396	581	503	367	359
4:20	455	401	334	533	449	380	558	483	352	345
4:30	438	386	322	513	432	367	538	465	339	332
4:40	422	372	310	495	417	353	519	449	327	320
4:50	408	360	300	478	402	341	501	433	316	309
5:00	394	348	290	462	389	329	484	419	305	299
5:10	381	336	280	447	376	319	468	405	296	289
5:20	369	326	272	433	364	309	454	393	286	280
5:30	358	316	263	420	353	300	440	381	278	272
5:40	348	307	256	408	343	291	427	370	270	264
5:50	338	298	248	396	333	283	415	359	262	256
6:00	328	290	241	385	324	274	403	349	255	249
6:10	320	282	235	375	315	268	393	340	248	242
6:20	311	274	229	365	307	261	382	331	241	236
6:30	303	267	223	355	299	254	372	322	235	230
6:40	296	261	217	347	292	246	363	314	229	224
6:50	288	254	212	338	285	241	354	306	224	219
7:00	281	248	207	330	278	236	346	299	218	214
7:10	275	243	202	322	271	230	337	292	213	209
7:20	269	237	197	315	265	224	330	285	208	204
7:30	263	232	193	308	259	220	322	279	204	199
7:40	257	227	189	301	253	215	315	273	199	195
7:50	252	222	185	295	248	210	309	267	195	191
8:00	246	217	181	289	243	206	302	262	191	187
8:10	241	213	177	283	238	202	296	256	187	183
8:20	236	209	174	277	233	198	290	251	183	179
8:30	232	204	170	272	229	194	285	246	180	176
8:40	227	201	167	267	224	190	279	242	176	173
8:50	223	198	164	262	220	187	274	237	173	169
9:00	219	193	161	257	216	183	269	233	170	166
9:10	215	190	158	252	212	180	264	228	167	163
9:20	211	186	155	248	208	176	260	224	164	160
9:30	207	183	152	243	204	174	255	220	161	157
9:40	204	180	150	239	201	171	250	217	158	155
9:50	200	177	147	235	198	168	246	213	155	152
10:00	197	174	145	231	194	165	242	209	153	150
10:10	194	171	142	227	191	162	238	206	150	147
10:20	191	168	140	224	188	159	234	203	148	145
10:30	188	166	138	220	185	157	230	199	145	142
10:40	185	163	136	217	182	154	227	196	143	140

Time (min. + sec.)	Selection Number									
	1	2	3	4	5	6	7	8	9	10
10:50	182	160	134	213	179	152	223	193	141	138
11:00	179	158	132	210	177	150	220	190	139	136
11:10	176	156	130	207	174	148	217	188	137	134
11:20	174	153	128	204	171	146	213	185	135	132
11:30	171	151	126	201	169	144	210	182	133	130
11:40	169	149	124	198	166	141	207	179	131	128
11:50	167	147	122	195	164	139	204	177	129	126
12:00	164	145	121	193	162	137	202	174	127	125
12:10	162	143	119	190	160	136	199	172	126	123
12:20	160	141	117	187	157	134	196	170	124	121
12:30	158	139	116	185	155	132	194	168	122	120
12:40	156	137	114	182	153	130	191	165	121	118
12:50	154	135	113	180	151	129	188	163	119	117
13:00	152	134	111	178	150	127	186	161	118	115
13:10	150	132	110	175	148	125	184	159	116	114
13:20	148	130	109	173	146	123	181	157	115	112
13:30	146	129	107	171	144	122	179	155	113	111
13:40	144	127	106	169	142	121	177	153	112	109
13:50	142	126	105	167	140	120	175	151	110	108
14:00	141	124	103	165	139	118	173	149	109	107
14:10	139	123	102	163	137	117	171	148	108	106
14:20	137	121	101	161	135	115	169	146	107	104
14:30	136	120	101	159	134	114	167	144	105	103
14:40	134	118	99	158	133	112	165	143	104	102
14:50	133	117	98	156	131	111	163	141	103	101
15:00	131	116	97	154	129	110	161	140	102	100

HOW TO USE THIS PROGRESS CHART

1. Find the point on the line that corresponds to your WPM. Use the column of figures under WPM to determine this.
2. Place an X on this point.
3. Find the point *on the same line* that corresponds to your comprehension score. Use the column of figures under % Comp. to determine this.
4. Place a 0 on this point.
5. Do this for each selection. As you do, you should joint WPM scores together. Also join % Comp. scores together. This will give you a line graph of your progress. It will be helpful if you use two different colors—one for WPM and one for % Comp.

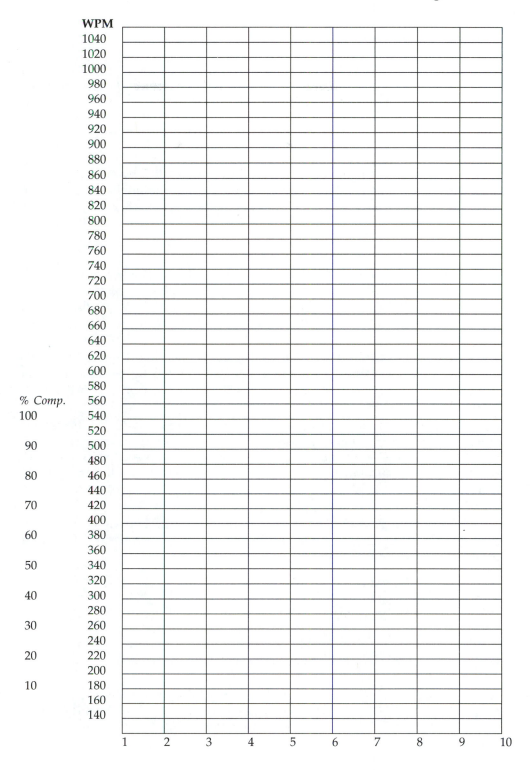

ACKNOWLEDGEMENTS

Selections in the Practice Exercises sections of this book are reprinted from the various sources listed below. (*Note:* The page on which a selection appears in this volume is listed in parentheses following the credit line.)

ADDISON-WESLEY PUBLISHING COMPANY, INC.:

(1) Excerpts from *Biology* by John Kimball. Copyright 1965 by Addison-Wesley Publishing Company, Inc. Reprinted by permission of the publisher. All Rights Reserved. (p. 27, item 10; p. 32, items 9, 10, 11; pp. 65–66, items 8, 9, 10; p. 168, item 15; p. 222, item 2; p. 228, item 19; p. 247, item 4; p. 274, item 2; p. 259, item 2; pp. 280–281, items 2, 3, 4)

(2) Excerpts from *Psychology* by W. J. McKeachie and C. L. Doyle. Copyright 1966 by Addison-Wesley Publishing Company, Inc. Reprinted by permission of the publisher. All Rights Reserved. (p. 51, item 15; p. 69, item 19; p. 167, item 12; p. 168, item 14; p. 233, item 10; p. 246, item 2; p. 278, item 4)

(3) Excerpts from *Mathematics for Liberal Arts* by Morris Kline. Copyright (© 1967 by Addison-Wesley Publishing Company, Inc. Reprinted by permission of the publisher. All Rights Reserved. (p. 55, items 28, 29; p. 241, item 4; p. 278, item 6)

(4) Excerpts from *Business Data Processing: An Introduction* by G. J. Wheeler and D. F. Jones. Copyright 1966 by Addison-Wesley Publishing Company, Inc. Reprinted by permission of the publisher. All Rights Reserved. (p. 235, item 13; p. 238, item 2; p. 240, item 2; p. 246, item 3, 5; p. 262, item 4; p. 278, item 5; p. 282, item 1)

(5) Excerpts from *A FORTRAN Primer* by E. Organick. Copyright © 1966 by Addison-Wesley Publishing Company, Inc. Reprinted by permission of the publisher. All Rights Reserved. (p. 181, item 9)

AMERICAN CANCER SOCIETY, INC.: Excerpts from *Cancer Source Book for Nurses*, American Cancer Society, Inc., 1963. (p. 50, item 11; p. 238, item 3)

AMERICAN TELEPHONE & TELEGRAPH COMPANY: Excerpts from *Alexander Graham Bell*, published by Bell Telephone System, 1963. (p. 249, item 6; p. 251, item 6)

ARCO PUBLISHING COMPANY, INC.: Excerpts from *How to Become a Successful Student* by Otis D. Froe and Maurice A. Lee. Copyright 1959 by Arco Publishing Company, Inc. Used by permission of Arco Publishing Company, Inc. (p. 167, item 11)

ARIZONA STATE UNIVERSITY: Excerpts from *Graduate Catalogue 1965–1966, 1966–1967*; Tempe, Arizona. (p. 226, item 14)

E. T. BARWICK MILLS, INC: Excerpt from *What You Should Know about Carpeting* by Dorothy Wagner, 1967. (p. 260, item 4)

BERKELEY PUBLISHING CORP:

(1) Excerpts from *The Blue Hotel* by Stephen Crane in *Eight Great American Short Novels*, 1963. (p. 168, item 16; p. 233, item 11)

(2) Excerpt from *A Study in Scarlet* by Sir Arthur Conan Doyle, copyright by Sir Arthur Conan Doyle Estates. (p. 225, item 10)

BROOKS/COLE PUBLISHING COMPANY:

(1) Excerpts from *Psychology of Human Behavior*, fourth edition, by Richard A. Kalish. Copyright 1977 by Wadsworth Publishing Company, Inc. Reprinted by permission of the publisher, Brooks/Cole Publishing Company, Pacific Grove, California. (p. 2, item 4; p. 41, items 1, 2, 3; p. 45, items 4, 5; p. 50, item 10; p. 53, item 21; p. 180, item 6)

(2) Excerpts from *Making the Most of College: A Guide to Effective Study*, second edition, by Richard A. Kalish. Copyright 1969 by Wadsworth Publishing Company, Inc. Reprinted by permission of the publisher, Brooks/Cole Publishing Company, Pacific Grove, California. (p. 131, item 1; p. 261, item 2)

(3) Excerpts from *The Search for Independence* by Joseph B. Cook, Marvin A. Hoss, and Robert Vargas. Copyright 1969 by Wadsworth Publishing Company, Inc. Reprinted by permission of the publisher, Brooks/Cole Publishing Company, Pacific Grove, California. (p. 5, item 15; p. 227, item 15; p. 253, item 6; p. 256, item 4; p. 258, item 5; p. 264, item 4)

(4) Excerpt from *Guide to Effective Study*, by Richard A. Kalish. Copyright 1979 by Wadsworth Publishing Company, Inc. Reprinted by permission of the publisher, Brooks/Cole Publishing Company, Pacific Grove, California (p. 42, item 6)

COOPER SQUARE PUBLISHERS, INC.: Excerpt from *Call It Sleep* by Henry Roth, Cooper Square Publishers, Inc., New York, New York, 1960. (p. 228, item 18)

THOMAS Y. CROWELL COMPANY: Excerpts from *General College Chemistry* by Joseph A. Babor and Alexander Lehrman, 1940. Reprinted by permission of the publisher. (p. 285, item 4)

(4) Excerpt from *A Night to Remember* by Walter Lord. Reprinted by permission of the publishers, Holt, Rinehart and Winston, Inc.; and Longman Group Limited, Burnt Mill, Harlow. (p. 240, item 1)

HOUGHTON MIFFLIN COMPANY:

(1) Excerpts from *Europe in Evolution* by Geoffrey Bruun (Houghton Mifflin Company, 1945). Reprinted by permission of Houghton Mifflin Company. (pp. 66–67, items 12 and 13)

(2) Excerpts from *Readings in American History* by James Richardson (Houghton Mifflin Company, 1956). Reprinted by permission of Houghton Mifflin Company. (p. 168, item 13; p. 274, item 1)

CHARLES A. JONES PUBLISHING COMPANY, INC.: Excerpts from *Career Perspective: Your Choice of Work* by Celia Denues. Copyright 1972 by Wadsworth Publishing Company, Inc. Reprinted by permission of the publisher, Charles A. Jones Publishing Company, Inc. (p. 49, item 8; p. 63, items 2 and 3; p. 233, item 8; p. 166, item 9)

JOSSEY-BASS INC., PUBLISHERS: Excerpts from *Stress and Campus Revolt* by G. Kerry Smith. Copyright 1968 by the American Association for Higher Education. (p. 258, item 4)

ALFRED A. KNOPF, INC.: Excerpt from *The Cruel Sea* by Nicholas Monsarrat. Copyright 1951 by Alfred A. Knopf, Inc. and Cassell & Company, Ltd. (p. 169, item 17)

LIFETIME LEARNING PUBLICATIONS: Excerpts from *Sweaty Palms* by Medley. Copyright 1978 by Wadsworth Publishing Company, Inc. Reprinted by permission of the publisher, Lifetime Learning Publications. (pp. 45–46, items 6, 7; p. 165, item 4)

J. B. LIPPINCOTT COMPANY: Excerpt from *Forbidden Area* by Pat Frank, 1966. (p. 223, item 6)

LITTLE, BROWN AND COMPANY:

(1) Excerpts from *Mythology* by Edith Hamilton, by permission of Little, Brown and Company. Copyright 1942 by Edith Hamilton. (p. 68, items 15, 16, 17)

(2) Excerpt from *Rats, Lice and History* by Hans Zinsser, 1935. Reprinted with permission of Little, Brown and Company. (p. 226, item 13)

(2) Excerpt from *Personnel Management and Industrial Relations* by Dale Yoder, fifth edition, copyright 1962. Reprinted by permission of Prentice-Hall, Inc., Englewood Cliffs, New Jersey. (p. 69, item 20)

SCIENCE RESEARCH ASSOCIATES: Excerpt from *Studying Students* by Clifford P. Froehlich. Copyright 1952, Science Research Associates, Inc. Reprinted by permission of the publisher. (p. 70, item 21; p. 242, item 1)

SCOTT, FORESMAN AND COMPANY:

(1) Excerpt from *Success in College* by Libaw, Martinson, and Goodman. Copyright 1960 by Scott, Foresman and Company. Reprinted by permission of the publisher. (p. 64, item 5)

(2) Excerpt from *A Tramp Abroad* by Mark Twain in *Factual Prose* by Walter Blair and John C. Gerber, 1955. (p. 218)

THE SETTLEMENT COOK BOOK COMPANY: Excerpt from *Settlement Cook Book* by Mrs. Simon Kandor. (p. 180, item 7)

SIMON & SCHUSTER, INC.: Excerpts from *Pocket History of the United States* by Allan Nevins and Henry Steele Commager, 1956. Used with permission of Simon & Schuster, Inc., and the Clarendon Press. (p. 54, item 24; p. 228, item 20)

H. S. STUTTMAN & COMPANY: Excerpts from *New Creative Home Decorating* by H. K. Rockow and J. Rockow, 1954. (p. 64, item 6; p. 70, item 22)

U.S. GOVERNMENT PRINTING OFFICE:

(1) Excerpts from 1969 *Yearbook of Agriculture (Food for Us All)*, U.S. Department of Agriculture. (pp. 47–48, items 3, 4, 5; p. 165, item 3; p. 181, item 10)

(2) Excerpts from *Transportation Occupations*, U.S. Department of Labor Bulletin No. 2001-8. 1979. (p. 48, item 6; p. 56, item 31)

(3) Excerpts from *Homemaking Handbook for Village Workers in Many Countries* 1971, Department of Agriculture. (p. 49, item 7; p. 54, item 26; p. 64, item 4; p. 166, item 7; p. 277, item 2)

(4) Excerpts from *Inaugural Addresses of the Presidents of the U.S.*, 1961. (p. 51, item 14; p. 227, item 17; p. 244, items 2, 3)

(5) Excerpt from *Facts About the U.S.*, Armed Forces Pamphlet, 1962. (p. 52, item 16)

(6) Excerpt from *Financial Recordkeeping for Small Stores*, 1966, Small Business Administration. (p. 240, item 3)

(7) Excerpt from *Removing Stains from Fabrics* by V. M. McLindon, Home and Garden Bulletin, 1942, Department of Agriculture. (p. 181, item 8)

(8) Excerpts from *Teaching Taxes*, Treasury Department. (p. 236, items 2, 3, 4)

(9) Excerpts from *In Time of Emergency*, 1968, U.S. Department of Defense, Office of Civil Defense. (p. 3, item 6; p. 165, item 5)

(10) Excerpts from *Family Guide: Emergency Health Care*, 1963. (p. 165, item 6; p. 182, item 13; p. 271, item 1; p. 284, item 2)

(11) Excerpt from *How to Prevent and Remove Mildew*, 1960, U.S. Department of Agriculture Home and Gardin Bulletin No. 68. (p. 164, item 2; p. 277, item 1)

(12) Chart from U.S. Weather Bureau records. (p. 205, figure 11.5)

(13) Excerpt from *Basic Fish Cookery* by Rose Kerr, 1961; Department of the Interior. (p. 280, item 1)

(14) Excerpt from *Counselors Handbook*, 1967, Department of Labor. (p. 274, item 3)

(15) Excerpt from *Pointing the Way to Success*, Army Recruiting Pamphlet. (p. 246, item 1)

(16) Excerpt from *Federal Textbook on Citizenship; Our Constitution and Government*, revised by Cathryn Seckler-Hudson, 1969, U.S. Government Printing Office. (p. 8, item 23; p. 292)

(17) Excerpt from *Characteristics of Persons with Corrective Lenses, United States, July 1965–1966*, National Center for Health Statistics, Series 10, Pamphlet No. 58; 1969, U.S. Department of HEW; U.S. Government Printing Office. (p. 8, item 24; graph, p. 302)

(18) *FDA Consumer*, January/February, 1995 edition. (Chart: p. 293; Chart: p. 295) *FDA Consumer*, March, 1995 edition. (diagram, p. 294)

(19) Map from *Historical Structures Report, Fort Smith Arkansas National Historic Site*. (p. 296)

(20) Tables from *National Survey of Worksite Health Promotion Activities*, U.S. Department of Health and Human Services. (p. 297; p. 298)

(21) Diagrams from *EER-2 Research Results*, Department of Housing and Urban Development, October, 1983. (p. 298; p. 301)

(22) Map from *A Market for U.S. Products in the Ivory Coast*, U.S. Department of Commerce, 1966. (p. 299)

UNIVERSITY OF ARIZONA COLLEGE OF AGRICULTURE: Excerpt from *Budding and Grafting Fruit and Nut Trees*, 1967, Cooperative Extension Service and Agricultural Experiment Station (issued in cooperation with U.S. Department of Agriculture). (p. 282, item 2)

WADSWORTH PUBLISHING COMPANY, INC.:

(1) Excerpts from *Fundamentals of Modern Business* by Robert Swindle. Copyright 1977 by Wadsworth Publishing Company, Inc. Reprinted by permission of the publisher. (p. 2, item 5; p. 72, item 25; p. 144; pp. 152–158, items A, B; p. 169, item 19; p. 213, item 10; pp. 222–224, items 1, 4, 8)

(2) Excerpt from *The Individual, Marriage, and the Family*, second edition, by Lloyd Saxton. Copyright 1972 by Wadsworth Publishing Company, Inc. Reprinted by permission of the publisher. (p. 132, item 2)

(3) Excerpts from *Beginning Golf* by Ben F. Bruce and Evelyn A. Davies. Copyright 1968 by Wadsworth Publishing Company, Inc. Reprinted by permission of the publisher. (p. 133, item 3; p. 169, item 18; p. 177, item 1; p. 271, item 3)

(4) Excerpt from *Body Conditioning, Figure, and Weight Control for Women* by Maryhelen Vannier. Copyright 1973 by Wadsworth Publishing Company, Inc. Reprinted by permission of the publisher. (p. 134, item 4)

(5) Excerpt from *Beginning Archery*, revised edition, by Roy K. Niemeyer. Copyright 1967 by Wadsworth Publishing Company, Inc. Reprinted by permission of the publisher. (p. 136, item F)

(6) Excerpt from *Of Children: An Introduction to Child Development* by Guy Lefrancois. Copyright 1973 by Wadsworth Publishing Company, Inc. Reprinted by permission of the publisher. (p. 51, item 13)

(7) Excerpts from *Anthropology: A Perspective on Man* by Robert T. Anderson. Copyright 1972 by Wadsworth Publishing Company, Inc. Reprinted by permission of the publisher. (p. 53, item 20)

(8) Excerpts from *Sociology: Concepts and Characteristics* by Judson R. Landis. Copyright 1971 by Wadsworth Publishing Company, Inc. Reprinted by permission of the publisher. (p. 53, item 23; p. 55, item 27; p. 253, item 5)

(19) Excerpts from *Remembering What You Read* by Irwin L. Joffe. Copyright 1971 by Wadsworth Publishing Company, Inc. Reprinted by permission of the publisher. (p. 10, item 27; p. 224, item 7; p. 261, item 3)

(20) Excerpt from *Reading and Interpreting* by Guerd G. Pagels, Wilson Pinney, and D. Robert Stiff. Copyright 1968 by Wadsworth Publishing Company, Inc. Reprinted by permission of the publisher. (p. 227, item 16)

(21) Excerpts from *Sociology*, second edition, by Earl Babbie. Copyright 1980 by Wadsworth Publishing Company, Inc. Reprinted by permission of the publisher. (p. 6, item 19; p. 236, item 1; p. 239, item 4)

(22) Excerpt from *Author's Guide*. Copyright 1978 by Wadsworth Publishing Company, Inc. Reprinted by permission of the publisher. (p. 177, item 2)

(23) Excerpts from *Introduction to Business*, 5th ed., by Theodore J. Sielaff and John W. Aberle. Copyright 1977 by Wadsworth Publishing Company, Inc. Reprinted by permission of the publisher. (p. 1, item 1; p. 6, item 18; p. 207, figure 11.8; p. 273, item 7; pp. 275–276, items 4, 5, 6, 7, 8; p. 279, items 7, 8)

(24) Excerpts from *Data Processing; Computers in Action, Second edition* by Edwards and Broadwell. Copyright 1982 by Wadsworth Publishing Company, Inc. Reprinted by permission of the publisher. (p. 41, item 4; p. 44, item 1)

WASHINGTON SQUARE PRESS: Excerpt from *Autobiography of Mark Twain*. Introduction by Charles Neider, copyright 1960 by Charles Neider. (p. 52, item 18)

H. H. WILSON COMPANY: Excerpt from *How to Use the Reader's Guide to Periodical Literature and Other Indexes*. (p. 245, item 5)

The reading selections of this volume are reprinted from the following sources:

PQ3R Practice Selections

From *Foundations of College Chemistry* by Morris Hein, Dickenson Publishing Company, Inc., a subsidiary of Wadsworth, 1967, pp. 295–299.

Reading Rate

SELECTION 1: "Becoming a Successful Student" by Irwin L. Joffe, from *Achieving Success in College*, Wadsworth, 1982.

SELECTION 2: "Improving Your Memory" by Irwin L. Joffe.